Stars in Modern French Film

Stars in Modern French Film

Guy Austin

ARNOLD

First published in Great Britain in 2003 by
Arnold, a member of the Hodder Headline Group,
338 Euston Road, London NW1 3BH

http://www.arnoldpublishers.com

Distributed in the United States of America by
Oxford University Press Inc.
198 Madison Avenue, New York, NY10016

British Library Cataloguing in Publication Data
A catalogue record for this book is available from the British Library

Library of Congress Cataloging in Publication Data
A catalogue record for this book is available from the Library of Congress

ISBN 0 340 76018 4 (hb)
ISBN 0 340 76019 2 (pb)

1 2 3 4 5 6 7 8 9 10

Typeset in 9½ on 12½ pt Baskerville Book by Phoenix Photosetting, Chatham, Kent
Printed and bound in England, by MPG Books Ltd., Bodmin, Cornwall

What do you think about this book? Or any other Arnold title?
Please send your comments to feedback.arnold@hodder.co.uk

For my mum and dad

ACKNOWLEDGEMENTS

Thanks to Alexia Chan, Maire Cross, Graeme Hayes, Susan Hayward, Di Holmes, Katharine Oakes, Martin O'Shaugnessy, Dave Platten, Lesley Riddle, Rob Sykes, and especially to Joanne Austin, Thomas Austin and Wendy Michallat.

The writing of this book was made possible by a research grant and a research leave grant from the Arts and Humanities Research Board.

In addition the author and publishers would like to thank the following for permission to include copyright illustrative material:

Nouvelles éditions de films for *Les Amants* (1959) on Pages 1 and 33; Channel 4 Television for *Et Dieu . . . créa la femme* (1956) – p.7; KG Productions for *Z* (1968) – p.17; MGM for *La Sirène du Mississippi* (1959) – p.47; StudioCanal Image for *Emmanuelle* (1974) – p.63; CAPAC for *Préparez vos mouchoirs* (1978) – p.77; Columbia for *Ishtar* (1987) – p.91; Cargo Films for *Betty Blue* (1986) – p.107; Pierre Grise Productions for *La Belle Noiseuse* (1991) – p.121.

BFI Collections supplied film stills on pages 1, 7, 17, 33, 47, 63, 77, 91 and 121; BFI Stills, Posters and Design supplied the image for page 107.

The photograph on page 133 is from the author's own collection.

Every effort has been made to trace copyright holders but this has not always been possible in all cases; any omissions brought to our attention will be corrected in future printings.

NOTE

All translations from French given in the notes are mine unless otherwise indicated.

CONTENTS

CHAPTER 1

What do stars mean? Jean Moreau considers her image in *Les Amants* (1959).

Introduction: star studies, star systems

WHAT DO 'STARS' MEAN?

Stars from such diverse realms as sport, politics, music, television and film are a ubiquitous feature of modern popular culture. They occupy spaces as varied as internet sites, adverts of all kinds, chat shows and magazines, as well as the original sources of their stardom (usually, but not always, distinct) such as films, songs, TV programmes. They feel known to us, and we often wish to be them or to be like them. Stars are not 'just' people, they are also commodities, brand names, whose capital is their face, their body, their clothing, their acting or their life style. They have been described as 'cult objects [that] condense audience fantasies', and as the embodiment of myths.[1] Of film stars it has been said that '*Leur vie privée est publique, leur vie publique est publicitaire, leur vie d'écran est surréelle, leur vie réelle est mythique*'.[2] In the modern era, stars are very much associated with the myth of the individual: finding yourself, being yourself, expressing yourself, fulfilling your potential.

Star studies is a relatively recent development within the study of film and media, and can be traced back to the publication of Richard Dyer's *Stars* in 1979, at least for an Anglophone readership. Like many who followed, Dyer looks almost exclusively at Hollywood stars: Brigitte Bardot, for instance, is only mentioned to cast light on the star image of Jane Fonda.[3] The principal tenets of his influential work are that stars possess a 'star image' made up of both on- and off-screen elements, and that these images reflect notions of identity that are relevant to the society which creates and consumes the stars. Moreover, Dyer suggests that most stars, by means of charisma, reconcile opposites within their persona and thus incarnate idealised solutions to ideological issues. Sometimes stars may 'subvert' such issues, but more usually they 'manage' or resolve them.[4] In Dyer's words, 'the theory of charisma advanced in this book places particular emphasis on the star as reconciler of contradictions'.[5]

---

[1] C. G. Crisp, *The Classical French Cinema, 1930–1960*, Bloomington, IUP, 1993, p.216; and E. Morin *Les Stars*, 3rd edition, Paris, Editions du Seuil, 1972, p.38.

[2] 'Their private life is public, their public life is all publicity, their screen life is surreal and their real life is mythic', ibid., p.13.

[3] See R. Dyer, *Stars*, New edition, London, BFI, 1998, pp.70 and 73. The link between Bardot and Fonda is made through their association with film director and svengali Roger Vadim.

[4] Ibid., p.34. See also p.26.

[5] Ibid., p.82.

Massive though Dyer's contribution to star studies is, his is not the first major intellectual investigation into how stars function and what they mean. That honour goes to Edgar Morin's *Les Stars*, first published in France in 1957 and acknowledged by Dyer as one of the key precursors to his own work. Like Dyer, Morin tends to concentrate on Hollywood stars, and takes Hollywood as the implicit model for film stardom generally, but he does also include analyses of French stars, albeit without noticeably differentiating between American and French modes of stardom. Apart from a section where he analyses fan letters to Luis Mariano, Morin makes Bardot the focus for most of his references to French stars. (Her star-making performance in *Et Dieu ... créa la femme* had come in 1956, just a year before the publication of his study.) Bardot, along with Marilyn Monroe, is given as an example of the reinvigoration of the star system in the 1950s and, like Monroe, Bardot reconciles opposites. By uniting innocence and eroticism both stars, in a clear anticipation of Dyer's 'charisma theory', embody '*la synthèse des qualités contraires*'.[6]

Although Morin makes few distinctions between America and France (or indeed Europe), he does historicise stardom to some extent by differentiating between the grand, god-like stars of the silent era and the more realistic, bourgeois and approachable stars of the 1930s, 1940s and 1950s. Before 1930, according to Morin, stars were perceived as other, as semi-divine beings who were not like mere mortals. They came from Olympus and kept to their own, either marrying other stars or retiring in haughty solitude. In the 1930s, thanks in part to the advent of sound cinema and a related trend towards realism in film, Morin detects an '*embourgeoisement*' of stars. No longer distant in castles or temples, they are seen to live in villas, apartments and ranches. Magazine spreads feature their homely lives, their bourgeois interiors, their ordinariness, so that '*La star est en effet devenue familière et familiale*'.[7] Thus begins the modern era of stardom, in which stars are not otherworldly creatures, but role models who are not only idealised but also emulated. Modern stars have come down to earth.

Recent developments in star studies include investigations into the relationship between audience and star, a concern to historicise stardom, an emphasis on the star body and star performance (often predicated on Judith Butler's theories of gender and performance),[8] and the description of stardom as work, as opposed to the more usual equation between stardom and leisure.[9] Much of this is a development of Dyer's work, some of it a critique. In *Heavenly Bodies*, his study of what Marilyn Monroe, Paul Robeson and Judy Garland signified for audiences in specific contexts, Dyer had attempted to show 'how people could make sense of the star', and thus to fill 'a major gap in work done on stars, and indeed in media and cultural studies generally'. But because Dyer privileges 'the idea of shared ways of reading'

6· 'the synthesis of opposing qualities', Morin, op. cit., p.32.

7· 'the star has become familiar and familial' – ibid., p.33.

8· See, for example, K. Reader, 'Mon cul est intertextuel?: Arletty's performance of Gender', in A. Hughes and J. Williams (eds), *Gender and French Cinema*, Oxford and New York, 2001, pp.63–76.

9· See P. McDonald, 'Supplementary Chapter: Reconceptualising Stardom' in Dyer, *Stars*, pp.175–200.

rather than 'individual readings', [10] *Heavenly Bodies* does not directly address how individual spectators interpret, understand and renegotiate star images. The fans that make up any star's key audience are addressed in a much more empirical, individualised way by Jackie Stacey in *Star Gazing*, her study of how British women identified with classical Hollywood stars. [11] No similar approach has yet been taken to French audiences (or to audiences for French stars), but this may be the next step in the gradual, belated entry of audience issues into the field of French film studies. As for star studies in France itself, this is a fragmented and neglected area. There are occasional essays in the more intellectual film magazines, like *Cahiers du cinéma* and *Positif*, but both titles tend to concentrate on actors rather than stars (thus avoiding the issue of celebrity which distinguishes the two), when they are not addressing their usual subject, directors. [12] This leaves stardom to the attentions of biographers, the popular film press and the press in general, while it is not yet a subject for concerted study in the academic sector. It seems that Morin's very early lead has not been followed, and that in France at present, stars definitely belong to popular rather than academic discourse.

IS THERE A FRENCH STAR SYSTEM?

From the silent period onwards, American films and American stars have proved extremely popular in France, but home-grown products have also been celebrated, and in some cases exported to Hollywood or the global market. In fact, France can claim 'the first international film star' in Max Linder, who was at his peak immediately before the First World War. [13] The post-war years saw a decline in France's position as the major power in world cinema (with Hollywood taking over), but also an expansion in cinema-going and in press publicity about cinema in France:

> The formation of a mass audience, while it might take other forms – such as posters, trailers, festivals – depended to some extent on those essentials of the Hollywood system, the generic replication of successes, and 'stars' who could attract recurrent audiences; and these in turn required a proliferation of fan magazines and 'photo-romans' to promote the industry's products as objects of desire. [14]

As Colin Crisp notes, stardom and genre cinema (the two mainstays of film as mass entertainment) informed each other, and proved mutually supportive – as they still do. While stars can embody and 'carry' genres on screen (Alain Delon the police thriller, Sylvia Kristel the soft porn film, Christian Clavier the comedy), their off-screen activities are assimilated to genres via the press, to form '*dramas* of poverty and riches, of chance

10· See R. Dyer, *Heavenly Bodies: Film Stars and Society*, London, BFI/Macmillan, 1986, p.ix.

11· J. Stacey, *Star Gazing: Hollywood Cinema and Female Spectatorship*, London, Routledge, 1994.

12· *Positif* in particular has run several special issues on actors (though not stars): see *Positif* 300 (February 1986), *Positif* 435 (May 1997) and *Positif* 495 (May 2002).

13· See G. Vincendeau, *Stars and Stardom in French Cinema*, London, Continuum, 2000, pp.42–58.

14· Crisp, op. cit., p.214.

encounters [...]; *sentimental romances* [...]; *adventure stories* [...] evocations of *spectacle*.[15] This is one key way in which the star's persona is represented as consistent, even though it occupies different cultural spaces: the cinema screen and 'real life'. We are often told that a star is the same on screen as off, adding to their sense of authenticity and our sense of familiarity with their persona. An eroticised or passionate star is often represented as having an equally turbulent personal life (Brigitte Bardot, Jeanne Moreau, Béatrice Dalle), while a joker apparently continues their stunts and gags after the camera stops rolling (Jean-Paul Belmondo).

The promotion of film products, stars included, has crystallised in France around the Cannes film festival. Launched in the late thirties, but only fully established in 1946, the festival has since been held annually almost without interruption (a famous exception being May 1968, when political protest forced its closure).[16] Cannes has since functioned as a site for the display and consumption of established stars and the discovery of new ones. Particularly during the 1950s and 1960s, Cannes was the crucible for the ambitions of embryonic or would-be stars. Hence Brigitte Bardot making a bikini-clad splash in 1953, or Alain Delon hanging around the festival in 1957, before he had shot a single scene, in the (successful) hope that he would be noticed. Although the films shown at Cannes are international, with Hollywood contributing an important share, numerous French stars have been cheered by the crowds and photographed by the paparazzi while ascending the famous red-carpeted steps to the Palais du festival.[17]

To Cannes one must add the Césars, the French equivalent of the Oscars, a televised award ceremony established in 1975 and presided over every year by a major French star. Just like Cannes, the Césars ceremony can consecrate a star, elevating them in the public consciousness, or confirming their dominance. In 1990, Gérard Depardieu and Isabelle Adjani shared the so-called Super-César for the actor of the decade. A more dramatic example of the ceremony's sacralising power dates from 1993 when, three days after the HIV-related death of the actor/director Cyril Collard, his film *Les Nuits fauves* won four Césars. In death, Collard had become a star. His journals were published, and he featured regularly on the cover of numerous magazines, including both film-specific (*Cahiers du cinéma*) and news/glamour (*Paris Match*). The following year, the televising of the Césars by Canal+ was followed by '*Une nuit fauve*', in which Collard's entire filmic output was broadcast.

So, does France have a star system? Confining himself to the classical period (1930–1960), Crisp says not, since French cinema did not have a studio system like Hollywood's: 'This relative absence of a star system in France is due primarily to the distinctive nature of its production system and the less developed form of capitalism of which that in turn was a symptom.'[18] As he goes on to explain,

---

15. Ibid., p.218, italics in original.

16. For more on the festival, see *Cahiers du cinéma*, 'Numéro spécial: Histoires de Cannes', April 1997.

17. In the 1990s, up to 500 films were shown annually at the festival, to an audience of around 40,000.

18. Crisp, op. cit., pp.224–5.

the [French] production companies had no vested interest in the merchandising of actors or actresses as stars, as did their Hollywood counterparts; the star was not their property, so his or her value would not reflect directly on the company's profit. [. . .] Moreover, without a studio base and associated support staff it was difficult for an actor or actress to become the focus of a fan system.

Crisp concludes that 'a full-fledged industrial capitalism such as existed in Hollywood is necessary to support the merchandising of actors central to the star system'.[19] But this account allows us to ask, in view of the fact that since the 1960s France has become a modern capitalist and consumerist society, whether it has also developed the kind of star system that depends on such conditions. Certainly this appears to be the case. René Prédal has observed (not at all approvingly) that since the late 1960s French cinema has seen the triumph of a Hollywood-style star system. He attributes this in part to a change in the ambition and financial power of French stars, who rarely produced or developed their own projects until the 1970s and 1980s, when films such as *Stavisky, Monsieur Klein* and *Camille Claudel* were financed by their stars (Belmondo, Delon, Adjani).[20] Prédal also remarks on the increasing need for French producers to have a star on board in order to finance their films or to find a distributor. If 'le cinéma français est un cinéma de stars', as Prédal claims,[21] this is surely also because the economic conditions now exist in France to enable the systematic creation and consumption of stars in ways that were only partially operative before the sixties.

The present study will look closely at sixteen major stars of modern French cinema, analysing their star images via forms such as on-screen performance, star bodies and star faces, and representations in the popular press, including generally approving film and celebrity titles (*Première, Paris Match*) and occasionally the more scandalous, muck-raking discourse of *Voici*. For the reasons sketched above, the starting point for this account of modern film stardom in France will be the late 1950s. This was a watershed in French political and cultural life, not just in terms of cinema (the advent of the new wave), cinema-going (which reached its peak in 1957 with 400 million spectators), film stardom (the emergence of Bardot as a new kind of star) and star studies (the publication of Morin's *Les Stars*), but also in broader terms with the beginning of Charles de Gaulle's presidency and of several social processes from decolonisation to the rise of the consumer society.[22] It is therefore with the 1950s and with Brigitte Bardot that this survey will begin.

19· Ibid., pp.225 and 226.

20· See R. Prédal, *Le cinéma français depuis 1945*, Paris, Nathan, 1991, pp.334, 337. With French film criticism's characteristic bias towards auteur cinema and against popular genres, Prédal supports the first two films and wishes that the third (by far the most successful) had never been made.

21· 'French cinema is a cinema of stars', ibid., p.333.

22· For an excellent evaluation of these trends, see K. Ross, *Fast Cars, Clean Bodies: Decolonization and the Reordering of French Culture*, Cambridge, Mass. and London, MIT Press, 1996.

CHAPTER 2

Sea, sex and sun: Brigitte Bardot in dominant mode in *Et Dieu . . . créa la femme* (1956).

And God created stars: Brigitte Bardot

NEW WAVE, NEW AUDIENCE, NEW STAR

French cinema in the 1950s saw a tension between the old and the new. This informed nearly all areas of film creation, from scriptwriting and shooting methods to production budgets and choice of stars. It can be encapsulated in the clash between two styles, *la tradition de qualité* (the tradition of quality) and *la nouvelle vague* (the new wave). Known more pejoratively as *le cinéma de papa* (daddy's cinema), so-called quality film making had been the dominant mode of French cinema since the end of the Second World War. It tended to rely heavily on literary adaptations, elaborate stage sets and theatrically trained actors. It also made use of increasingly large budgets, and generated stars such as Gérard Philipe and Martine Carol. High production values, popular stars and familiar narrative material allowed the format to flourish and contributed to domestic cinema's resurgence against Hollywood in post-war France.[1] In terms of performance style, the class archetypes and 'extrovert expressiveness' favoured in the 1930s had given way to 'anguished interiority' and a stress on the psychological make-up of characters.[2] This was far from the Method, however, a much more in-depth and ostensibly naturalistic performance style which was being articulated in America at the same time, and which came to international recognition with Marlon Brando's performance in *On the Waterfront* (1954).[3] French cinema was still waiting for its own encounter with fresh, innovative and shocking forms.

Those forms arrived – or at least seemed to arrive – with the new wave of film makers in the late 1950s. Filming original and often self-penned scripts on location, using small budgets, hitherto unknown young actors and at times innovative techniques, the new wave represented itself (and was duly represented by others) as a revolution in cinema.[4] Several actresses have been proposed as the face of the new wave, among them Anna Karina, Jeanne Moreau and Jean Seberg,[5] but during the mid and late 1950s, the key star

1. The average film budget doubled between 1950 and 1955. Whereas American films had accounted for half of the French box office in 1948, and home product for only a third, by 1957 the situation had been reversed. See G. Sadoul, *Le Cinéma français*, Paris, Flammarion, 1962, pp.103 and 145.

2. C. G. Crisp, *The Classical French Cinema, 1930–1960*, Bloomington and Indianapolis, I.U.P., 1993, p.365.

3. For more on Method acting, see S. M. Carnickie, 'Lee Strasberg's Paradox of the Actor', in A. Lovell and P. Kramer (eds), *Screen Acting*, London and New York, Routledge, 1999, pp.75–87.

4. For a careful consideration of just how innovative the new wave really was, see Crisp, op. cit.

5. See G. Vincendeau, *Stars and Stardom In French Cinema*, London, Continuum, 2000, pp.111–13.

in France was Brigitte Bardot. Although she starred in only two new wave films – Louis Malle's *Vie privée* (1961) and Jean-Luc Godard's *Le Mépris* (1963) – and these after the early days of her own stardom and of the movement itself, Bardot can be seen as emblematic of the freshness, youth and disregard for convention which characterised this moment in French cinema. A star at the Cannes film festival before she was twenty, Bardot connected with a new, youthful audience in fifties France, as Colin Crisp notes:

> No better example of new audiences with new values could exist than the young Brigitte Bardot, at once voluptuous and naïve, animal and (as her initials imply) babyish. Her rise parallels the growth of the pop music industry and of youth culture in general, as the most evident cultural manifestation of that ethic of instant gratification promoted by consumerism and now extended to the increasingly affluent younger generation.[6]

Bardot's breakthrough performance came at the age of twenty-two, in her husband Roger Vadim's first feature, *Et Dieu créa . . . la femme* (1956). Although not traditionally considered part of the new wave canon, the film was a crucial precursor to the movement, proving that a first-time director working on location with a small budget could create a big commercial success. But the film belongs to Bardot, not Vadim. Showcasing her body in dance sequences and beach scenes, *Et Dieu . . . créa la femme* made Bardot an international star. In the United States, the film was marketed with the line 'God created woman . . . but the devil invented Brigitte Bardot'. A year later, François Truffaut (soon to become the most popular director of the new wave) wrote that 'without realising it [Bardot] is busy saving French cinema'. Even a predictable 'quality' costume drama, such as *Une Parisienne*, he explained, could have its stifling 'unity of tone destroyed' by Bardot's 'lack of sophistication and refusal of convention'.[7] The young star's raucous voice, her everyday speech patterns, the open and graceful way that she seemed to inhabit her body, and her relaxed candour about nudity all contributed to her image as sexy but natural, erotic but artless (and hence the opposite of the *tradition de qualité*). Above all, Bardot was simple.[8] By 1958 Bardot worship or 'bardolâtrie' was at its height. *Paris Match* magazine was typical in publishing apparently unposed, 'natural' photos of Bardot out shopping, or sitting on the pavement barefoot, strumming a guitar. Here was a star who had come down from her pedestal and was just like her own fans:

> *Elle est coiffée à la diable, à peine maquillée, vêtue comme n'importe quelle autre fille de son âge, et elle se comporte avec la même spontanéité qu'à l'écran. [. . .] Des milliers de jeunes femmes s'identifient à elle, la copient.*[9]

6· Crisp, op. cit., p.366. In French, Bardot's initials (BB) give the sound *bébé*, meaning 'baby'.

7· Truffaut writing in *Arts*, 15 May 1957, cited in ibid., p.364.

8· It was her simplicity that apparently endeared Bardot to President Charles de Gaulle.

9· 'Her hair's a mess, she wears hardly any make-up, she dresses like any girl her age, and she behaves with the same spontaneity that you see on screen. Thousands of young women identify with her and copy her', – Anon., 'Et un monde qui commence', *Paris Match: Souvenirs*, 1988, hors série, p.97.

It is this identification between Bardot and her fans which makes her a more accessible star and adds to the discourse of authenticity and naturalness which surrounds her. *Positif* magazine recently asserted that '*Dans le cinéma français, peut-être en raison d'une habitude issue du théâtre, les comediennes ont longtemps répondu à des "emplois": l'ingénue, la garce, la femme fatale, la grande dame*'.[10] Bardot does not inhabit any of these archetypes. She is simply BB. Despite her overt sexuality, she is neither a *femme fatale* nor a tart, and despite her youth, she is not an *ingénue*. She does seem to combine elements of various types, and hence to reconcile opposites as true stars are said to do.[11] In this she is comparable to Marilyn Monroe, whose attitude to nudity and to sex was famously 'Guiltless [and] natural, not prurient'; in her final interview Monroe stated that 'sexuality is only attractive when it is natural and spontaneous'.[12] The same 'natural' view of sexuality was ascribed to Bardot, who became a major star only three years after Monroe did.[13] Bardot is also an example of a historical moment in post-war France, a 'trend in characterisation away from myths, types and conventional categories' and towards 'the myth of the unique individual'.[14] It is this myth, and in particular its youthful incarnation in the new phenomenon of the teenager, that Bardot incorporates. As Juliette in *Et Dieu ... créa la femme* she dramatises the need for the individual to express and, if possible, satisfy their desires. Juliette is an orphan, and is hence largely untouched by family structures. She lives for the moment, deriding the future and celebrating the immediate pleasures of '*la mer, le soleil, le sable, et la musique*',[15] to which one should add sex. Voraciously consuming pop music (by means of the radio and the jukebox), she dreams of owning a sports car. Like the off-screen Bardot (at least of the fifties) and her own fans, she has one goal in mind above all others: to have fun.

SEX KITTEN

As Edgar Morin has remarked, the young Bardot (already famous at Cannes before she had starred in any well-known films) combined extreme innocence with extreme eroticism, and was thus '*la plus sexy des vedettes bébé, le plus bébé des vedettes sexy*'.[16] Morin locates this mixture of the innocent child and the sexual animal in Bardot's appearance, especially her face:

10• 'Perhaps because of a tradition taken from the theatre, actresses in French cinema have always played certain types: the *ingénue*, the tart, the *femme fatale*, the grand lady' – M. Ciment and Y. Tobin, 'Actrices françaises', *Positif*, 495, (May 2002), p.5.

11• See Chapter 1. For a discussion of what these opposites are in Bardot's case, see below.

12• R. Dyer, *Heavenly Bodies: Film Stars and Society*, London, BFI/Macmillan, 1986, pp.31 and 32.

13• Bardot's breakthrough was in 1956 with *Et Dieu ... créa la femme*. In 1953 Monroe had her first three starring roles and was voted top female box office star by American film distributors. See ibid., p.27.

14• Crisp, op. cit., p.366.

15• 'the sea, the sun, the sand, and music' – Juliette to Carradine (Curt Jurgens) in the film.

16• 'the most sexy of the baby stars, and the most babyish of the sexy stars' – E. Morin, *Les Stars*, 3rd edition, Paris, Editions du Seuil, 1972, p.31.

En effet son visage de petite chatte est ouvert à la fois sur l'enfance et sur la félinité: sa chevelure longue et tombante par derrière est le symbole même du déshabillé lascif, de la nudité offerte, mais une frange faussement désordonnée sur le front nous ramène à la petite collégienne. [. . .] la lèvre inférieure très charnue fait une moue de bébé mais aussi une invitation au baiser.[17]

Youthful innocence and animal sexuality combine in the image of the sex kitten. Morin's opening phrase above recalls Michel's description of Juliette in *Et Dieu . . . créa la femme* as '*un petit chat*', or the priest calling her '*un jeune animal*'.[18] Throughout the film, Bardot is identified alternately with animals and with childhood. At times the two tropes coexist, as in the scenes showing Juliette tending to her pets, and later letting them go (a symbol of lost innocence when she realises the depth of her desire for Antoine). More often there is a contrast between the child and the sexual animal. Several times Antoine dismisses Juliette as '*une gosse*', although he also admits that '*C'est une vraie femme maintenant*'.[19] The sexually charged confrontation between Juliette and Antoine on the beach, one of the climaxes of the film, is sandwiched between scenes infantilising Juliette. In the first, she struggles weakly in the sea after her boat catches fire, and begs Antoine '*Ne me laisse pas*'.[20] Yet once he has helped her ashore, she stands over him in a magnificent display of sexual power, grinding his head into the sand with her bare feet. She proceeds to stretch out languorously on the sand to show him her body, barely contained by her dripping wet dress. But the sexual predation apparent here is disavowed in the scene that follows, with Juliette cast as a little girl again, in bed with a fever and talking about her fears in a childish voice to Antoine's little brother. Like these sequences, Bardot's star image itself oscillates between infantile helplessness (BB as baby) and sexual dominance (BB as sex bomb).

BARDOT AND NATURE

A modern avatar of the Venus myth, Bardot is often represented as an ideal beauty rising from the waves. Before the beach scene in *Et Dieu . . . créa la femme*, she had made a famous appearance at the Cannes festival in 1953, recounted thus by Vadim:

First they saw her long tresses floating on the surface of the water; then the face, streaming with drops of water, glistening in the sun [. . .]. Her innocent, sensual mouth [. . .], her cheeks as round as a child's, were made for pleasure and laughter. [. . .] The apparition hoisted herself on board [. . .]. A little bikini, a shadow rather than a garment, hid nothing of this sensual, glorious body.[21]

17• 'In fact her kittenish face is both childlike and feline: her long hair, falling down behind, symbolises lasciviousness and nakedness, but her deceptively untidy fringe recalls the little schoolgirl. Her thick lower lip forms a babyish pout, but also invites a kiss', ibid., p.31. One could add that Bardot's blondeness (ironically, not natural) is both sexual and juvenile.

18• a little cat'; 'a young animal'. Michel (Jean-Louis Trintignant) marries Juliette despite this.

19• 'a kid'; 'She's a real woman now'. The film concerns Juliette's desire for her brother-in-law Antoine.

20• 'Don't leave me'.

21• R. Vadim, *Bardot, Deneuve and Fonda: The Memoirs of Roger Vadim*, London, New English Library, Hodder and Stoughton, 1986, p.13.

The tropes mobilised here informed Bardot's star image throughout her career. We recognise the mixture of the adult ('made for pleasure', 'this sensual, glorious body') and the childlike ('innocent mouth', 'cheeks as round as a child's'). Vadim also introduces the association between Bardot and the sea, an image of freshness and purity, but also of elemental power. Elsewhere he describes the young actress as 'all spontaneity, like a running brook'.[22] In only her second film, *Manina, fille sans voiles* (1952), Bardot had been portrayed emerging from the waves wearing a bikini, and as late as 1974, at the age of forty, she was photographed nude on the beach at La Madrague, with her hair falling down in its usual wild way over her shoulders and breasts. The accompanying feature recalled her early star image, established '*en se déshabillant simplement au soleil des vacances*'.[23] It also noted that her acting style seemed entirely natural, rendering that of her 1950s colleagues (such as Edwige Feuillère, who had appeared nude on screen before Bardot did) all the more theatrical and artificial.

The imagery of simplicity, youth and naturalness, so central to Bardot's persona, is here elevated to such an extent that she is declared the opposite of a star, since

> *Son emprise magique sur des des centaines de millions d'hommes et de femmes, elle ne l'a pas fondée sur le mystère, sur la sophistication, sur la gloire solitaire et sur le mal de vivre, mais sur le naturel. Sa légende n'était pas celle d'une grande reine mais d'une gentille gosse qui régnait sur une bande de copains farceurs.*[24]

According to this (reductive) reading, Bardot is – until the age of forty! – a young girl who refuses to grow up, but whose pleasures we share. This image of Bardot as a fun-loving girl is above all parochial. As *Paris Match* noted, contrasting her with grandiose and distant Hollywood stars, '*C'est tellement français*'.[25] Bardot is typically French, we are told, in her attitude to money (she likes it, but spends it carefully) and to seclusion (she wants peace and quiet, but not a proud withdrawal from the world, like that of Greta Garbo). And it is a measure of Bardot's parochial image that, despite being a global star, she seeks mature seclusion in exactly the same place that she sought youthful amusement: the beaches of the Riviera. Bardot has always been associated not with Paris, but with the Côte d'Azur. This association is anchored in her screen roles (notably *Et Dieu créa . . . la femme,* set in St Tropez), her house at La Madrague, and her regular appearances at the Cannes film festival from the early fifties to the late sixties. By incarnating the Riviera, Bardot celebrates the pleasures of leisure time, of consumption and, above all, of holidays in the

---

22· Ibid., p.22.

23· 'by undressing simply in the holiday sunshine', F. Caviglioli, 'Etre Brigitte à 40 ans', *Paris Match*, 28 September 1974, p.57. Bardot thus appears as a kind of naturist. Compare Jayne Mansfield's remark about Marilyn Monroe being a naturist, cited in Dyer, op. cit., p.32.

24· 'Her magical hold over hundreds of millions of men and women wasn't based on mystery or sophistication, on lonely glory or world-weariness, but on being natural. Her legend wasn't that of a great queen, but of a sweet kid who reigned over a band of playful pals', Caviglioli, op. cit., p.59.

25· 'It's all so French', ibid., p.59. Bardot also rejected several offers to work in Hollywood.

sun, which became increasingly available to the French middle classes during the years of her stardom.

Despite Juliette's aspiration to own a car in *Et Dieu créa . . . la femme*, she is never seen in one, and goes everywhere on foot or by bike. She links two opposed worlds: the tamed nature of the port, or of Carradine's luxury yacht, and the wild nature of the outdoors and of her own self. The latter is signified by her disdain for dress codes: she sits around the house in just a shirt, showing off her long legs; she sunbathes completely naked in the opening sequence; she wears her skirts and dresses unbuttoned to reveal her crotch; and she goes everywhere in bare feet. Wild nature is also expressed in the film by the dance sequences, most particularly the climactic mambo, whose Afro-Caribbean rhythms bring Juliette's illicit desires to the fore. Bardot's performance of this dance will be analysed shortly, but it is worth noting here that there are allusions to Africa as a traditional metaphor for unexplored (sexual) territory in the choice of the music and in the images of Juliette dancing erotically in tandem with the black percussionist. Four years after *Et Dieu . . . créa la femme*, a *Paris Match* feature showed Bardot in a hammock, wearing safari suit and pith helmet, while the text announced: '*Dans la jungle du cinéma, la rencontre d'une exploratrice et de son sauveur*'.[26] The reference here to Bardot as an explorer in the jungle mobilises again the metaphor of the dark continent, the mysterious uncharted area of female sexuality. Yet this is balanced by the familiar, infantilised cry for help which is the other side of Bardot's image. Hence she needs rescuing from the jungle by her saviour and supposed creator, Vadim, just as Juliette needs rescuing from the sea by Antoine.

THE SPECTACLE OF THE BODY

Bardot's image is centred on the display of her star body, but do her famous nude scenes and dance sequences position her as an object of desire for the (supposedly male) audience, or as a desiring subject with whom (supposedly female) fans can identify?[27] Recent accounts of Bardot's star image have emphasised the latter reading. An essay by Philippe Fraisse in *Positif* magazine describes Bardot's body as '*le représentant du désir féminin, [. . .] un corps désirant*'.[28] Fraisse contrasts the 'heroic' display of Bardot's nude body (in films such as *Et Dieu . . . créa la femme*, *En cas de malheur*, *Le Repos du guerrier* and *Le Mépris*) with the convention whereby the face is the index of stardom: '*au visage [. . .] de la Star, Brigitte Bardot oppose son corps nu, attitude indigne justement d'une star, mais [. . .] qui signifie: [. . .] je désire*'.[29]

26• 'In the film jungle, here's the meeting between a female explorer and her saviour', Anon., 'Brigitte: "Au secours Vadim!"', *Paris Match*, 24 December 1960, pp.128–9. The article went on to explain that Bardot had asked Vadim to direct her next film.

27• The description of viewing positions as inherently male or female is a problematic convention within film studies. For an excellent account of how viewing positions should not be held as gender specific, see C. Clover, *Men Women and Chain Saws: Gender in the Modern Horror Film*, London, BFI, 1992.

28• 'the representation of female desire, a desiring body', P. Fraisse, 'Toutes nues! Essai de théorie-fiction sur la nudité des comédiennes françaises', *Positif*, 495 (May 2002), p.16.

29• 'Bardot pits her naked body against the face of the Star. This attitude, unworthy of a star in fact, signifies "I desire"', ibid., p.16.

He concludes: '*Face au corps héroïquement dénudé de Brigitte Bardot, nous ne sommes plus face à un objet désirable fabriqué pour notre satisfaction égotiste, mais [. . .] à un autre être de désir comparable à nous*'.[30] A similar argument is made by Sarah Leahy when analysing Bardot's dance scenes in *La Femme et le pantin* (1959), *La Vérité* (1960) and *Et Dieu . . . créa la femme*. For Leahy, 'Bardot's dancing body refuses the objectification of the camera and the male gaze [. . .] so as to constitute herself as subject'.[31] Bardot's dances are 'expressions of her agency' and resist objectification because it is Bardot herself who, via her performance, controls the music and the camera work, both of which adapt themselves to her desires. Hence, in the celebrated mambo at the end of *Et Dieu . . . créa la femme*, she joins in the percussion, and leads the camera round the performance space, from one end of the room to the other, from dance floor to table and back again.

Leahy notes that in both *La Femme et le pantin* (for the flamenco) and *La Vérité* (for the jive) Bardot is filmed from the waist up, with the focus on her arms, breasts and hair.[32] The close-ups during the mambo from *Et Dieu . . . créa la femme*, however, are often shot lower down, showing Bardot's hips and legs, but also her crotch, which is displayed by her unbuttoned skirt. The erotic spectacle concludes with a pan up Bardot's body from her bare legs to her face, which is flushed and sweaty, her hair dishevelled. She shakes her head, grimaces, and makes biting motions with her mouth. Leahy remarks that 'the expression is one of pure *jouissance*', and that Bardot is here performing the orgasm displaced from the elided sex scene between Juliette and Antoine earlier in the film.[33] More generally, Bardot's dances function 'to express aspects of her star persona (sexual spectacle, challenge to bourgeois values, youthful rebellion)' and as 'an expression of frustration at [her] character's inability to make herself heard or understood [. . .] within the discourse of patriarchy embodied in the hero'.[34] Returning to the mambo in *Et Dieu créa . . . la femme*, we can read in Bardot's performance not just sexual pleasure but also a sense of distress, expressed facially rather than bodily. Her expression at the climax of the dance, directed towards Michel, is one of despair as well as ecstasy – despair that her ecstasy has no place in the married life that he represents: '*Affirmant son désir de manière directe, son insatisfaction fait le constat d'un monde dystopique [. . .] où les corps désirants n'ont pas de place*'.[35]

30· 'Confronted with the heroically bare body of Brigitte Bardot, we are no longer faced by a desirable object made for our own satisfaction, but by another desiring being, comparable to us', ibid., p.16.

31· S. Leahy, 'Bardot and dance: representing the real?', *French Cultural Studies*, 13:1, no.37 (February 2002), p.50.

32· See ibid., p.57.

33· Ibid., p.59.

34· Ibid., p.54.

35· 'Unambiguously affirming her desire, her dissatisfaction charts a dystopian world where desiring bodies have no place', Fraisse, op. cit., p.16.

CONCLUSION: PROBLEMATISING BARDOT

Bardot's star image is not entirely straightforward. Even if we accept that her 1950s persona was a 'simple' resolution of innocence and sex appeal, encoded as natural and joyful, it must be said that this image changed over time. It was complicated by controversies and renegotiations during the 1960s, so that by the time Bardot quit the cinema in 1973, it meant something rather different. When Bardot turned forty a year later, *Paris Match* reported that the only TV crew to be seen at her house were repairing the aerial. No longer able to prolong the summer of youth and fame, she was now associated with rain, winter, and the passing of time, even while she posed naked on the beach. [36] Her own brand of sunny outdoors eroticism, perceived as old fashioned, was contrasted with the colder, darker eroticism of the mid-1970s.[37] It was felt that in a time of political and social troubles in France (as well as elsewhere, notably the USA), Bardot's simple pleasures no longer held a meaning for her audience: '*Elle n'a rien à dire et rien à montrer à ceux qui doutent. Et nous doutons*'.[38]

However, the reading of Bardot as a sex kitten who couldn't grow up glosses over the renegotiation of her image during the 1960s. From the very start of the decade, her persona became darker and more troubled. In *La Vérité* (1960), she played a woman accused of murder, who ultimately kills herself. Later that year, and two years before Monroe's death, Bardot herself attempted suicide. Her characters in *Vie privée* (1961) and *Le Mépris* (1963), new wave reflections on the Bardot persona, die at the end of each film. Even the opening sequence of *Le Mépris*, with the camera celebrating her naked form in a reprise of the sunbathing scene from *Et Dieu ... créa la femme*, adds a questioning note as Camille (Bardot) asks Paul (Michel Piccoli) if he likes the various parts of her body. The star body itself no longer seems such a simple, innocent signifier. Morin has described *La Vérité* and *Vie privée* as demonstrating Bardot's '*ascension vers la spiritualité*'.[39] This was certainly a move away from her established star image, which dictated that BB was not spiritual or complex, but earthy and straightforward.

By 1962, her adult roles, erotic image and suicide attempts were interpreted by her younger fans as a betrayal. She was no longer a teenage idol.[40] The schoolgirl fringe, last seen in the 1950s, was a thing of the past. During the 1960s, Bardot had a second child, a second suicide attempt and a third husband. She made her last appearance at the Cannes film festival in 1967, before switching her focus to pop music. That same year Bardot, an international icon of female beauty, began a relationship with Serge Gainsbourg, a national icon of male ugliness, nick-named *L'homme à la tête de chou*.[41] This 1960s pairing of

---

36• See Caviglioli, op. cit., p.58.

37• See ibid., p.58. For more on erotic stars of the seventies, see Chapter 6.

38• 'She has nothing to say and nothing to show to those who feel doubt. Like us', ibid., p.59.

39• 'ascension towards the spiritual', Morin, op. cit., p.32.

40• See Anon., 'BB a-t-elle trahi la jeunesse?', *Age tendre, tête de bois*, 1 (November 1962), pp.34–9.

41• 'Cabbage Head'. Gainsbourg's affair with Bardot led to an eroticising of his own star image.

beauty and the beast resulted in the recording of several duets, including *Bonnie and Clyde*, *Initials BB* and the original version of *Je t'aime … moi non plus*. During this period, her liaison with Gainsbourg saw Bardot's celebrated 'natural' sexuality renegotiated via sado-masochistic imagery, notably her chained performance of *Harley Davidson* recorded with Gainsbourg for her television programme *Le show Bardot*. Once more, she was apparently trying to escape the constraints of her star image, and to reassert some kind of agency in its production.[42] The final step in this attempt to control her own image was, of course, to leave cinema altogether. That step means that Bardot's mature star image is not related to on-screen performance, but to activism in the field of animal rights. As early as 1962, she had denounced the cruelty of killing methods in French abattoirs, and campaigned successfully for the implementation of more humane practices. In 1986 she established her Foundation for animal rights. With her youth gone, Bardot has dissociated herself from the cult of the sex kitten, and has shifted the focus of her animalistic star image from herself to the animals themselves.

42· An example of this agency is the fact that the Bardot/Gainsbourg version of 'Je t'aime … moi non plus' was not released until 1986, at her request. The 1969 hit version was made with Jane Birkin.

CHAPTER 3

A glamorous political icon: Yves Montand's image paraded in Z (1968).

Politics and glamour: Yves Montand and Simone Signoret

MYTHS AND PROBLEMS OF STARDOM

Edgar Morin has noted that, under the classical star system, film stars were perceived as other, as a race apart, with a semi-divine glamour. '*Au zénith mythique du star system*,' it was understood that these gods and goddesses would stick to their own, and that '*La star doit, de préférence, aimer la star.*'[1] Hence, the mythic couples formed by Clark Gable and Carole Lombard, Elizabeth Taylor and Richard Burton, Alain Delon and Romy Schneider, Simone Signoret and Yves Montand.[2] The latter couple were married in 1951 and remained so until Signoret's death in 1985. When they met, each was already an established star in their own field – Signoret as a screen actress, Montand as a popular singer. As a star couple, they therefore combined the glamour of cinema with that of *la chanson*. Their first meeting was presented in entirely mythic terms, as a moment of timeless innocence and romance (see below). But their star images did not remain in the realm of the mythic, for two reasons. Firstly, their careers, although begun in the 1940s, outlived the classical period of film stardom to enter the more troubled, contested period of the sixties and seventies, when stardom became, according to Morin, less mythic and more problematic. Secondly, and perhaps related to the former, politics was a crucial factor in their activities and image.

Morin states that the period of classical film stardom, from 1930 to 1960, was characterised by '*la mythologie du bonheur*'.[3] From the 1960s onwards, with the deaths of James Dean and Marilyn Monroe, and the suicide attempt of Brigitte Bardot, this was replaced by '*la problématisation du bonheur*'.[4] It was in this problematic period that Hollywood stars became more politicised, most notably Jane Fonda, Montand's co-star in *Tout va bien* (1972). In France this tendency appears most clearly in the personae of Montand and Signoret, but it is important to note that their star images were, in fact, already politicised

---

1· 'At the mythic zenith of the star system, a star must, if possible, love another star' – E. Morin, *Les Stars*, third edition, Paris, Editions du Seuil, 1972, p.61. The subsequent examples are given by Morin.

2· The mythic status of these couples is such that even when they broke up (as with Taylor and Burton, or Delon and Schneider), they remained linked in the public perception.

3· 'the mythology of happiness' – Morin, op. cit., 146.

4· 'the problematising of happiness' – ibid., 146.

in the early 1950s, and hence are not limited to the 'counter-culture' and the issues of the 1960s and 1970s in the way that Fonda's political image is.[5] From their first months together, Signoret and Montand shared a very public commitment to politics. In 1950 they signed the *Appel de Stockholm* calling for the nuclear bomb to be banned. A year later they made public statements supporting the Rosenbergs,[6] and in 1956 Signoret accompanied Montand on his controversial singing tour of the USSR and the Eastern Bloc. Of course, their political activity (as with other elements of their star images) was individual as well as shared – for example, Signoret's signing of the *Manifeste des 343 salopes*, to declare that she supported the right to abortion at a time when this was still illegal in France. But their public image was one of mutual support and of political solidarity. Unable to join Signoret in signing the *Manifeste des 121* against the Algerian war because he was filming *Sanctuary* in Hollywood, Montand made his support for the manifesto clear on his return to France. Only in the closing years of their marriage did a political split appear between the two, when Signoret distanced herself from Montand's public attacks on the hard-line left in 1983. Although their disagreement was ideological, it was reported in terms associated with the end of romance or with separation.[7] This was an exception, however, to the strong solidarity which tended to characterise the public image of the couple. They were often pictured together, and their journeys, whether geographical (the USSR, Hollywood) or political (their move from supporting to rejecting Soviet communism) were generally made as a couple. When Signoret died of cancer, Montand's absence from her side was not interpreted as a sign of distance or disregard, but as melodramatic and even romantic, via her self-sacrifice and his suffering, as if Signoret were a romantic heroine sparing her lover the sight of her death: '*Dans sa douleur, Yves n'a pas même la consolation d'avoir été près de sa femme au moment du grand départ. "Pars sans crainte", lui avait-elle dit!*'.[8] Moreover, Montand's decision to continue filming *Jean de Florette* after her death was interpreted as a sign of common purpose with his wife, since '*elle tenait justement à ce que l'homme de sa vie, seule vraie star de la chanson française, soit également un grand acteur. En étant fidèle à un film, il semble l'être aussi à la volonté de Signoret.*'[9] Thus, solidarity is the watchword for this star couple even at its dissolution. And yet this is, in a sense, another myth which attaches to the star couple. For some commentators at least, the Signoret/Montand couple was destroyed by Montand's affair with Marilyn Monroe in 1960.[10] We shall see below how far this event

---

5· For more on Jane Fonda and politics, see R. Dyer, *Stars*, new edition, BFI, London, 1998, pp.77–83.

6· American communist sympathisers who were accused of treason and executed.

7· See the photo of the couple (torn in two) and the article 'Montand/Signoret: Leurs idées ne divorcent pas, elles font chambre à part', *Le Point*, October 1983, reproduced in M.Giniès, *Montand*, Paris, Vade Retro, 1995, p.158.

8· 'In his grief, Yves doesn't even have the consolation of having been at his wife's side during her final moments. "Go without fear", she had told him!' – *France-Dimanche*, 30 September 1985, reproduced in Giniès, op. cit., p.162.

9· 'she wanted the man in her life, the one great star of French song, to also be a great actor. In being faithful to a film, it seems that he is also being faithful to Signoret's wishes' – 'Montand: et maintenant', *VSD*, 10-16 October 1985, reproduced in Giniès, op. cit., p.162.

10· See, for example, S.Hayward, 'Simone Signoret 1921-1985: the star as sign – the sign as scar', in D. Knight and J. Still (eds), *Women and Representation*, Nottingham, WIF Publications, 1995, pp.57–74.

problematised Signoret's image in particular, and also that of the star couple she formed with Montand.

MONTAND: SOLIDARITY AND THE STAR

For Montand as an individual star, the question of solidarity is crucial, since it raises issues related not only to politics generally, but specifically to class. His social origins and his move away from them, thanks to international stardom, are succinctly expressed by Montand himself in an interview from 1974:

> *Fils d'émigrés italiens, ayant moi-même été ouvrier, pauvre petit Rital, je pouvais alors exprimer le peuple. Je ne me reconnais plus ce droit. Les ouvriers, je ne suis plus des leurs. Reste la solidarité . . .*[11]

As an Italian immigrant growing up in Marseilles, Montand (then called Ivo Livi) witnessed union solidarity in the factory where he worked at the age of twelve: '*c'est là que j'ai découvert la solidarité, la chaleur humaine*'.[12] His early career as a singer in the music-hall tradition saw him pejoratively defined by his class when nicknamed '*le prolo chantant*'.[13] As an established star of *la chanson*, his repertoire included pacifist songs (*Quand un soldat va-t-en guerre*), vignettes of urban alienation (*Luna Park*) and '*un disque à tendance progressiste*',[14] the 1955 album *Les Chansons populaires de France*. It was as a singer that he became famous in America, after the McCarthyite ban on himself and Signoret visiting the USA was lifted in 1959. His singing tour was celebrated by reference to the glamour of Hollywood's biggest female stars, with endorsements from Marilyn Monroe ('*Quel homme! Il me donne la chair de poule!*'), Marlène Dietrich ('*Il est beau . . . et sensuel*') and Paulette Godard ('*Sa voix . . . j'en rêve!*').[15] Unsurprisingly, his subsequent film performances in Hollywood – as a millionaire opposite Monroe in *Let's Make Love* (1960), as a racing driver in *Grand Prix* (1966) and as a hypnotist in *On a Clear Day You Can See Forever* (1970) – often relied on his singing, and tended to situate Montand far from his roots. Even in France, his film work very rarely placed him in relation to the working class. When it did so, the relation could be problematic, as in *Tout va bien* (see below). The role which was deemed by the press to be most authentically 'true' to Montand's own personality was that of a troubled, bourgeois romantic in *César et Rosalie* (1972). But his solidarity with political causes, and

---

11· 'As the son of Italian immigrants, having myself been a worker, a poor little Wop, I could embody the people. I no longer feel that I have that right. I'm no longer a worker. But the solidarity remains . . .' – Montand cited in C. Mauriac, 'Chris Marker filme Yves Montand', *Le Figaro*, 18 December 1974, reproduced in Giniès, op. cit., p.119.

12· 'that's where I discovered solidarity, humanity and warmth' – 'La peine et l'argent', *Candide*, 22 May 1967, reproduced in Giniès, op. cit., p.5.

13· 'the singing pleb'.

14· 'a progressive album' – Montand cited in F. Granier, 'Confession sensationnelle d'Yves Montand', *Cinérevue* (1955), reproduced in Giniès, op. cit., p.36.

15· 'What a man! He gives me goose-pimples!'; 'He is handsome . . . and sensual'; 'His voice . . . I dream of it!' – *Paris Jour*, 5 May 1959, reproduced in Giniès, op. cit., p.70.

above all his desire to speak a language of politics that a working-class audience could understand, were an essential part of his mature star image, as we shall see.

Sound cinema had precipitated the advent of the singer as film star, with Bing Crosby in the USA and Luis Mariano in France,[16] but Montand's efforts to make the same transition were, for a long time, unsuccessful. For the twenty years between *Les Portes de la nuit* (1946) and *Compartiment tueurs* (1965), Montand felt that his cinema career was that of a dilettante.[17] The closing years of classical cinema – when Signoret was at the height of her fame – saw Montand undertake only two important starring roles, in *Le Salaire de la peur* (1953) and *Let's Make Love* (1960). The vast press interest in the latter was due not to Montand's performance, but to rumours of an affair with Monroe which may have contributed to the break-up of her marriage with Henry Miller.[18] In the United States, Montand remained a singer who also acted. His star image there was thus noticeably lighter and less serious than in France, as is clear from the report on his return to Hollywood to shoot the musical *On a Clear Day You Can See Forever* in 1968: '*C'est en chantant et en dansant qu'Yves Montand va faire sa rentrée à Hollywood*.'[19] While he sang and danced in France too, Montand added to this a political gravitas which reflected his activities both on and off screen. When he finally became a star of French cinema in the late 1960s, it was largely thanks to a series of films for the Greek émigré director Costa-Gavras: *Compartiment tueurs* (1965), *Z* (1968), *L'Aveu* (1969), and *Etat de siège* (1973). Apart from the first, a whodunnit, the latter three films are explicitly political. Thus, Montand's ascension to film stardom – at least in France – was *directly* associated with politics, in a way that Signoret's was not.

Before making the political trilogy with Costa-Gavras, Montand gave his first explicitly political performance in Alain Resnais's *La Guerre est finie* (1966), a film written by the exiled Spaniard Jorge Semprun, who went on to write *Z* and to become a close friend of Montand. In *La Guerre est finie*, Montand stars as a Spanish radical based in France, who organises covert activity in Spain against Francos's fascist dictatorship. The film foregrounds Montand's performance by reiterating the multiple identities assumed by his character, Diego (also known in the film as Domingo, Carlos and René). There are repeated shots of Montand looking in the mirror, preparing his various roles, while the dialogue emphasises the formation and delivery of identity.[20] In this way, the performance comments not only on an underground world of danger and subterfuge, but also obliquely on Montand's own star image, in which the role of Diego is an identity-defining moment, suggesting a move towards an on-screen politics to match his off-screen politics. This trend continues in *Z*, the

---

16• See Morin, op. cit., p. 29.

17• See F. Roche, 'Yves Montand', *France-Soir*, 8 June 1965, reproduced in Giniès, op. cit., p.78.

18• See, for example, S. Groueff, 'Beauté et intelligence divorcent: pourquoi', *Paris Match,* 607 (26 November 1960), pp.46–55.

19• 'Yves Montand will return to Hollywood singing and dancing' – *France-Soir*, 12 June 1968, reproduced in Giniès, op. cit., p.114.

20• One could compare Montand's performance in the gangster thriller *Le Cercle rouge* (1970) which, although in a very different context, again stresses mirror compositions and the repeated transformation of Montand's character into various alternative selves (drunkard, marksman, gentleman, gangster).

first and most successful of the Costa-Gavras trilogy, but what distinguishes *Z* from *La Guerre est finie* is the glamour of Montand's role. In the earlier film, Montand is physically restricted, almost always seen in a shirt, tie, jumper and jacket. His face is consistently tense, his movements stiff and careful, as if always thought out as part of a plan of action. Although politically committed to a dangerous cause, his character is a thinker above all else. The two sex scenes in the film almost ignore Montand to concentrate on the female characters (he is invisible in the first, and only glimpsed, half-naked, towards the end of the second). By contrast, *Z* posits Montand's character as a multifaceted star, a man of glamour, physical prowess and sex appeal as well as political intellect. These were already attributes of Montand as a singer and public figure, but had not yet been incarnated by him on screen with any success. *Z* changed that and crystallised the image of Montand at the end of the sixties as a political *and* glamorous film star.

The identification of Montand with his role in *Z* is illustrated by a headline from *Paris-Jour*, which shrieked, in April 1968: '*Yves Montand assassiné comme John Kennedy*'.[21] Moreover, the analogy with JFK succinctly equips Montand the political actor/activist with the youthful charisma and sex appeal that were part of the Kennedy myth. These elements are stressed throughout the film. If in *La Guerre est finie* Montand was an underground militant, here he is a celebrity. He plays the leader of the democratic opposition movement in Greece, confronting a military clique. Known simply as 'Z' or 'the Doctor', he is a media star who combines bravery with brains (hence his two nicknames, one recalling the bandit Zorro and the other revealing his intellectual credentials). He dresses in a suit and has gravitas, yet he also experiences sexual desire (in a fantasy/flashback sequence). Like a film star or a president, he makes his entrance descending the steps of a jet (in a sequence later reworked, ironically, throughout *Etat de siège*). As a journalist helpfully explains while the camera tracks forwards and then zooms in on Montand,

C'est le nouveau visage de l'opposition. Avant lui, c'était le désert. Les jeunes sont avec lui, et les jeunes filles en fleur. [. . .] Champion olympique dans sa jeunesse, médecin, professeur à l'université, et il est plutôt honnête – parfait![22]

The stress on athleticism offsets the political gravity, and revivifies an element of Montand's early star image – one of his songs, *Battling Joe*, was about a boxer, and a 1948 headline called him '*Athlète de la chanson*'.[23] Physical prowess is also reiterated in the compositions showing Montand taller than his colleagues, and in the references to his exceptional heart – attacked by thugs, he is left brain-damaged and clinically dead, but his heart is still beating. In other words, the Doctor's politics, like Montand's, are characterised by solidarity and warmth: he is all heart. Flashbacks after his death

---

21· 'Yves Montand assassinated like John Kennedy', see Giniès, op. cit., p.109.

22· 'He's the new face of the opposition. Before him there was nobody. The young men and women all support him. He was an Olympic champion in his youth, now he's a doctor, a professor at the university, and honest with it – he's perfect!'

23· 'The athlete of song', cited in Giniès, op. cit., p.11.

strengthen the impression by showing Z smiling with his wife and children (another cliché given a bitter twist in *Etat de siège*). His supporters parade iconic posters showing Z's photo through the streets; the film ends with a still of his face and the slogan '*il est vivant*'.[24] In sum, *Z* mythologises Montand as a political celebrity with everything, including the immortal glamour of the true star.

Z is a rare case in Montand's filmography. His other political roles, including two more for Costa-Gavras, are much more problematic. For *L'aveu* he lost twelve kilos in six weeks to play Arthur London, victim of the communist regime in Czechoslovakia. The performance required a political realignment as well as a physical one, since it was only now that Montand and Signoret (who played London's wife, Lise) were fully confronted with the excesses of Stalinism. As Signoret herself said, '*Montand se sentait très culpabilisé*'.[25] In *Etat de siège* Montand was the villain, a CIA agent named Santore operating in a South American country. The romanticised representation of Montand as a political star in *Z* was now turned on its head, with various sequences throughout *Etat de siège* formally repeating the shots of Montand descending from a jet or relaxing, posing with his family. But these images were now shown to be rhetoric, propaganda, and were demythologised by the running commentary in the film provided by the freedom fighters who kidnap Santore and question him. Thus, *Etat de siège* tends to interrogate the iconic images of stardom that had been so effective in *Z*.

Montand's political commitment continued to inform his film work even when the roles themselves were in no way politicised. Thus, his successful comic performance opposite Louis de Funès in *La Folie des grandeurs* (1971) only took place after Montand had refused to travel to Spain to star in the film unless nine Basque militants, facing execution, were pardoned. It is a measure of Montand's stardom, and of his political influence, that General Franco agreed to his terms and the film went ahead. A year later Montand starred opposite Jane Fonda in Godard and Gorin's *Tout va bien* (1972). A reflection on the aftermath of the events of May '68, the film has a left-wing bourgeois couple, Jacques (Montand) and Susan (Fonda) caught up in a factory occupation which serves as a reminder of the spirit of '68. Significantly, the couple are locked up with the boss by the striking workers, an act which categorises Jacques and Susan as the class enemy of the proletariat. When the strike ends, the film explores how Jacques and Susan have been led to rethink their relation to one another, to work, and to May '68 by their experience in the factory. Godard and Gorin's declared intention is to urge individuals to '*se penser historiquement*'.[26] For Susan, a journalist, this involves a determination to re-politicise her reporting and to place her relationship with Jacques in the context of work, rather than simply one of sex/romance/leisure. For Jacques, it means rethinking his own passivity

---

24• 'he is alive'. We are told that this is the meaning of 'Z' in ancient Greek. Compare the refusal on the part of some fans to acknowledge that stars such as James Dean and Elvis Presley are actually dead.

25• 'Montand felt very guilty', *France-Soir*, 18 November 1976, reproduced in Giniès, op. cit., p.114.

26• 'think of themselves historically'.

during the factory occupation and since May '68. The character of Jacques obviously reflects some of Godard's political concerns and compromises: like Godard, Jacques is a filmmaker who abandoned cinema in 1968 and now shoots commercials while ruminating on various vague political projects.[27] But many of the concerns expressed are also relevant to Montand's politics: like Montand, Jacques supported the Rosenbergs and campaigned against the Algerian War. He is a sympathiser with various causes rather than an agent of political change. Hence, he confesses to using his fame and behaving like a intellectual – signing manifestoes but never immersing himself fully in political struggle. This self-criticism reflects the fraught position of the bourgeois radical (shared by Godard, Montand and Fonda),[28] and is a key example of how Montand's star image problematises his relation to his own class origins and to political struggle.[29]

However, while *Tout va bien* could thus be said to dramatise Montand's relation to political struggle, it also confirms his stardom in terms that are, in some ways, comparable to those established by his iconic performance in *Z*. Those terms were athleticism, sex appeal, physical strength and intellect. To these one might add the power of the voice, represented in *Z* by the Doctor's political speeches, and a fundamental part of Montand's star image as both actor and singer. *Tout va bien* catalogues these components of Montand's stardom. An early sequence introduces Montand and Fonda as the film's stars. In a parody of the famous introduction to Bardot in Godard's *Le Mépris* (1963), Montand tells Fonda, *'J'aime tes yeux, j'aime ta bouche, j'aime tes genoux, j'aime ton cul, j'aime tes cheveux, j'aime tes mains.'*[30] Fonda then tells Montand, *'J'aime ton front, et j'aime tes jambes, et j'aime tes couilles, et j'aime tes épaules, et j'aime ta bouche.'*[31] While Fonda's attributes here signify the romantic or the sexual (thus recalling her early star image, which was comparable to Bardot's and in no way political), Montand's are clearly more diverse: intellect (*'ton front'*), but also athleticism (*'tes jambes'*), sex (*'tes couilles'*), work/physical strength (*'tes épaules'*) and language (*'ta bouche'*). The complete image combines the power of intellect and language with physicality and the world of work. Like his character in *Z*, Montand appears to have everything. A star feature from *Candide* magazine in 1967 constructs a similar image. Montand is photographed playing *boules* and cards, relaxing with his wife after a meal, and splashing in the pool, as well as reading or talking with the poet Jacques Prévert.[32] The intellectual connotations here (literature, poetry) are balanced by an emphasis on the less rarefied pleasures of life. The same effect is achieved by the text, which matches intellectual activity with the more 'ordinary' pursuits of leisure and romance: *'Entre deux recitals, deux*

27• This is a rather self-deprecatory caricature of Godard, who had actually made several political film-tracts with Gorin in the early 1970s, as well as the infamous adverts for Dim tights.

28• For an account of Fonda's star image in relation to 'white radicalism', see Dyer, op. cit., pp.78–9.

29• Montand's performance in *Tout va bien* only deepened the political conflict between himself and his brother, Julien Livi, an official in the (communist) union the CGT. See Giniès, op. cit., p.117.

30• 'I love your eyes, your mouth, your knees, your arse, your hair, your hands'.

31• 'I love your forehead, and your legs, and your balls, and your shoulders, and your mouth.'

32• See *Candide*, 25 May 1967, reproduced in Giniès, op. cit., pp.82–4. Note that the overly cerebral connotations of literature are offset by the fact that Montand is shown reading in his swimming trunks!

tournages, aujourd'hui, Montand sait savourer les moments de détente et même prendre le temps pour lire, jouer, ou aimer.'[33] As regards politics, Montand restates his solidarity with various causes (and his own independence from political parties), but does so in an everyday language that *Candide* contrasts with the usual 'empty phrases' of politicians.[34]

Montand's use of language consistently displays a common touch, which obviates any danger of his star image being limited to the ghetto of the intellectual. This is apparent even after he entered the realm of 'official' politics in the mid-1980s, with a series of interviews and TV broadcasts in which he outlined his alarm at events in the USSR, Poland and Afghanistan. In 1983, *Le Point* magazine praised Montand for expressing himself with '*une verve gourmande et vengeresse qui fait voler en éclats la langue de bois de la classe politique*',[35] and characterised him as a superstar who was also a man of the people. For the next three years, Montand was regarded as a potential presidential candidate.[36] The phrase '*appeler un chat un chat*'[37] was used repeatedly to describe his down-to-earth language. His ability to talk directly to the people was famously evident when, during an interview, he turned to address the TV audience as '*Vous*', in a gesture that recalls similar scenes from *Z* and *Tout va bien*. Although he never actually ran for office, Montand campaigned on various causes and continued to sing and to act. An indication of his popularity is given by a *Paris Match* survey from 1982, which saw him voted favourite actor of 1981, ahead of Jean-Paul Belmondo in second and Gérard Depardieu in third.[38] But Depardieu – Montand's co-star in *Le Choix des armes* (1981) and *Jean de Florette* (1986) – was critical of Montand's entry into politics:

Je peux vraiment pas rentrer dans l'image Montand-politique. [. . .] Je connais le Montand d'entre deux prises, avec sa force méditerranéenne, sa bonté, ses angoisses, ce Montand qui n'a pas d'âge. Le Montand de la politique est automatiquement plus restreint.[39]

The Mediterranean Montand evoked here by Depardieu, is closely associated with the land and the nostalgic myth of 'the 'ordinary' Frenchman whose roots are in his ancestors'

33• 'These days, Montand knows how to savour the relaxing moments between two recitals or two film shoots, taking the time to read, to play, to love', P. Giannoli, 'Yves Montand dit tout', *Candide*, 25 May 1967, reproduced in Giniès, op. cit., p.84.

34• See ibid., p.84.

35• 'a hungry and vengeful verve which shatters the stiff language of the political class', P. Billard, 'La Vedette politique de septembre est un chanteur-comédien', *Le Point*, 3 October 1983, reproduced in Giniès, op. cit., p.156.

36• See, for example, M. Gonod, 'Montand en première ligne', *Paris Match*, 20 June 1986.

37• 'to call a spade a spade'. See for instance C. Sarraute, 'Montand president?', *Le Monde*, January 1984, reproduced in Giniès, op. cit., p.159.

38• See V. Merlin, 'L'Année Montand', *Paris Match*, 5 March 1982, p.40.

39• 'I can't really relate to the image of the political Montand. I know the Montand between takes, with his Mediterranean strength, his generosity and his anxieties, the ageless Montand. The Montand of politics is automatically more limited', O.Dazat, 'Gérard Depardieu en liberté', *Cinématographe*, 121 (July/August 1986), p.22.

terroir.[40] Like Jean Gabin, and later Depardieu, Montand bought himself a farm, declaring: '*Je suis fils de paysans et j'avais toujours rêvé d'avoir un lopin de terre.*'[41] His link to the land was most strongly expressed in his great late performance in two Pagnol adaptations, *Jean de Florette* and *Manon des sources* (both 1986). Marcel Pagnol, a film maker and novelist strongly associated with Marseilles and Provence, had attended Montand and Signoret's wedding at St Paul de Vance in the same region. Montand himself had grown up in Marseilles and had retained a slight southern accent, which was exaggerated in his performance as the peasant patriarch César, a character he likened to his Italian grandfather. Yet even this sense of rootedness in '*la France profonde*' did not go unquestioned, since *IP5* (1991) saw him play an elderly mystic who wanders in the woods but is in many ways a flawed and decrepit figure. In his final film role, Montand's glamorous and rooted star body is dismantled and revealed to be ageing, frail and vulnerable.[42]

Montand's star image (as an actor, not a singer) is principally about contestation, about politics, solidarity and struggle. In the words of Pierre Billard, '*Héros de la mauvaise conscience moderne, Montand est porteur de plus d'exigence que d'espérances, de plus de lucidité que de promesses.*'[43] To return to Edgar Morin's terminology, Montand personifies '*la problématisation du bonheur*' (the problematisation of happiness). This appears, at first, to hold less true for Signoret, whose early star image is classical, and can seem mythic rather than problematic. However, as we shall see, Signoret's late image in particular tends to call into question several of the codes of classical female stardom.

SIGNORET: GLAMOUR DECONSTRUCTED

Signoret is a classical film star in a way that Montand is not, since her film career was at its height in the period 1945–1960, when Montand was still known primarily as a singer. Susan Hayward has called this period 'the "beauty" years' as far as Signoret's star body is concerned.[44] We can also apply to this period Morin's phrase '*la mythologie du bonheur*' (the mythology of happiness). A key moment in this mythologising of happiness and of the beautiful star body is the account of how Signoret and Montand met and fell in love. As told by Montand, the anecdote centres on Signoret, and introduces the symbolism of doves, a figure of innocence which recurs in photos of Signoret from this period:

40• G. Vincendeau, *Stars and Stardom in French Cinema,* London & New York, Continuum, 2000, p.72.

41• 'I'm from peasant stock, and I always dreamed of having a plot of land', Montand cited in Granier, op. cit., p.36. Montand's farm was actually in Normandy (as was Gabin's), not in Provence.

42• Montand died on the last day of the shoot. For a reading of *IP5* as dismantling Montand's star body, see P. Powrie, *Jean-Jacques Beineix*, Manchester, Manchester University Press, 2001, pp.184–195.

43• 'A hero of the modern bad conscience, Montand is more demanding than hopeful, more lucid than promising', cited in Giniès, op. cit., p.124.

44• S. Hayward, 'Setting the Agenders: Simone Signoret – The Pre-Feminist Star Body', in A. Hughes and J.S.Williams (eds), *Gender and French Cinema*, Oxford and New York, Berg, 2001, p.109.

Au milieu de la cour, entourée d'impondérables colombes, il y a une jeune femme [...]. Elle sourit comme les jeunes filles des peintres italiens d'autrefois. Je sais qu'elle s'appelle Simone Signoret, je n'ai jamais vu ses films, je ne la connais pas, mais je sais que je vais marcher vers elle, en essayant de ne pas soulever les colombes, et lui dire deux ou trois phrases comme ça, n'importe lesquelles ...[45]

As Montand himself acknowledged, this idyllic moment was, in fact, a myth, a romantic picture that he and Signoret fed to the press. But this of little importance. As regards Signoret's star image, this moment's power is associated not with any claim to veracity, but with the symbolising of abstracts such as youth, classical beauty, happiness and innocence in the person of a young actress. This is reinforced, moreover, by the repeated symbolism of the doves, prominent in at least three publicity photos of Signoret at this period (including one actually taken at the wedding in 1951),[46] and present in the name of the restaurant (*La Colombe d'Or*) where the couple often met and where the wedding reception took place.

This off-screen image of romantic innocence, under the sign of the dove, contrasts quite markedly with Signoret's on-screen performances of the time, which saw her consistently cast as 'a prostitute or a scheming woman'.[47] The received image of Signoret in her 'beauty years' is one of seduction and power, even cruelty. Montand calls her '*radieusement belle*' but also '*parfois cruelle*';[48] Hayward notes that, 'In fanzines of the time [...] her gaze is often described as ironic, volcanic, cruel and disturbing'.[49] Roles such as that of the scheming manipulator, Nicole, in *Les Diaboliques* (1954) seem to reinforce the elements of control, power and cruelty in her star image. But this image is also softened in 1950s representations of her romance and married life with Montand, which include photo spreads of the couple in rustic clothes on their farm in Normandy, or coping with the everyday pressures of stardom in their Paris apartment.[50] In some of these features, Signoret is associated with motherhood and domesticity. This association is largely spatial (she is seen in a domestic space, at the table, or cooking in the kitchen), but despite the references to Catherine Allégret, Signoret's daughter from her first marriage, there are very few images of mother and daughter together. Catherine was largely shielded from

---

45• 'In the middle of the courtyard, surrounded by innumerable doves, is a young woman. She smiles like the young girls in Italian paintings from long ago. I know that she's called Simone Signoret, I've never seen her films and I don't know her, but I know that I'm going to walk towards her, trying not to startle the doves, and I'm going to say something to her, anything , it doesn't matter what ...', Montand cited in Giniès, op. cit., p.33.

46• See ibid., pp.34, 47, and 48. Montand is present in two of these photos but the focus is on Signoret and the doves are most clearly associated with her (she is holding, releasing, or feeding them).

47• Hayward, 'Setting the Agenders', p.109. Roughly half of the films Signoret made from 1945 to 1960 saw her play a 'tart' character, as in *Dédée d'Anvers* (1948), *La Ronde* (1950) and *Casque d'or* (1952).

48• 'radiantly beautiful, sometimes cruel', Montand cited in Granier, op. cit., p.36.

49• Hayward, 'Setting the Agenders', p.113.

50• See, for example, Giniès, op. cit., pp. 98 and 38–9.

the media, and was rarely photographed until the sixties. Thus, the maternal facet of Signoret's persona remains peripheral, and tends to be obscured by other facets.

The absence of a strong maternal image for Signoret adds weight to Susan Hayward's view that in 'the beauty years', Signoret 'communicated not myths of woman but something else'.[51] This 'something else' can be summarised as various forms of resistance: political resistance to the Cold War, the Algerian War, and certain domestic policies (such as the denial of abortion rights); historical Resistance in representing the French struggle against Occupation; and a 'resistance to the ideological construction of the gendered subject'.[52] The first form is evident in her political activism, often alongside Montand. The second is evident in her performances in *Les Démons de l'aube* (1946), *Against the Wind* (1947), and *L'Armée des ombres* (1969), wherein she embodies 'the female presence within the Resistance'.[53] The third form is the least explicit, but can be read in the lesbian subtext of films such as *Les Diaboliques* and *Les Mauvais Coups* (1961).[54] It also informs the representation of her star body, which did not conform to the conventional objectification of film actresses in the fifties, as Hayward observes:

> Because of the metonymic, erotic power of her eyes and lips, Signoret's *body* was not fetishized [. . .] as Martine Carol's and Brigitte Bardot's bodies were. Signoret is never shot in the nude (Carol and Bardot were). [. . .] She embodied the freedom of a sexually-potent woman, as opposed to the infantile-nubile sexuality Bardot conveyed.[55]

The emphasis on Signoret's eyes at the expense of her (unseen) body is evident in *La Ronde* and *Room at the Top* (1959), even though in both films she plays sexualised women and appears in love scenes. Publicity photos from the 1950s and 1960s also tend to obscure her body, which is habitually covered up by coats, suits, trousers and jackets.[56]

Signoret had always opted out of the ritual of identification that informs stardom:

> Hordes of young girls never copied my hairdoes or the way I talk or the way I dress. I have, therefore, never had to go through the stress of perpetuating an image that's often the equivalent of one particular song that forever freezes a precise moment of one's youth.[57]

51· Hayward, 'Setting the Agenders', p.109.

52· Ibid., p.112.

53· Ibid., p.112.

54· For more on a possible 'queer reading' of these films, see ibid., pp.114–19.

55· Ibid., pp.113 and 120, italics in original.

56· See for example Giniès, op. cit., pp.33, 38–9, 46–7, 49, 61, 62, 65, 69, 73 and 80.

57· Quotation from Signoret at www.http://us.imdb.com/Bio?Signoret,+Simone. For more on patterns of identification between fans and stars, see Morin, op. cit., p.90, and J.Stacey, *Star Gazing: Hollywood Cinema and Female Spectatorship*, London, Routledge, 1994.

This ability to move on from a previous image is characteristic of Signoret, and is a sharp contrast with the 'eternal' image cultivated by stars like Catherine Deneuve and Isabelle Adjani. Signoret's (willing) loss of youth, beauty and glamour is dramatised in very tragic and pessimistic terms by her performance in *Le Chat* (1971), but the actual process began at least ten years earlier in her career. According to Hayward, 'Signoret's stunning looks "deteriorated" in a rapid five-year period (1961–66) – her body, many film critics asserted, having become the site of emotional scars.' By the late 1960s, 'her body was showing all the signs of being ravaged by the consequences of her assuming the right to auto-determination/destruction', and 'she had progressed from the "flawless" French beauty of the 1950s to a different set of signs: woman as the site of suffering/ageing.'[58] Hayward cites the beginning of these changes in 1960, with the affair between Montand and Monroe and hence Signoret's supposed sense of betrayal. When Montand returned to Signoret, there was a perception that French womanhood had defeated American womanhood, but 'the betrayal left its scars', and 'in five years' time – at the age of 45 – Signoret's looks had radically altered'.[59] Hayward is certainly right to mention the role that cancer played in Signoret's visible deterioration, and to point out the increased popularity that the mature roles of the 1970s brought her, but the Montand/Monroe affair is perhaps not the crucial turning-point. For the shift in Signoret's star image (from youth and beauty to age and suffering) can be identified a year earlier, in a key performance from 1959, her Oscar-winning role as Alice in the British 'kitchen-sink' drama *Room At the Top*. As Signoret herself acknowledged, this performance (given at the age of thirty-seven, but representing a woman well into her forties) marked a watershed in her career.[60]

What distinguishes Signoret's performance in *Room at the Top* is not that it is in English, or even that she won an Oscar for it, but that it centres on her character's age and the anxiety this creates (for her and for others). Signoret plays Alice, an unhappily-married French woman living in the North of England. She becomes a friend and then a lover of Joe (Laurence Harvey), who is at least fifteen years younger than her. Alice is characterised in two distinct ways. Firstly, she is an eroticised older woman, an object of exotic attraction and fantasy, whose nationality signifies sex. A minor character declares that 'Alice is all woman', and she is first introduced with the words 'Sex! Terrific! Alice Aysgill – she's French.' Alice's charisma and sex appeal are linked not just to her place of birth, but also to her brand of amateur stardom: she is the leading lady of the local dramatic society. In an early sequence, we see her in front of her dressing-room mirror – an association with the glamour of 'real' stardom – but as the film develops, the symbolism of the mirrored compositions changes and her powerful, exotic image is gradually obscured by one of age and vulnerability. She is repeatedly called 'an old whore' and when Joe breaks with her, he sarcastically asks 'What did you do 50 years ago back in the Great War?' The dichotomy within her character is reflected in the lighting for the film: at times Signoret is

---

58• Hayward, 'Simone Signoret 1921–1985', pp.59 and 60.

59• Ibid., p.62.

60• See A. Carbonnier, 'Simone, Signoret: les deux images', *Cinéma*, 323 (October 1985), p.3.

lit with a bright glow that makes her blonde hair shine and erases any lines on her face (as in the still for the film poster, and the scene of her first kiss with Joe). At other times, however, and even within the same sequence, Signoret's face is shown in half-shadow or in contrastive lighting which reveals the lines on her forehead and around her mouth. The discourse of ageing is most insistently represented, however, in the mirror scenes that recur throughout the film.

Where the mirrored compositions of Signoret in *Les Mauvais Coups* seem to reflect 'a lesbian narrative',[61] here they have a more negative function: to underline Alice's insecurity about her appearance and her age. Alice contradicts her claim to be proud of her own body when she tells Joe, 'I'm too old to walk about in my girdle.' As Hayward notes, the sexualised body was never part of Signoret's star image, but here its absence from view is related to Signoret's performance of anxiety. Alice retires behind a screen to dress after sex; later she surreptitiously looks at herself in a compact mirror, trying to smooth the lines on her neck. After her final rejection by Joe she stands, drunk, in a pub and stares at her image reflected *ad infinitum* by multiple mirrors. She then staggers off screen, having been unable to change or accept what she saw. The next we hear of Alice, she has died horrifically in a suicidal car crash, which left her 'totally mutilated'. Thus, in *Room at the Top* Signoret enacts the despair of ageing and the destruction of the star body a year before the Montand/Monroe affair, and long before her related roles of the 1970s.[62]

Key among these late roles is Signoret's performance in *Le Chat*. She and Jean Gabin star as Clémence and Julien, an elderly couple locked in a miserable and hate-filled marriage. The destruction of their earlier selves, their previous love for each other, and their physical capacities, is symbolised in the film's setting, as the old housing around them is demolished to make way for the construction of a new Paris of concrete and glass. Their own house is condemned, and they are served with a notice of eviction. If the wrecking ball that Clémence watches from behind her curtains is an image of the devouring power of time, so too is the sinister black garbage lorry, which makes its way slowly up the street towards her, grinding and growling. It is no coincidence that the cat of the title (her husband's pet and hence, in a sense, her rival for his love) ends up dead in the rubbish that is consumed by the lorry. This is Clémence and Julien's destination too, since the lorry signifies death, and they both die at the end of the film.

Playing Julien, Gabin is white-haired and crotchety, but has a sturdy appearance even at 67. The signs of ageing and physical collapse are in fact more marked in Signoret's performance, given at the age of only fifty. As Clémence, she limps and coughs in an

---

61. Hayward,, 'Setting the Agenders', p.117.

62. Her performance can be linked to Montand's affair in that it dramatises insecurity within a romantic couple. A similar insecurity may perhaps be detected in the photos of Signoret and Montand from this period, which tend to show Montand as the object of Signoret's desire: she is often looking at him, while he fails to return her gaze. This is most evident in an informal photograph of the couple with Arthur Miller and Marilyn Monroe in April 1960: while Montand and Monroe face each other across the table, Signoret is caught running her hand through her hair and glancing at Montand with an expression of apprehension and anxiety. See Giniès, op. cit., p.91 and also p.98.

exaggerated manner. Her heavily-lined face is frequently shown in close-ups as Clémence (like Alice in *Room at the Top*) looks anxiously in the mirror. She is repeatedly reminded by Julien of her age and ugliness, and yet Clémence, rather like Alice, could almost have been a star. In this case, the hint at stardom comes from the circus, not the theatre troupe. Framed photos on the walls and occasional flashbacks reveal the young Clémence, a beautiful and athletic trapeze artist with whom Julien fell in love. But these images are contained, fixed in the past, held tight in the photographic frames or the irises that close the flashbacks. The only vestiges of her faded glamour that remain are to be found in Clémence's dress (a red kaftan) and her gestures (drinking rum, smoking black cigarillos). As in *Room at the Top*, the character's deterioration is signalled by the lighting. Flashbacks to a relatively recent period show Signoret herself playing the middle-aged Clémence in a golden haze, the glow acting as a figure for idealising memory and also softening the lines on Signoret's face. In contrast, the present of the narrative, lit in duller tones, repeatedly shows a heavy, wrinkled and puffy face, scowling in the mirror, the eyes full of hurt. At one point, when she and her husband are still talking, Clémence says, '*J'étais belle, tu te souviens?*', to which he replies '*Je me souviens, oui. [. . .] T'étais parfaite*'.[63] But for Clémence, as for Signoret, the youthful image is lost in the past, to be replaced by age, ugliness and infirmity. It is a loss that kills Clémence, but which allows Signoret to live fully in her mature roles from the seventies and early eighties.

CONCLUSION: GENDER AND AGEING, GLAMOUR AND POLITICS

In film stardom, as elsewhere, there is a double standard about ageing and gender. Age is presented as a problem for women, but not for men. This has been a convention throughout film history and is still apparent in cinema today (most notably in Hollywood, but also in France). A female star is always under threat from ageing, since, as Morin puts it,

Un jour les rides et les bouffissures [. . .] seront ineffaçables. La star livrera son ultime combat, à la suite duquel elle devra se résoudre à cesser d'être amoureuse, c'est-à-dire d'être jeune, belle, c'est-à-dire d'être star.[64]

By contrast, visible ageing in a male star is a sign of rugged authority: '*Gary Cooper, Clark Gable, Humphrey Bogart, qui avaient la soixantaine, sont morts en pleine jeunesse cinématographique [. . .] marqués par des rides, non de délabrement, mais de souci et d'expérience*.'[65] One could easily

---

63• 'I was beautiful once, do you remember?'; 'Yes, I remember. You were perfect.'

64• 'One day the wrinkles and the puffiness will become permanent. The star will give up her last battle, after which she will have to resign herself to no longer being in love, that's to say, no longer being young or beautiful, that's to say no longer being a star', Morin, op. cit., p.45.

65• 'Gary Cooper, Clark Gable and Humphrey Bogart, who were all about sixty, died in their filmic youth, not crumbling and wrinkled but marked by the lines of anxiety and experience', ibid., p.45, n.1.

add Montand to this list: dead at 67, with a three-year-old son by his new partner, and only one performance as an old man (in *IP5*, his final film). Signoret, however, left numerous performances – including *Le Chat*, *Madame Rosa* (1977) and *L'Etoile du Nord* (1982) – that centre on her aged body. As she herself remarked, '*Je suis grosse et moche, je vais m'en servir*'.[66] It is, of course, much more usual for film actresses to feel they have to perpetuate a frozen image of youth and beauty, either by retiring from the cinema or by relying on make-up and lighting to maintain their appearance.

If the eternal youth of the star actress is one myth that Signoret rejects, another is the myth of an eternal political struggle (towards an endlessly deferred utopia?). For Montand, political struggle is the story of his life. He said of his visit to Israel in 1986: '*il se place dans la continuité de la lutte que je mène depuis l'âge de onze ans et demi*',[67] but Signoret refutes such a reading of her own activities:

> *Arrêtez de me parler de mon combat politique, ça n'a jamais été un combat politique. Ce sont des coups de coeur humanistes, de la façon la plus démodée, et qui n'ont rien à voir avec la politique. Je refuse cette expression.*[68]

If we accept Signoret's point here, then neither politics nor glamour are crucial to her star image. For Montand, however, they seem to be omnipresent. In the final analysis, then, Signoret is less mythologised than Montand, who, for all his problematic performances of the late sixties and early seventies, is a star whose image is an eternal amalgam of myths and types: the song-and-dance man, the romantic, the intellectual, the worker, the athlete, the sex symbol, the peasant and the man of politics. For Signoret, comparable elements might be the beauty, the mother, the *femme fatale*, the political activist, the jilted wife, and the aged, suffering woman. But these are stages in her stardom rather than permanent features of it. Montand's star image is synchronic, immutable, combining all things at once, and is ultimately, therefore, mythic. Signoret's is diachronic, mutable, shifting, discontinuous and degenerating, and is therefore more human – less of a myth, more of a problem.

66• 'I'm fat and ugly, and I'm going to put that to use', cited in Hayward, 'Simone Signoret', p.65, n.7.

67• 'It's part of the continuous battle that I've been fighting since the age of eleven and a half', cited in M. Gonod, 'Montand: "Mon seul parti sera celui du coeur"', *Paris Match*, 20 June 1986.

68• 'Stop talking to me about my political combat; it wasn't political combat. They were just humanist reactions, of the most outdated kind, and they had nothing to do with politics. I reject that expression', cited in Hayward, 'Simone Signoret', p.67, n.10.

CHAPTER 4

The Red woman on top: Jeanne Moreau with Jean-Marc Bory in *Les Amants* (1959).

Red woman/white woman: Jeanne Moreau and Catherine Deneuve

FANTASIES OF WOMEN

As Bardot's case demonstrates, female stars are often used to incorporate abstract values. These values tend to be organised in a series of binaries that inform western culture and the function of women within that culture. In *Male Fantasies*, Klaus Theweleit states that 'The urge to see women in images seems irresistible.'[1] He goes on to explore the diverse forms that images of women have taken in modern Europe. He has called the two key forms the 'Red woman' and the 'white woman'.[2] The former tends to be demonised, the latter idealised; one is corporeal, the other ethereal, but both derive their prevalence and their power from fears of femininity and of the unconscious. The Red woman is explicitly sexualised, usually as a prostitute. She is associated with communism and the working classes, and is often represented as a 'Red flood' or 'an infernal maelstrom of terrifying desires'. The white woman, on the other hand, is a shining bastion against such filth: 'Mother, sister (-of-mercy, nurse), and countess all in one person. Such is the holy trinity of the "good woman", the nonwhore.'[3] The white woman is impassive, her face 'a cold (nobly beautiful) mask', while the Red woman gives full vent to her excessive emotions, as she 'swears, shrieks, spits [and] scratches'.[4] These are the moulds into which the star images of many star actresses have been poured, but they seem to fit most resonantly with two stars whose long and successful careers may be due, in part, to the persistence of these very archetypes: Jeanne Moreau and Catherine Deneuve.

Deneuve is the white woman, a figure of control, of unattainable beauty, refinement and rigidity, pallor and poise. In his memoirs, Roger Vadim contrasts her with the 'aggressive

---

1• K. Theweleit, *Male Fantasies, I: Women, floods, bodies, history*, Cambridge, Polity Press, 1987, p.168.

2• The term 'red' is capitalised by Theweleit to reflect its political connotations. Although his study is initially of fascism in 1920s Germany, he states that his subjects are 'equivalent to the tip of the patriarchal iceberg' (p.171), and that 'the relationship of the twentieth-century soldier males to white and Red women [...] represents a segment within the continuum of bourgeois patriarchy' (p.362).

3• Ibid., p.95.

4• Ibid., pp.95 and 67.

sensuality' of Bardot or the 'earthy' appeal of Moreau.[5] He describes Deneuve as an idealised source of illumination ('pale and radiant', even after giving birth to their son) and also as a controlling 'domestic tyrant'.[6] Her image is maternal yet cold, as symbolised in the final, snowy scene of *Les Parapluies de Cherbourg* (1964), the film that made her a star. In contrast to 'the glacial Catherine Deneuve', Moreau exudes a 'fluid' and 'primal sexuality'.[7] Her eroticised performance in *Les Amants* (1958), including a famous scene where cunnilingus is implied, made this 'the film that shocked the world'.[8] Like the Red woman, Moreau 'can be very volatile, very capricious, [and] swear like a truck-driver when her temper erupts'.[9] If Deneuve personifies serene beauty, Moreau embodies passion and pleasure. Where Deneuve freezes, Moreau flows.

MOREAU AND THE RED FLOOD

The archetype of the prostitute – an avatar of the sexualised, threatening woman – has consistently informed Jeanne Moreau's star image. She has played prostitutes, strippers or madams in numerous films, including *Touchez pas au grisbi* (1954), *Eva* (1962), *The Trial* (1963), *Le plus vieux métier du monde* (1967), *Joanna Francesca* (1975) and *Querelle* (1982). Part of her childhood was spent in a cheap Parisian hotel 'with whores and so on'; when she told her father she wanted to act, he replied that 'To be an actress was to be a whore'.[10] Later, as a successful star in the 1960s, she felt herself to be demonised by the French press for her frank attitude to sex both on and off screen: 'they think I'm some kind of monster, the scarlet woman of Babylon'.[11] The term 'monster' implies that Moreau can not only be seen as violent or cruel, but also as formless, uncontrolled, inhuman. This amorphous threat is associated, in Theweleit's terminology, with class, and forms part of the nexus '*Erotic woman – unfeeling woman – vulgar woman – whore/proletarian woman [. . .] woman on the attack*'.[12]

When the young Moreau was asked what her ideal theatrical role would be, she chose Eliza in *Pygmalion*: an unruly working class woman who is trained to pass as a 'white countess'. If she had not made a career in acting, she claims that she would have worked 'in the fields, on a farm'.[13] This association with rural, working-class origins (her father's background) was later partially obscured by her status as a fashion icon in the 1960s and early 1970s. But her lover of that time, fashion designer Pierre Cardin, still referred to her as 'a simple farming

---

5. R. Vadim, *Bardot, Deneuve and Fonda: The Memoirs of Roger Vadim*, London, Hodder and Stoughton, New English Library, 1987, p.214.

6. Ibid., pp.209 and 205. For more on 'radiance' and female stars, see Chapter 8.

7. M. Gray, *La Moreau: A Biography of Jeanne Moreau*, London, Warner Books, 1995, pp.viii–ix.

8. Ibid., p.viii.

9. Ibid., p.ix.

10. Moreau cited in ibid., pp.6 and 11.

11. Moreau cited in ibid., p.90.

12. Theweleit, op. cit., p.79, italics in original.

13. Moreau cited in Gray, op. cit., p.20.

girl'.[14] Moreau can also be seen to embody the land via her acting style, which is often referred to as natural or earthy. Her rasping, cigarette-stained voice, which made her a singing star in the sixties, also contributes to the warmth of her persona and to her 'visceral' appeal.[15] She is thus linked to the guts, the inner workings of the body, but not explicitly to motherhood. In fact, Moreau is very far from being an earth mother. Maternity is not part of her persona, while eroticised bodily display definitely is. Already in the fifties, she appeared naked or semi-naked in films such as *Les Amants* (1958) and *La Reine Margot (1954)*, and in the sixties she posed nude for *Playboy*.[16] Yet, in marked contrast to Deneuve, an icon of beauty, Moreau has been described by press, actors and directors as ugly, with her down-turned mouth and baggy eyes.[17] In the sixties, American *Vogue* described her as 'Sexy, smouldering, yet "plain"'.[18] Historically, her eroticised image, although first established in the fifties, has most often been taken as evocative of the 1960s. One of the faces of the French new wave, she is also considered an embodiment of women's liberation (despite never presenting herself as directly interested in feminism). She was one of many French actresses, including Signoret and Deneuve, to sign the 1971 'Manifeste des 343' in favour of the right to legal abortion. However, although there is a specific context for Moreau's star image (see below), it also conforms to a pervasive and largely dehistoricised myth of Woman. Writing about her most celebrated and controversial film, *Les Amants*, François Truffaut declared that *'il s'agit moins ici d'une femme d'aujourd'hui que de la femme en général'*.[19]

From the very first sequence, *Les Amants* mobilises water imagery as a symbol for female sexuality. During the opening credits, the camera moves slowly across a map depicting several waterways. Following the line of a stream, it passes the *'Lac d'indifférence'* and comes to rest on a confluence, where three tributaries run into a large river bearing the legend *'Dangereuse'*.[20] Both linguistically and topographically, the map suggests the development of sexual awareness, from a still and circumscribed space (the lake) and a tidy, channelled stream, to a large and threatening body of water. The figuring of the female body and its desires as a series of waterways is maintained throughout the film, in which Moreau plays Jeanne, a bored bourgeois wife and mother. At the start of the film, Jeanne occupies the position of the white woman: we see her embracing her daughter, visiting her husband's workplace, wearing white. But the narrative charts her sexual awakening and her abandonment of house, husband and daughter in the throes of desire and passion. The white woman will reveal herself to be the locus of unsuspected depths and powerful floods. As Theweleit notes, the metaphor of the flood 'engenders a clearly ambivalent

14• Ibid., p.x.

15• Ibid., p.36.

16• A body double was used for some scenes in *La Reine Margot*.

17• See, for example *Paris Match*, 4 June 1960, pp.24–35.

18• Cited in Gray, op. cit., p.25.

19• 'it's not about a woman of today so much as woman in general', F. Truffaut, writing in *Arts*, September 1958, cited in *Fil à Films: Les Films de ma vie*, publicity material for video of *Les Amants*.

20• 'Lake of indifference'; 'Dangerous'.

state of excitement. It is threatening, but also attractive'. Against the intoxicating but wild flood stands the monolith of patriarchy, controlling and reactionary: 'Nothing is to be permitted to flow, least of all "Red floods"'.[21] It is notable, in this context, that in Germany the scenes showing Jeanne's daughter were cut, since 'it was not acceptable for a married mother to have an affair'.[22] The white woman should be sacrosanct and should not deviate from her idealised, desexualised status.

We can chart Jeanne's sexual awakening by means of the water imagery which, none too subtly, runs through *Les Amants*. When Jeanne, dressed in white, first meets Bernard (Jean-Marc Bory), the man with whom she will have an affair, her car has broken down by a canal. This smooth and constrained waterway is followed by a trickling stream, into which she drives Bernard's car. The feelings which were held in check are gradually un-dammed. Hence Jeanne's hysterical laughter when she returns home with Bernard, a laughter which is uncontrolled and exaggeratedly sustained in Moreau's performance, as if an internal check has been broken. She is, moreover, laughing at her husband, in a repudiation of his authority over her body.[23] Moreau's performance here, with the emphasis on repetition and a loss of control, prefigures her performance of orgasm in the film's most controversial sequence. In the build-up to that moment, we are presented with more water imagery: Jeanne running a bath, Jeanne and Bernard meeting at night by a roaring water wheel in the garden, the two of them draining their glasses simultaneously, and then crossing a bridge over a waterfall, where they kiss for the first time. The water symbolism in effect narrates Jeanne's shift from white woman to Red, and the dissolution of her previous inhibitions in ever-increasing streams of desire. She and Bernard drift down the millstream in a boat, and later (after the central sex scene) take a bath together in the house. The bath scene is a final repudiation of the constraint and control of the white woman. Again, Moreau laughs, this time as Bernard joins her in the water. Bathing, with its connotations of cleanliness and purity, has become a sexualised experience, just as tap water, 'the material incarnation of the antisexual abstraction "white woman" ("pure mother"; "white countess-nurse")',[24] here becomes a flood of liberating waves. The timid, controlled streams of the canal or the tap have given way to the 'oceanic feeling' of orgasm,[25] a kind of universalised image of the flowing, sexually uninhibited woman.

The identification of Moreau's star image with sexual pleasure and 'oceanic feeling' originates above all in her performance of orgasm in *Les Amants*. Lying naked on a bed while Bory's head disappears off screen in a suggestion of cunnilingus, Moreau repeatedly gasps 'Mon amour', louder and louder, her eyes shut and her mouth half open, in a pose

---

21. Theweleit, op. cit., p.230. The 'Red floods' spoken of here are communist uprisings, but also more generally, images of the working class as a flood, a tide or a stream.

22. Gray, op. cit., p.40. Gray continues: 'Luckily Hitler's decree that a woman unfaithful to her husband must die before the end of the film had lapsed!' Other countries, including Britain, cut various scenes.

23. Theweleit describes the Red woman as laughing uncontrollably at men in op. cit., p.67.

24. Ibid., p.422.

25. See ibid., pp.251–4. Theweleit takes the term from Romain Rolland and Wilhelm Reich.

that prefigures Sylvia Kristel's enacting of orgasm in soft porn cinema.[26] The cunnilingus implied here is reiterated, along with the fluid figuring of Moreau's body, in the later scene where Bory dips his face into the cold bathwater. Moreau is, in this film, quite simply a body of water.

The 'oceanic' or orgasmic within Moreau's star image was still being evoked over thirty years after *Les Amants*, in *La Vieille qui marchait dans la mer* (1991), a performance that won Moreau her first César for best actress. Playing the supposedly aristocratic con artist Lady M., Moreau gives vent to a stream of brilliantly vulgar insults and jokes, and speaks of life as being 'beau comme un orgasme'.[27] At the start and the conclusion of the film, we see her walking in the sea in an attempt to rejuvenate her ageing body. Like Jeanne in *Les Amants*, Lady M. is an embodiment of 'the woman-in-the-water; woman as water; [. . .] woman as the enticing (or perilous) deep'.[28] But the film is also a knowing and affectionate reflection on stardom, and on Moreau's persona as the Red woman of post-war French cinema. Seated in front of a mirror at the start of the film, Moreau declares, '*Je suis une vieille salope*'.[29] We are later shown photos of her at various points in her career (aged seventeen, twenty-three and forty-two). Dressed in red, with red hair and lipstick, she gropes, cackles and swears her way through the film. In a clear reference to *Les Amants*, she grins broadly as her equally aged companion, Pompilius (Michel Serrault), goes down on a young woman. The taboo theme of elderly sexuality is energetically explored, either as pathetic (Lady M. shows signs of senility and confuses present men with lovers of the past) or, more often, as grotesque: Pompilius declares, '*Vous êtes une truie en chaleur [. . .]. Votre sexe rassis se met à capoter devant les jeunes mâles*'.[30] Despite her age, Lady M. is nonetheless a powerful, manipulative and, at times, threatening character. The violence associated with the castrating ferocity of the Red woman is evoked when, lost in a crowd of men at the close of the film, she rages, '*Je voudrais leur couper la queue à tous, et former un Himalaya de bites*'.[31] But for the most part, Moreau's star image remains 'oceanic' rather than explicitly castrating. At the close of *La Vieielle qui marchait dans la mer*, the street full of men swiftly dissolves into a shot of blue seawater and the film ends, as it began, with Lady M. walking in the sea in Guadeloupe. Beside her is a young companion, of whom she wonders, '*Je me demande le goût qu'elle a, la queue de mon petit Lambert*'.[32] Even at the age of 63, Moreau is here associated with voracious (oral) sexuality, with bodily fluids and streams of desire.[33]

26• See Chapter 6.

27• 'beautiful as an orgasm'. We might note the identification between star and role implied here by the name of her character (M), as is also the case in *Les Amants* (Jeanne).

28• Theweleit, op. cit., p.283.

29• 'I'm an old tart'.

30• 'You are a sow in heat. Your stale sex flaps open whenever you see a young male'.

31• 'I'd like to cut off all their cocks and make a Himalaya of pricks'. As Julie in *La Mariée était en noir* (1967), Moreau pursues and murders several men. For an account of the Red woman as threatening castration, see Theweleit, op. cit., pp.70–79.

32• 'I wonder what my little Lambert's cock tastes like'. This perhaps has a hint of castrating menace.

33• Compare the sexual energy of her performance as Lili in *The Clothes in the Wardrobe* (1992).

The eroticisation of Moreau's image is clear, but what is her class status? Does that also conform to the archetype of the Red woman? Both on and off screen, Moreau's social image is ambiguous. Despite her rural, working-class origins, she has enjoyed the lifestyle of a global celebrity, including being chauffeured around in a Rolls-Royce, wearing high-fashion clothes (designed by Cardin) and collecting *objets d'art*. Her large farmhouse, bought in 1963 and sold in the eighties, was featured in several magazine spreads, yet the house signifies not only luxury (the magazine features, the setting near St Tropez, the fashion and art kept within), but also a kind of return to the land and to Moreau's roots (she often cooked for guests herself, roamed the garden in bare feet, and shopped very carefully for produce).[34] On screen, her roles have included the aristocratic and the bourgeois, as well as the proletarian. Her most iconic performances, however, have either emphasised sexuality over class codes (*Les Amants, Jules et Jim, La Vieille qui marchait dans la mer*) or have positioned her character as working class. Among the latter we find her role as the aspirational laundry worker Berthe, in *Souvenirs d'en France* (1975) and her triumphant return to the theatre as *La Servante Zerline* in 1986, but Moreau's most famous working-class incarnation is as the maid in Buñuel's *Le Journal d'une femme de chambre* (1964).

In a reversal of the narrative from *Les Amants*, as Célestine in *Le Journal d'une femme de chambre* Moreau plays a Red woman who becomes white. The transformation here is both social and sexual, as the unsettlingly erotic chambermaid ends up a bourgeois wife. In so doing, she channels and tames the working-class sexuality that flows in dangerous streams through the film. Male working-class desire is portrayed as sadistic and violent, as personified by the fascistic gardener Joseph, who rapes and murders the young orphan Claire. Female working-class sexuality is in some ways comparable (Joseph tells Célestine that they are both alike, and she initiates sex with him before betraying him to the police), but is characterised above all as dirty. The aristocratic household that Célestine enters is a temple to obsessive cleanliness, where working-class women represent a form of contagion. From the outset, dirt is associated with both Claire and Célestine: Madame Monteuil, the frigid 'white countess' of the house, asks Célestine '*Est-ce que vous êtes très propre?*', while her aged father, Monsieur Rabour, tells Claire '*T'es bien sale, tu sais*'.[35] On her arrival, Célestine is asked to remove her dirty boots, which the old man later fantasises about cleaning. Hence 'the bodies of erotic women, especially proletarian ones, become so much wet dirt'.[36]

Célestine's 'Red' sexuality threatens to destabilise bourgeois codes of behaviour, particularly when she coyly teases Monsieur Monteil or insists on sleeping with Joseph before their proposed marriage. The threat represented by the body of the Red woman is most strikingly conjured up in the sequence where Célestine reads to Monsieur Rabour. The passage chosen concerns the Salome myth and, as such, evokes the castrating violence of the erotic woman. Moreover, although the text describes the head of John the

---

34• See Gray, op. cit., pp.74–5.

35• 'Are you very clean?'; 'You're really dirty, you know.'

36• Theweleit, op. cit., p.421.

Baptist, it does so by mobilising images of blood and hair which we can interpret as a hysterical and fearful reference to the female genitalia: '*L'horrible tête flamboie, saignant toujours, mettant des caillous de pourpre sombre aux pointes de la barbe et des cheveux*'.[37] The association with Célestine's sex is reinforced by the fact that while she reads this passage aloud, the camera shows Monsieur Rabour's hand caressing her stockinged legs, an object of fetishistic representation throughout the film and a part of the body contiguous with the invisible site of her own desire. Ultimately, however, the threat of Célestine's potentially savage sexuality is contained, and by marrying out of her class (the captain next door), she concludes the film as a white woman. The final image of Célestine shows her dressed in white, sitting by a window where snow is falling – a rare image in Moreau's filmography of the assumption of pure, cold, bourgeois sexuality. For once, the flow has been frozen.

DENEUVE AND THE WHITE MASK

Deneuve's star image, as one might imagine, is diametrically opposed to Moreau's. This is why the films each actress made with Buñuel move in opposite directions: the premise of *Le Journal d'une femme de chambre* is inverted three years later in *Belle de jour*, where Deneuve plays a white woman who turns Red (see below). Where Moreau is compared to streams and storms, metaphors of frigidity and whiteness have always accompanied Deneuve. She is the cold beauty, the ice maiden, the snow queen. While Moreau and Simone Signoret have repeatedly played tarts, Deneuve has been relentlessly typecast as the elegant and expressionless bourgeois woman. As *Télérama* magazine notes, even when her characters are thrust into difficult or destabilising situations – the prostitution of *Belle de jour* (1967), the wartime tensions of *Le Dernier Métro* (1980) – Deneuve remains essentially the same, impassive, beautiful, untouched: '*Avec toujours, quelle que soit la situation, le cheveu impeccable, le maquillage parfait, l'élégance indiscutable*'.[38] Her restrained acting style and conventional appearance have been condemned as '*l'embourgeoisement du jeu de l'acteur*'.[39] Clad in Yves Saint-Laurent, seemingly ageless in her beauty, always blonde (though this is not her natural colour), Deneuve seems the perfect incarnation of the white woman. In this regard, she presents a clear contrast not just with Moreau, but with her older sister, the warm, red-headed, expressive Françoise Dorléac, with whom she starred as twins in *Les Demoiselles de Rochefort* (1967) shortly before Dorléac's death.[40] Deneuve and Dorléac were indeed twins, in the sense that they functioned as two sides of the same coin, as two

---

37• 'The horrible head blazes, still bleeding, sprinkling beard and hair with dark crimson cinders'. Compare the association between blood, sex and the female body in *Les Valseuses* (1974) where, after sex, Moreau's character shoots herself in the vagina and bleeds to death.

38• 'Whatever the situation, her hair is always impeccable, her make-up perfect, her elegance beyond question', M. Amar, 'Le jeu discret de la bourgeoise', *Télérama*, 2262 (19 May 1993), p.40.

39• 'the embourgeoisement of acting style', ibid., p.40.

40• For a comparison of the two, see M. Anderson, 'A la Recherche de la Soeur Perdue: The Stardom of Françoise Dorléac', *Studies in French Cinema*, 2:1 (2002), pp.14–22.

related abstractions, the white woman and the Red. Hence their reported comment that '*A nous deux, nous ferions une femme parfaite*'.[41]

This division of women into binaries – the corporeal and the ethereal, the Red and the white – also informs Deneuve's individual star image. In *Belle de jour* the division is between the conscious and the unconscious. Deneuve plays Séverine, an elegant bourgeois wife who dreams of giving free reign to her masochistic desires. She submits to her unconscious and becomes a prostitute, working in the daytime to satisfy herself sexually, but Deneuve's image is not radically challenged – her appearance, her acting style, her hair, are all unscathed. Buñuel's purist, restrained film style maintains an envelope of coldness and distance around her cool performance. There is no hysterical evocation of Deneuve/Séverine's sexuality in *Belle de jour* to match that of Moreau/Célestine in *Le Journal d'une femme de chambre*. The closest we get are the fantasy sequences in which Deneuve, dressed in white, is brutalised with whips or pelted with mud. However, although this would seem to suggest the dirtying of Deneuve's clean image, the effect is shortlived. Even here, in the realm of the unconscious, Deneuve's acting style is typically minimalist and impassive. Her perfect, stainless persona emerges paradoxically even more elegant from the mire of taboo desires: '*en avilissant son image, [Buñuel] la magnifie encore plus*'.[42] A similar logic lies behind Truffaut's casting of Deneuve as the *femme fatale* Marion in *La Sirène du Mississippi* (1969). Despite her delinquent past, her criminal associations and her incessant manipulation of her husband, Marion is ultimately encoded as the idealised white woman. The cold radiance of Deneuve's persona wins through, so that even the private detective who is tracking Marion has to admit that all who see her are struck by '*la pureté de son visage*'.[43]

The separation of the self in Deneuve's star image, and the casting off of the Red woman, begins with *Les Parapluies de Cherbourg* (1964), her star-making performance and a film that dramatises the establishment of her cool, restrained, bourgeois persona. In Demy's confectionary-coloured musical, Deneuve plays Geneviève, a provincial teenager who is transformed at the end of the film into an elegant Parisienne. This process is most apparent in terms of her appearance: originally dressed in cardigans and jumpers, with her hair in a ponytail, Geneviève ultimately appears in a fur coat with coiffed hair and discreet jewels. Even more telling is Deneuve's performance of emotion, and the concomitant representation of her face. On several occasions in the first half of the film, she cries uncontrollably over the call-up and apparent disappearance of her fiancé Guy: in these scenes (including sequences where she is heavily pregnant with Guy's child), Deneuve's face is pink, livid, blotchy. But as Genviève learns to forget Guy and marries Roland instead, so she masters her emotions, and Deneuve's white mask appears. The corporeal

---

41• 'Between us we would make a perfect woman', 'Deneuve déjà star', *Paris Match: Souvenirs* (hors série), 1988, p.22.

42• 'by debasing her image, Bunuel just glorifies it even more', F. Ozon, 'Femmes sous influence', *Télérama*, 2717 (6 February 2002), p.40. Ozon directs Deneuve in *8 Femmes* (see Chapter 11).

43• 'the purity of her face'.

woman (getting pregnant, fainting, crying) has been replaced by the star face, flawlessly made up and coolly composed. It is a measure of the control associated with Deneuve as a star that a performance in which she cries in close-up (*Ma saison préférée*) should be deemed noteworthy as a watershed in her portrayal of emotion[44] – thirty years after *Les Parapluies de Cherbourg*.

The change in Geneviève/Deneuve's face is mirrored by the change in her social status – from unmarried, pregnant shop girl to the wife of a successful diamond merchant. It is Roland, her future husband, who sees the idealised white woman in Geneviève, and compares her to the Sleeping Beauty and the Madonna. After his proposal, we see Geneviève framed between mannequins in bridal veils, signifying the rigidity that she is being asked to adopt. The film further dramatises the separation of the Red woman from the white by means of Jenny, a red-clad prostitute who sleeps with Guy after his return from Algeria and who reveals that her real name is Geneviève. This Red woman symbolises the young, carnal Geneviève who Guy once knew, and who is replaced by the cold *bourgeoise* of the final sequence. Where once Geneviève cried without restraint at Guy's absence, when she finally meets him again, four years later, her face remains pale and composed. As Guy and Geneviève part once more, the emotion of the moment is signalled not by anything in Deneuve's performance, but in the swirling snow and in the hysterical crescendo of the music. Deneuve drives out of the film a star, the white woman incarnate, with her mask in place.

The mask has served her well. Deneuve has long been celebrated as an eternal beauty, a star out of time. This myth informs not just verbal descriptions of the star, but also photographic images of her face, which maintain the impression by using overexposure to soften her features and, in one instance, by recycling photos taken years earlier.[45] Apparently ageless, Deneuve becomes an ideal, an abstract. Between 1985 and 2000, she was the model for Marianne, embodiment of the French Republic. Her function as an icon of the French nation is also reinforced by her association with the fashion products of Chanel and Yves Saint Laurent, and by several performances in which she personifies France – including *Fort Saganne* (1984) and *Indochine* (1991). The latter in particular casts her as the motherland: she is France, while her adopted daughter represents the (ex)colony of Vietnam.[46] Both of these films evoke a nostalgia for the French colonial empire, and suggest that Deneuve evokes not only spatial distance (she is unattainable, out of reach), but also temporal distance. In 1993, the magazine *Le Mensuel du cinéma* noted that four of her five most successful films were set in the past.[47]

44· See Amar, op. cit., p.41.

45· See the cover of *Télérama*, 2 August 2000, which replicates an image of Deneuve used on the cover of the same magazine in August 1996.

46· See G. Austin, *Contemporary French Cinema*, Manchester, MUP, 1996, pp.150–152, and S. Ravi, 'Women, Family and Empire-building: Régis Warnier's *Indochine*', *Studies in French Cinema*, 2: 2 (2002), pp.74–82.

47· See Y. Alion, 'Box-office de Catherine Deneuve: La distance du temps', *Le Mensuel du cinéma*, June 1993, p.17.

The maternal element of Deneuve's persona evoked in *Indochine* connects with the related image of the 'white countess-nurse'.[48] According to Theweleit, the nurse is 'an emblem for the bourgeois woman's renunciation of her female body. The nurse's is a dead body, with no desires and no sexuality'.[49] Playing the nurse Hélène in *Hôtel des Amériques* (1981), Deneuve gives one of her more desperate, brittle performances, as a character who is detached from her present lover (an equally tormented Patrick Dewaere) and haunted by death (her ex-lover's suicide). Although the film charts a doomed romance, neither protagonist is eroticised: Dewaere plays a zombie, and Deneuve is possessed by ghosts.[50] The association between symbolic whiteness, 'cool blankness'[51] and the renunciation of the body as a form of death, reaches its apogee in *Repulsion* (1965), where Deneuve plays a frigid, neurotic woman driven to murder by her fear of sex. Certainly, films such as *Repulsion*, *Hôtel des Amériques*, *Drôle d'endroit pour une rencontre* (1988) and *Les Voleurs* (1996), have suggested cracks in Deneuve's mask, flaws and tensions beneath the ice. These seem to have broken though the polished surface of her star image in the late nineties with a revisiting of her sister's death. In December 1996, the television station Canal+ held a 'Deneuve-Dorléac Night', broadcasting several of their films, including *Les Demoiselles de Rochefort*, and a specially commissioned documentary, *Elle s'appelait Françoise*, on Dorléac's life. Deneuve broke her long silence on her sister's death (and on her private life in general, which she had long refused to discuss in the press) by contributing to the documentary and to a book of the same title. The effect was finally to establish an emotional connection between Deneuve and her audience. The star noted that her suffering was understood by her fans, '*qui m'ont envoyé beaucoup de lettres pour me raconter leurs propres deuils*'.[52] Yet, as Deneuve also acknowledged, there remained a sense of restraint, a threshold placed between herself and the public that even grief was unable to dissolve.

Despite the tenacious fixity of her star image, Deneuve has continued the efforts made in the nineties to question and qualify it. In *Place Vendôme* (1999) she plays an alcoholic, ironically called Marianne, a vulnerable and ageing character who has little of the glamorous serenity usually associated with Deneuve. The eruption of previously unseen depths, of the red stream of bodily fluids, is literalised when at one point her nose begins to bleed uncontrollably. If *Place Vendôme* replaces the ageless Marianne of the French Republic with a much more corporeal, compromised Marianne, *Dancer in the Dark* (2000) replaces the image of the cool, bourgeois mother at the end of *Les Parapluies de Cherbourg*

48• Theweleit, op. cit., p.422.

49• Ibid., p.134.

50• For more on Dewaere's performance in the film, see Chapter 7. Deneuve's more eroticised roles tend to be for Hollywood, where rather than being an icon of whiteness, she is the exotic/erotic other, in films like *Hustle* (as a sex worker) and *The Hunger* (as a lesbian vampire). The latter was instrumental in establishing Deneuve as a lesbian icon, particularly in the USA. This status is playfully alluded to in *8 Femmes* (2002), where Deneuve literally fights against lesbian desire (personified by Fanny Ardant) before succumbing to it – lying on the ground, she and Ardant grapple before passionately kissing.

51• This term is used to described Deneuve's performance in *Repulsion* in Anderson, op. cit., p.17.

52• 'who sent me lots of letters to tell me about their own bereavements', Deneuve cited in J. Garcin, 'La double vie de Catherine Deneuve', *Le Nouvel Observateur*, 20–26 March 1997, p. 53.

with a working-class avatar in a headscarf. Both films are musicals, but although Deneuve's character, Cathy, does reluctantly dance and sing a little in *Dancer in the Dark*, she is not the focus of the musical numbers. She is identified less with music than with class (her work in the factory) and with motherhood (her relationship as surrogate mother to both Selma and Gene). This is a rare proletarian role for Deneuve, and allows her to give an unusually warm and emotional performance. It is also a film which, due to the technical conditions under which it was made, does present Deneuve's image in a literally new light. But, like other films she has made in America – *Hustle* (1975) and *The Hunger* (1983) – it remains a renegotiation of her star image which does not seem to have fundamentally changed how she is represented and understood in France.[53]

CONCLUSION: HISTORICIZING MOREAU AND DENEUVE

Thus far, we have interpreted Moreau and Deneuve in terms of well-established western archetypes of women, but can we historicize their star images more precisely? In other words, was there anything specific about the period in which they became stars that facilitated imagery of the Red and the white, the dirty and the clean, in female stars? The answer lies in *Fast Cars, Clean Bodies*, Kristin Ross's excellent analysis of French culture in the fifties and sixties. Ross reveals in great detail the extent to which post-war France was obsessed with the discourse of cleanliness. The origins of this 'deep psychological need [. . .] to be *clean*'[54] can be located in a resolve to purify and modernise France after the trauma of the Second World War (the German Occupation, collaboration by the Vichy state, civil war of a kind). In the months and years following the Liberation, efforts were made to cleanse France of various 'stains', including purges of collaborators (*l'épuration*), and a campaign for 'moral cleanliness', which culminated in the closing down of all 177 brothels in Paris, via the law of 13 April 1946. It is no accident that such measures were aimed principally at women. The representation of the nation by means of female figures (Marianne, for example) is a key factor here, but so is the psychological effect of decolonisation in the post-war years. As Ross puts it,

> If the woman is clean, the family is clean, the nation is clean. If the French woman is dirty, then France is dirty and backward. But France can't be dirty and backward, because that is the role played by the colonies. But there are no more colonies. [. . .] France must, so to speak, clean house.[55]

Hence the establishment or re-launching of women's magazines in the fifties, with their emphasis on the need to 'clean house'. In 1951, an investigative survey by *Elle*, called '*La Française est-elle propre?*', discovered that '25 per cent of French women never brushed their

---

53· See Chapter 11 for an account of digital technology's impact on the representation of Deneuve.

54· K. Ross, *Fast Cars, Clean Bodies: Decolonization and the Reordering of French Culture*, Cambridge, Mass., October Books, MIT Press, 1996, p.73. Italics in original.

55· Ibid., p.78.

teeth, and that 39 percent washed themselves once a month'.[56] This was not good enough for a country that was trying to wash away the past and reinvent itself as a modern, urbanised nation. The dirt had to be scrubbed off.

As a star, Deneuve embodies perfectly the cultural project of post-war France. Even her (stage) name suggests the new and the modern: De-*neuve* (new). Her star image crystallises the process identified by Ross, which, in the decade from 1955 to 1965, 'saw both the end of the empire and the surge in French consumption and modernization'.[57] The attendant discourse of whiteness, cleanliness, and timelessness reads like a definition of Deneuve-as-star. Her whiteness (the blonde hair, the pale, flawless face, the associations with snow and ice) conforms not just to the archetype of the white woman, but also to the aspirations of French women in the fifties and sixties, who were encouraged to surround themselves with white goods: *Marie-Claire* magazine marked its relaunch in 1954 by celebrating 'the age [...] of the refrigerator, pasteurised milk, the washing machine', while in 1955, *Elle* published an issue devoted entirely to whiteness.[58] With its celebration of the new, clean, modern woman, *Elle* was aimed at a female readership from the provinces, 'the reader from Angoulême'.[59] Deneuve plays precisely this kind of woman as Geneviève in *Les Parapluies de Cherbourg*. Beginning as a young, slightly wild provincial, she ends the film a modernised *bourgeoise*, driving her own car and presumably living in Paris, having left her origins far behind. Her symbolic identification with white goods and with cleanliness is made clear when the umbrella shop she leaves behind is re-equipped as a store selling brand new washing machines.[60] Moreover, the shiny new car she drives in the closing sequence is itself a metaphor for modern France. As Roland Barthes noted in 1963 (a year before *Les Parapluies de Cherbourg*), the shining car and its ritualised cleaning symbolises a need 'to remake the virginity of the object over and over again', an 'obsession with cleanliness' which aims at 'immobilizing time'.[61] Deneuve is the human face of this desire: apparently ageless and eternal, she is always modern and yet always the same (remade over and over again, as in the identical *Télérama* covers).

Deneuve's 'clean' image is also a salient example of the 'domesticated sublime' identified by Henri Lefebvre in sixties France.[62] She is both domestic (white goods, maternal imagery) and a goddess (divine, unattainable, idealised). Her reticence, the distance she maintains between self and audience, her inwardness and coolness all chime with the

---

56• Ibid., p.209, n.11. The survey's title translates as 'Is the French woman clean?'.

57• Ibid., p.77. Deneuve, of course, later played the role of France giving up her colonies in *Indochine*.

58• See ibid., p.84.

59• Ibid., p.79.

60• The shift in the film from 'artisanal' umbrella shop to modern white goods store is noted by Ross in ibid., p.98. She does not, however, consider Deneuve's image.

61• R. Barthes, 'La voiture, projection de l'égo', *Réalités*, 213 (1963), cited in ibid., pp.105–6.

62• See H. Lefebvre, *Critique de la vie quotidienne* (volume 2), Paris, Arche, 1961. Deneuve is repeatedly described as clean. See, for example, D. Roth-Bettoni, J. Valot and Y. Alion, 'L'autre Deneuve', *Le Mensuel du cinéma*, June 1993, p.15.

concept of introversion and the privatisation of space, a 'movement of retreat, or *repliement* ("folding back inward")' noted by Lefebvre and others as 'the dominant social movement' of the late 1950s and early 1960s.[63] Among the things apparently left behind by this modernised, privatised vision of France were not just previous formations of public or social space, but also a previous formulation of Woman, to be discarded and replaced by the new, clean *bourgeoise*. In the words of Edgar Morin, France was seeing the 'decolonisation of the peasant woman'.[64] The first step to achieving this was the development of a 'filth complex' on the part of working-class women. In 1964, the very same year that *Les Parapluies de Cherbourg* dramatises this process, so too does Moreau's performance as Célestine in *Le Journal d'une femme de chambre*. At first, she is identified with the working class and with what lies outside (or beneath) a facade of domestic order and purity. Although set in the 1930s, the film can in fact be seen to reflect the 1960s trend towards

the Manichean division of the interior from the exterior, the latter now viewed as sordid, dirty, and repellent to the woman, who vigilantly policies its various invasions into her realm in the form of grime and odors tracked in from the outside on bodies and hands.[65]

By the close of the film, Célestine has internalised the values of cleanliness and order.

However, the success of Moreau's shocking, sexualised, non-bourgeois star image suggests that the internal decolonisation sought by Morin and achieved by Célestine was not total. In modern France there remain elements that have not been fully expunged, and which demand to be expressed. Hence, there is Moreau the star, swearing, laughing, coming. Despite her Rolls-Royce and her Cardin clothes, she is rooted and dirty in a way that Deneuve is not. No one could accuse her of being ageless, and she refuses to be domesticated, decolonised or cleaned up. Thus, we return to the polarised archetypes of the Red woman and the white, but anchored in a precise historical moment:

All of the new repulsions and aversions coalesce into a 'filth complex' that accompanies the definitive eruption of the new domestic model into the female psyche and which in turn translates into a global repudiation of the peasant condition.[66]

If Deneuve represents the triumph of the 'filth complex' in France, then Moreau represents what this apparent triumph represses: dirt and sex, streams and floods.

63∗ Ross, op. cit., p.106.

64∗ E. Morin, *Commune en France: La metamorphose de Plodémet*, Paris, Fayard, 1967, cited in ibid., p.91.

65∗ Ibid., p.92. And on feet, one might add.

66∗ Ross, op. cit., p.92.

CHAPTER 5

Which one will wear the trousers? Jean-Paul Belmondo and Catherine Deneuve in *La Sirène du Mississippi* (1969).

Macho men: Jean-Paul Belmondo and Alain Delon

MASCULINE STARS IN A FEMININE JOB

There is a hidden contradiction in the existence of macho film stars. Despite the perennial appeal of action heroes and tough guys, gangsters and cops, ultra-masculine male stars are, to an extent, feminised by the nature of their work. It is no coincidence that in French, stars are feminine (*la star* or *la vedette*). Acting is a profession of display, and hence ranks as ornamental, a masquerade, and no job for a 'real' man:

> There is no passage to manhood in such a world. A man can only wait to be discovered; and even if he lucks out, his 'achievement' is fraught with gender confusion for its 'feminine' implications of glamour and display.[1]

The anxiety that this generates in macho male stars is evident in their comments about acting and stardom. At the start of his career, Hollywood tough guy Robert Mitchum told his wife, 'Your husband is going to be a movie actress.' Macho French stars such as Jean Gabin and Lino Ventura felt a similar unease: *'[Ventura] était honteux qu'on le regarde dans la rue, qu'on le reconnaisse, comme si ce n'était pas un métier honorable, d'être acteur! Exactement comme Gabin!'*[2] Ironically, playing macho characters and possessing a star body encoded as vigorously masculine only makes matters worse, since the 'feminised muscle man'[3] is as much an object of display as the beauty queen. The sense of inauthenticity and feminisation is perhaps strongest in those actors who had previously undertaken work in an unambiguously masculine sphere, such as sport or the armed services: for example, Ventura, a former wrestler, Alain Delon, a sailor who had seen active service, or the ex-boxer Jean-Paul Belmondo. There is a clear ontological distinction between being an athlete or a soldier, and playing one for the camera. No matter how macho the role, acting

---

1· S. Faludi, *Stiffed: The Betrayal of the Modern Man*, London, Vintage, 2000, p.39.

2· 'Ventura was ashamed to be looked at in the street, to be recognised, as if being an actor wasn't an honest profession! Exactly like Gabin!', Pierre Granier-Deferre cited in G. Durieux, *Lino Ventura*, Paris, Flammarion, 2001, p.274.

3· Faludi, op. cit., p.591. She takes Sylvester Stallone as her main example of this.

is a performance of masculinity, and as such it 'turns manliness into a detachable entity, at which point it instantly becomes ornamental, and about as innately "masculine" as fake eyelashes are inherently "feminine"'.[4]

The ornamental nature of acting is heightened by the apparently feminising forms of masquerade used by actors, notably make-up: '*Lino refusait aussi presque toujours le maquillage, où il voyait une coquetterie féminine*.'[5] Delon too, especially in the mature years of his career, has been reluctant to wear make-up. Similar anxieties were voiced by one of Delon's early girlfriends, who felt that an acting career threatened his masculinity and would lead to him becoming both prostituted and feminised as '*une pute*'.[6] Even his most ultra-masculine behaviour (acts of violence, a fascination with women, fast cars and guns) could be seen, she insisted, as a masquerade: '*Je pense qu'il y a une part de comédie dans tous ses outrances. Alain a besoin de jouer de la comédie, de paraître*'.[7] As we shall see, Delon's star image in fact involves an energetic denial of the supposedly inauthentic and compromised masculinity of the actor, and the ceaseless reiteration of Delon's supposedly innate and authentic machismo.

DELON VERSUS BÉBEL

Along with Ventura and the mature Gabin, Belmondo and Delon are the key macho stars in modern French film. For the period 1956–1992, cumulative box office figures in France rank Belmondo at number 3, Gabin at 4, Delon at 6 and Ventura at 7.[8] Hence, four of the top ten stars of that period have a macho image, suggesting that machismo appeals to a vast number of cinemagoers. Certain ultra-masculine archetypes, most notably expressing the ideals of independence and authority, are mobilised by these stars. There is also a historical specificity fuelling such archetypes, as we shall see. The appeal of Belmondo and Delon can, moreover, be attributed to their association with popular genres, the thriller in particular, and appears related to the gender identity of their audience (see below).

Born in 1933 and 1935 respectively, Belmondo and Delon are of the same generation. They both came to prominence in the new wave period of French film making, although while Belmondo appeared in films by Godard, Chabrol and Truffaut, Delon worked with the *tradition de qualité* directors attacked by the new wave (notably René Clément), as well as with more fashionable directors such as Visconti and Melville. Co-stars in the classic gangster film *Borsalino* (1970), Belmondo and Delon have often been bracketed together by the French press, usually as rivals, but occasionally as colleagues and friends. A *Paris Match* feature of 1982 presents them as engaged in a friendly 'duel' for the hearts of the French

---

4• Ibid., p.607.

5• 'So Lino almost always refused make-up, which he saw as a feminine coquetry', José Giovanni cited in Durieux, op. cit., p.284.

6• 'a whore', B. Auber, cited in B. Violet, *Les Mystères Delon*, Paris, Flammarion, 2000, p.61.

7• 'I think there is an element of acting in all of his excesses. Alain needs to play a role, to seem to be', ibid., 66.

8• See G. Vincendeau, 'Gérard Depardieu, the axiom of contemporary French cinema', *Screen*, 34:4 (Winter 1993), p.344. Numbers 1, 2 and 5 are comic stars (de Funès, Bourvil and Fernandel). For more on comedy and stardom, see Chapter 11.

public, and appears to draw a line under the spats of the sixties and seventies (including a lawsuit brought by Belmondo against Delon for taking first billing on *Borsalino*),[9] but a review of *Les Acteurs* (2000) suggested that

> *certains comédiens ne se mélangent pas (Delon et Belmondo ont chacun leur scène, comme Mickey et Bugs Bunny devaient avoir par contrat, dans* Qui veut la peau de Roger Rabbit?*, le même temps d'apparition à l'écran).*[10]

Both men, as we have seen, began their working lives outside the cinema. Their star images are in many ways similar: athletic, muscled, determined, authoritative, yet sufficiently versatile to shift successfully between popular genres and art cinema. Both played boxers in early screen roles, Belmondo in *Un coeur gros comme ça* (1961) and *L'Aîné des Ferchaud* (1963), Delon in *Rocco and his brothers* (1960). Belmondo and Delon also became associated with distinct sub-genres of the French thriller: Belmondo with the flamboyant comedy/action thriller, Delon with the harder, tougher format of the gangster movie and the police thriller. There was some overlap (Belmondo appeared, at times, to alternate between the two styles) but the distinction between their star images remained clear. Speaking of the French thriller, Jean-Pierre Melville could say that 'There are only two formats here: Delon and Belmondo'.[11] They are both macho men, but in Ginette Vincendeau's formulation, 'One smiles, the other doesn't'.[12]

Another distinction between the two lies in their training, or lack of it. Delon has often alluded to Belmondo's professional training at the Paris Conservatoire and his own total absence of such. More generally, Delon has repeatedly asserted his independence from the screen acting profession in France, its unions, rituals, ceremonies and awards, expressing his isolation in an originally contemptuous and defiant, but increasingly bitter and lonely tone. In 1964, preparing for what would prove to be an abortive move to Hollywood, he attacked French cinema and Belmondo's primacy within it:

> *Qu'est-ce que cela veut dire que Belmondo est le champion du box-office de l'année? La France ne compte pas dans le marché mondial du cinema. Je me moque de la France! C'est moi qu'on connaît aux Etats-Unis et au Japon. [. . .] On ne m'aime pas en France, je suis trop indépendant. Je n'appartiens pas à l'Union des acteurs, ni à autre chose de semblable.*[13]

9. *Paris Match*, 26 February 1982. For an account of the lawsuit, see J. Strazzula and S. Leduc, *Belmondo: L'histoire d'une vie*, Paris, Ramsay, 1996, pp.121–3.

10. 'certain actors don't mix (Delon and Belmondo each have their own scene, just as Mickey and Bugs Bunny were contracted to have the same amount of screen time in *Who Framed Roger Rabbit?*)', G. Valens, 'Les Acteurs', *Positif*, 471 (May 2000), p.39.

11. Cited in J. Forbes, *The Cinema in France After the New Wave*, London, BFI, 1992, pp.53–4.

12. See G. Vincendeau, *Stars and Stardom in French Cinema*, London and New York, Continuum, 2000, p.158.

13. 'Who cares if Belmondo is number one at the French box office this year? France doesn't count in the global market for cinema. I don't care about France! I'm the one they know in the USA and Japan. They don't like me in France because I'm too independent. I don't belong to the Actors' Union, or to anything like that', cited in Violet op. cit., p.191.

Despite his own insistence that the public (not critics or the acting profession) were his only focus, Belmondo was, in fact, at this stage the president of the SFA, the French actors' union, and thus on the inside, while Delon projected himself as an outsider. Delon has also continued to emphasise the distinction between *un acteur* and *un comédien*.[14] A *comédien* (Belmondo) plays a role, but *un acteur* (Delon) simply *is*:

je vis mes roles, je ne les joue pas. Si j'étais un comédien, j'aurais appris le métier [. . . mais] je ne cherche pas à être autre chose que moi. Etre acteur, c'est une personnalité forte au service du cinéma.[15]

In this repect, Delon compares himself repeatedly to Burt Lancaster, Gabin and Ventura, pointing out that each of these actors arrived fully formed on screen, without training, from their previous jobs as a trapeze artist, a music-hall artist, and a wrestler.[16] Delon's previous job was famously as a sailor on active service during the war in Indochina. Belmondo also served briefly in the French armed forces, during the Algerian War, but this never became an essential part of his star image in the way that Indochina did for Delon. The latter's three years in the navy, from the age of seventeen to twenty, have been frequently celebrated by him as a formative experience, teaching him to be a man, and also acting as a crucible for the star image that followed: 'ma période militaire [. . .] m'a permis d'être tout ce qui a suivi et ce que je suis aujourd'hui. [. . .] J'ai appris à me battre, à me défendre, à être un homme'.[17] Similar masculine metaphors, expressing independence and strength via images of fighting, are also part of Belmondo's star image, but have a pugilistic rather than a military quality. His teenage years as a boxer have generated a frequent use of fighting metaphors in accounts of his legal battles (with the press and the police),[18] as well as informing his athletic image, and providing him with the broken nose which remains a visible symbol of his authentic macho origins.

Belmondo's second childhood ambition, other than boxing, was to be a clown. He has the face of a boxer, but also the elastic, rubbery features of the funny man, best displayed in his trademark grin. It is the clowning flamboyance of his performances that tends to soften the harder elements of his star image and demarcate him from the cold, authoritarian image of Delon. Interestingly, however, Belmondo's flamboyance and warmth seem to endear him to male fans, while Delon's icy aloofness and exceptional good looks endear

---

14· See T. Jousse and S. Toubiana, 'Mystère Delon', *Cahiers du cinéma*, 501 (April 1996), p.20. Both words mean 'actor' in French, but the latter derives from the name of France's premier theatrical establishment, La Comédie française, and is thus rooted in the history of the profession. It also has connotations of play-acting and artifice.

15· 'I don't play my parts, I live them. If I was a trained actor, I would have learnt the craft, but I don't seek to be anything else but me. Being a film actor means putting a strong personality at the service of the cinema', C. Schwab, 'Alain Delon, Christine Angot: Aveux intimes', *Paris Match*, 2784, 3 October 2002, p.26.

16· See for example, Jousse and Toubiana, op. cit., pp.20–21.

17· 'my time in the services allowed me to be everything which followed and what I am today. I learnt to fight, to defend myself, to be a man', Violet, op. cit., p.48.

18· See, for example, Strazzula and Leduc, op. cit., pp.34, 107.

him to female fans. This is certainly the impression given by the *Paris Match* survey of 1982, undertaken at a time when the two could reasonably be described as the two greatest stars of French cinema, and when a television screening of *Borsalino* had just scooped an astounding 92 per cent of the available audience.[19] The survey concludes that the French public love Belmondo but are seduced by Delon: '*Le premier plaît; l'autre séduit. Delon trouble, Belmondo attire*'.[20] Responses to the series of comparative questions asked about the two stars are broken down by gender and show a decisive split: ten times out of eleven, there is a clear majority of men in favour of Belmondo and a clear majority of women in favour of Delon. The overall responses also underline established aspects of the stars' public images: hence, Delon is cast as the best seducer (58 per cent to Belmondo's 28 per cent), while Belmondo triumphs as an entertainer (dinner guest, stage star, or song and dance man).[21] The latter also wins out in the final total, by five to three (with three draws). The adoption by the popular press of the diminutive '*Bébel*' is a further indication of the warmth and affection felt for the approachable Belmondo, while Delon has continued to appear aloof and solitary, '*Delon-le-solitaire*'[22].

ON THE OUTSIDE: MUSCLES AND MARGINALITY

Two key performances may serve to show, however, that the stars shared a common function in the early part of their careers. Both performances – Belmondo's as the intruder Laszlo in *A double tour* (1959) and Delon's as the psychopath Ripley in *Plein soleil* (1960) – centre on the physical appropriation of space, on a display of confidence and mastery served by a very mobile, fluid and natural acting style which contrasts with the formality of the bourgeois settings for these films and, in Belmondo's case, with the more restrained and stiffer performances of the other actors. Laszlo declares that he has nothing but vices, eats noisily, drinks to excess, appears naked, swears, cajoles and literally wrestles with his social betters. As Ripley, Delon is also a social outsider, but one who slowly and deliberately appropriates the identity of the friend that he murders. In the sequence following Philip's murder (and to a lesser extent, Freddie's, later in the film) the camera follows Delon's every move as he launches himself into his plan, struggling with the body and the boat, darting in and out of the cabin, and then occupying the clothes, the spaces, the voice and, eventually, the identity left by Tom with rapid, easy gestures. The animalistic grace and speed of Delon's movements was to become attenuated and stylised in the spare performances he gave in Melville's gangster movies later in the sixties, as indeed his voice was to become more sparingly used, as his roles became increasingly taciturn or morose. But in *Plein soleil* Delon's acting style is at its most exuberant. His performance even includes two escapes out of windows or over rooftops, rather gentle

---

19• Jean Cau, 'Vingt cinq ans de métier et toujours un seul maître: le public', *Paris Match*, 26 February 1982, p.52.

20• 'The former is pleasing, the latter seductive. Delon is troubling, Belmondo attractive', ibid., p.52.

21• Scoring 48%, 47% and 46% respectively against Delon's 31%, 30% and 29%. See ibid., pp.54–6.

22• 'lonely Delon', Jousse and Toubiana, op. cit., p.19.

stunts which are also present in Belmondo's early work (*A bout de souffle*, for instance) and which were to become a celebrated and ever more dangerous part of Bébel's star persona.

The outward display of physical prowess can be interpreted as the pitting of the male ego against nature (external or internal). Herbert Marcuse writes in *Eros and Civilisation* that 'nature (its own as well as the external world) was "given" to the ego as something that had to be fought, conquered and even violated – such was the precondition for self-preservation and self-development'.[23] Mastery of the self (self-control) and of the outside world (by means of athletic feats) is a sign of masculine authority and is essential to the star personae of both men. The development of Belmondo's star persona in particular was predicated on his own physical prowess, manifest in his famous insistence on performing all his own stunts (Delon, by contrast, worked with stunt doubles). These feats began in earnest with *L'Homme de Rio* in 1964 and continued until Belmondo suffered a serious injury while filming a television show in 1985. Among the more famous on-screen examples are the sequences where Belmondo parachutes towards a river full of piranhas (*L'Homme de Rio*), runs along the roof of a speeding metro train (*Peur sur la ville*), and hangs from a helicopter above Venice for five full minutes (*Le Guignolo*). Belmondo also undertook elaborate practical jokes and scaled high buildings when off screen.[24] As Martin O'Shaughnessy says of such stunts, 'Masculinity has nothing to prove yet somehow needs constantly to prove itself'.[25]

In *Le Marginal* (1983), Belmondo's character is seen driving an armour-plated Mustang, a car which deflects the villains' bullets and thus functions as 'an embodiment of a male fantasy. It confers limitless power and invulnerability and hides the male's softer, inner self behind an impenetrable boundary'.[26] The armour-plated car can also be seen as a hypostasised male body. Like the Mustang, the male star's muscular and tanned torso demonstrates strength and invulnerability. The muscular body is a fixed and polished surface which, unlike the face or voice, betrays no emotion; hence it displays external prowess and serves to deflect attention from any potential inner weakness. It is body armour, a 'male exterior' that functions to control the 'female interior'.[27] Of course, in Delon's case, the famously expressionless face and the neutral tone of voice also have this effect. Belmondo's voice and facial expressions are much more lively, and at times even camp, but they are grounded and rendered less transgressive by the hypermasculine body which is repeatedly displayed in his films, as well as in publicity photos.[28] For both stars,

---

23• H. Marcuse, *Eros and Civilization*, Boston, Beacon Press, 1955, p.110, cited in V. J. Seidler, 'Fathering, Authority and Masculinity' in R. Chapman, and J. Rutherford (eds), *Male Order: Unwrapping Masculinity* (London, Lawrence and Wishart, 1988), p.301, n.32.

24• For examples, see Strazzula and Leduc, op. cit., pp.102 and 105.

25• M. O'Shaughnessy, 'Jean-Paul Belmondo: Masculinity, Violence and the Outsider', in R. Gunther and J. Windebank (eds), *Violence and Conflict in Modern French Culture*, Sheffield, Sheffield Academic Press, 1994, p.224.

26• Ibid., p.224.

27• See K. Theweleit, *Male Fantasies, I: women, floods, bodies, history*, Cambridge, Polity Press, 1987, p.434.

28• See, for example, *Paris Match*, 26 February 1982, p.57, and *Paris Match*, 23 August 2001, p.51. Stills from both men's boxing movies are reproduced in *Paris Match*, 26 February 1982, p.56.

this kind of display continued into middle age and beyond: Delon begins his performance in *Parole de flic* (1985) with a virtuoso bout of half-naked wrestling; Belmondo's athletic physique was celebrated even when he suffered a collapse at the age of 67. [29]

Traditionally, solitary self-reliance has been associated with masculinity: 'Learning to be independent and self-sufficient [... men] pride themselves on the fact that they do not have emotional needs, [... and] assume an instrumental relationship to themselves.'[30] Thus, the male body becomes an instrument that can be controlled at will (to perform stunts, to hide emotion), but self-sufficient hypermasculinity is also expressed by assuming a position outside society. Even when playing detectives, Belmondo and Delon are often represented as rogue males, as loners who despise the bureaucracy of their superiors (*Peur sur la ville*) or who have left the force in disgust (*Parole de flic*). The outsider theme is repeatedly expressed in the titles of Belmondo's films (*Le Marginal, Flic ou voyou*),[31] and is comically literalised in the latter, when Belmondo's character sleeps under the stars, or in a tiny one-man tent, only to emerge in a pristine dinner suit for an evening engagement. Marginality appears even more urgent in Delon's star image, since despite his success, Delon has always felt excluded from the French film industry itself.[32] His performance as Ripley in *Plein soleil* is emblematic of his outsider status. He is a poor but gifted autodidact who believes that '*Tout s'apprend*'.[33] Yet even when he has entered the inner sanctum (achieving wealth and social position), there remains a hidden insecurity (manifested in the film by Ripley's perpetual deceit and repeated violence). Delon has spoken of his own feelings of isolation and exclusion, of his original lack of wealth, social standing and education, his sense of not belonging to his family. Like Ripley, this apparently uncontrolled outsider has taught himself to occupy the centre (stardom, fame, wealth, but also the role of producer, businessman and art connoisseur), but still feels ill at ease. This is exemplified by Delon's relationship with Romy Schneider, his fiancée of the late 1950s, who helped him to develop skills such as good reading and conversation. For all that, Delon remained painfully aware of the social contrast between them: '*Elle vient de la classe sociale que je hais le plus au monde*'.[34] While this may have contributed to Delon's break-up with Schneider, it may also have helped secure his image as a seducer whose appeal, as we have seen, is to a female rather than a male fan base. Much more than Belmondo, Delon fits the romantic paradigm of the wild, savage male who may one day, fans hope, be domesticated by love.[35]

29• See *Paris Match*, 23 August 2001, pp.48–9. The reporting of Belmondo's collapse is countered by an emphasis on his eternal physique and unceasing exercise. The threat to his health is one more 'battle' which Bébel will win (p.44) – the boxing analogy invokes a fantasy of youth and invulnerability.

30• Seidler, op. cit., p.281.

31• *Flic ou voyou* means simply 'Cop or yob', a confusion that informs Belmondo's performances as early as 1959, with *A double tour*, where Laszlo is described as being a *voyou* despite in effect solving a murder and effecting justice. For more on *Le Marginal*, see O'Shaugnessy, op. cit., pp.223–8.

32• For instance, he refers to himself three times as a marginal in Jousse and Toubiana, op. cit., and compares his apparent neglect in France with an ecstatic reception at the Berlin film festival.

33• 'Everything can be learnt'.

34• 'She comes from the social class that I hate more than anything in the world', cited in Violet, op. cit., p.177.

35• For more on this romantic model, see J. Radway, *Reading the romance: women, patriarchy and popular literature*, London, Verso, 1987.

The ideal of taming the wild male is mobilised by the animal imagery used frequently to describe Delon: he is a cat, a dog, a wolf, but always untamed and therefore potentially violent.[36] These connotations are only emphasised by Delon's associations with the criminal underworld in Marseilles, which have provided an undercurrent of controversy throughout his career, particularly in the Markovic affair of 1968, when his bodyguard was murdered.[37] Belmondo, too, has at times been represented off screen as a kind of outlaw: in 1965 the star won a case against a policeman who had assaulted him, but not before the judge had asked him if his own behaviour had been influenced by his habitual gangster roles. Both Belmondo and Delon sought to maintain their lawless images by attempting to buy the rights to the autobiography of Mesrine, the charismatic and extremely popular bank robber of the early seventies who was eventually killed in a police ambush. (Although Belmondo beat Delon to the punch, the film was never made.) Ultimately, however, both stars occupy a paradoxical position, on the outside and the inside simultaneously. According to Richard Dyer, such reconciling of opposites is what characterises stardom.[38] As stars, Belmondo and Delon oscillate perpetually between the terms *flic* and *voyou*. They played outsiders while remaining central, as star actors and as producers, to French cinema over at least two decades. However marginal some of their characters or performances may have been, there was often another grouping – a racial or sexual other, most notably women in the macho thrillers – that was genuinely excluded.[39]

THE LAW OF THE FATHER

The authority of the lone male star is often sharply contrasted with impersonal authority systems, such as governments, all forms of bureaucracy, hierarchies and even police procedures. It is pitted against both fascistic (para)military regimes (*Le Professionnel*, *Parole de flic*) and permissive, libertarian attitudes to sex and drugs (*Le Marginal*, *Flic ou voyou*). The authority embodied by Belmondo and Delon is thus generally represented as reasonable, a kind of middle path between extremes, and although it often operates outside the letter of the law, it is authorised by an appeal to an apparently eternal, natural law: that of fatherhood. It is out of paternal grief for his murdered daughter that Pratt (Delon) exercises his revenge in *Parole de flic*. Similarly, in *Flic ou voyou*, Borowitz (Belmondo) is motivated to act increasingly violently by the kidnapping of his daughter. In both cases, the hero is the law (a police officer) but most importantly, he is the father.

Paternal authority is not, however, a natural given. It is an essential part of western culture, a construct derived from Enlightenment thinking, which holds that reason and authority are masculine, while nature and emotion are coded as feminine. This has

---

36• Delon's character in *Le Samouraï* is described as a 'lone wolf', while Schneider compares him to a young dog in Violet, op. cit., p.175.

37• See ibid, pp.231–48 for more on the Markovic affair.

38• R. Dyer, *Stars* (new edition), London, BFI, 1998, p.82.

39• See O'Shaugnessy, op. cit., p.226, for an account of this process in *Le Marginal*.

important repercussions in terms of gender roles, particularly within the heterosexual family where, according to the Enlightenment tradition, 'the father is to be the source of reason. He is also to be the source of discipline for, as Kant says [. . .], "Discipline changes animal nature into human nature"'.[40] One could say that the importance of fatherhood in Delon's star image shifts him from 'animal nature into human nature'. Belmondo's juvenile clowning is also in part authorised by the paternal discipline and authority that his off-screen persona possesses. He is often represented as a patriarch in the popular press, an image which is strengthened by reference to his Italian roots and the traditional family structures which he has inherited and seeks to maintain (for example, naming the eldest son of each generation Paul). In its 1982 'duel' feature, *Paris Match* described both stars as marvellous fathers, noting in particular that Anthony Delon was the double of his dad.[41] There remains, however, a fragility and even a kind of desperation in Delon's relation to fatherhood. His bonding with Anthony is balanced by his rejection of Ari (his son with the singer Nico). Delon's own father abandoned him twice – first when his parents' marriage broke up, and again when, at the age of eighteen, Delon's request to join the navy was authorised with alacrity. The armed forces, as Delon has admitted, gave him the sense of inclusion and the patriarchal authority absent from his own family. In his subsequent film career, he appears to have sought out collaborations or confrontations with male directors who might act as powerful surrogate fathers (Clément, Visconti and Melville, followed later by Godard and Lévy). Hence, also, his fixation with acting as a test of strength: '*j'ai besoin d'une force que j'admire. [. . .] il y a toujours ce putain de bras de fer*'.[42]

If Delon's entire approach to acting can be characterised as a son's search for the absent father, a key performance by Belmondo dramatises the rejection of the bad father/s by the rebellious son. According to the theorists of the Frankfurt school, 'the just and moral father [. . .] teaches the sons to revolt'. In this process, the sons 'first internalise the father's principles and prohibitions and then challenge him for his failure to live up to them. This legitimates their revolt against him.'[43] Such a pattern is articulated in two massively popular films of the early eighties, *Rambo* (1985) and *Le Professionnel* (1981). Susan Faludi has written that the *Rambo* series 'reclaimed the virtue of the solitary American man'.[44] The second of the series, *Rambo: First Blood II*, was by far the most successful, although all three starred the action hero Sylvester Stallone. In *Rambo*, Stallone's war veteran returns to Vietnam to rescue the mythologised lone soldiers who are still missing in action – long-time POWs who have been abandoned by their military superiors. As Faludi notes,

---

40· Seidler, op. cit., p.274.

41· *Paris Match*, 26 February 1982, pp.58–9. Note the use of animal imagery (Anthony is described as having the same catlike walk as his father). For more on Delon and doubles, see below.

42· 'I need someone strong who I can admire. It always comes down to that fucking trial of strength', cited in Schwab, op. cit., p.28. The struggle is physical (*bras de fer* can also mean arm-wrestling).

43· Seidler, op. cit., p.287.

44· Faludi, op. cit., p.364.

> The POW became a stand-in for all the ways the postwar sons had been deserted by
> their 'commanding officers' [. . .]. For many of the men who responded so dramatically
> to the Rambo myth, those 'stinking bureaucrats' may have brought to mind [. . .] all
> the anonymous post World War II fathers [. . .] who had abandoned them on the fields
> of masculinity.[45]

The exception that proves the rule is Colonel Trautman, the one good father who has not
betrayed John Rambo. The idealised father–son bond between Trautman and Rambo is
all that stands against the generalised collapse of paternal authority in the film, and the
replacement of traditional fathering by impersonal, cynical systems of hierarchy and
command. The same drama is played out in *Le Professionnel*, one of Belmondo's biggest
(and last) hits at the box office, a film seen by over five million spectators and which, like
Rambo, seems to address a predominantly male audience in its depiction of the hero's
revolt against corrupt paternal authority.

In *Le Professionnel* Belmondo plays Major Joss Beaumont, a secret service agent sent on a
mission to assassinate the dictator of an African country (the fictitious Malagawi, for
which we might read the French ex-colony of Mali). He fails, is imprisoned, but eventually
escapes and returns to France. In the meantime, government policy towards Malagawi has
changed, and the mission has been suppressed. The suits in Paris (like the 'stinking
Washington bureaucrats' in *Rambo*) have abandoned our hero to his fate. Just like Rambo,
and the post-war generation of men surveyed in Faludi's study, Beaumont has been
'stiffed'. However, although alone and hunted by the secret service, he is a professional
with pride in his abilities. Thus the individual working man goes to battle against the
impersonal forces of the state. Beaumont is determined to carry out the contract, and
indeed succeeds in assassinating the dictator at the close of the film. His resourcefulness
and refusal to play by the rules enable him to outwit the apparatus of the state. His
enemies are all middle-aged authority figures, from the dictator to various French
politicians and the officers who originally trained and employed him. Captain Valera
alone, like Rambo's Colonel Trautman, stands out as a potential ally or a good father.
Although of a junior rank to Beaumont, Valera looks older, and has a sedentary,
avuncular appearance. He remains loyal to Beaumont and defends him at every
opportunity, eulogising his old friend in similar terms to those Trautman will use for
Rambo ('the best combat vet I've ever seen'). But where *Rambo*'s revisionism is ultimately
optimistic – the Vietnam war can be won this time; a good father can still be found – the
vision in *Le Professionnel* is much bleaker. Under pressure from his superiors, Valera betrays
Beaumont. The revolt of the son ends in death (very rare for a character played by
Belmondo), reinforcing the sense of betrayal that permeates the film.

Le Professionnel is not entirely downbeat. Belmondo's performance lightens the mood with
one-liners and clowning routines (for example, rolling around in the street disguised as a
drunken tramp). But in comparison with his other successes of the same period (*Flic ou*

---

45. Ibid., p.366.

voyou, L'As des as), the film is pessimistic, even tragic in tone, with poignant inevitability expressed in Morricone's famous score. Why, then, was *Le Professionnel* so popular? Another way to phrase the question is to ask why paternal authority was perceived as corrupt, and in need of a new, rebellious avatar like Joss Beaumont. The place of the father in twentieth-century society had been rendered increasingly problematic by the flourishing of modern capitalism, and the collapse of paternal traditions in the workplace (for example, the passing on of skills from father to son).[46] What has been termed an 'instrumentalised' culture saw 'the internalisation of authority' in imitation of the father replaced by 'conformity to external standards'.[47] Authority was no longer embodied by individual fathers, but was expressed via impersonal, systematised forms, such as management structures. In France, the development of modern capitalism took place in the post-war years, and reached a peak during the period when Belmondo and Delon became stars.

Kristin Ross has traced this process in detail, and has identified the late 1950s and early 1960s – the moment of Belmondo and Delon's entry into stardom – as crucial in the formation of a new technocratic and corporate vision in France. The process found expression in the figure of the executive, whose qualities – 'adaptability bordering on passivity, serviceability, [...] and being on the whole devoid of singularity – amounted to a distinct loss in virility'.[48] Hence the need for Delon and Belmondo to preserve singular machismo. With 'subjectivity' and 'agency' being replaced in the workplace (and the academy) by 'rules, codes, and structures',[49] it is no surprise to see actors who embodied these threatened, traditional masculine values coming to the fore as stars. Heroes were going to be needed in a society apparently 'composed of agentless structures', where 'unchecked bureaucratic growth meant that institutions [...] no longer put humans first', and people felt 'that the future was not in their control'.[50] Belmondo in particular incarnates an appealing alternative to 'the ideology of technocracy', since in a world where 'those "in the know" are adults, and everyone else is a child',[51] Bébel is always on the side of the child (and hence of the public, of 'everyone else'). Finally, if the new technocratic and bureaucratic France denied 'the outside itself',[52] then the stars who compensated for this state of affairs were sure to be found on the outside (of buildings, bureaucracies, the law). Later social factors contributing to Delon and Belmondo's mature stardom might include the economic crisis of the 1970s, mass unemployment, and a sense of the modern city as a threatening and violent place, all of which contribute to 'male identification with

46· See Seidler, op. cit., pp.293–4.

47· Ibid., p.279.

48· K. Ross, *Fast Cars, Clean Bodies: Decolonisation and the Reordering of French Culture*, Cambridge, Mass. and London, MIT Press, 1996, p.175.

49· Ibid., p.161.

50· Ibid., p.177.

51· Ibid., 178.

52· Ibid., p.195.

invulnerable hero figures'.[53] These heroes are often rebellious sons who can also be seen as new father figures, capable of reintroducing a charismatic form of masculine authority while flouting the law of the absent or impersonal father. Belmondo and Delon both manage to incarnate paternal discipline while transgressing the rules that govern social conformity and hierarchy (notably going against superiors, condemning bureaucracy and breaking the law – often while playing policemen). The physicality of their performances (Delon's natural grace and rapid appropriation of space, Belmondo's theatrical gestures and dangerous stunts) reanimate masculine authority, making it dynamic and personal where it had become impersonal and alienating.

CONCLUSION: BEYOND MACHISMO

So far, so macho. But are there elements within the star images of Belmondo and Delon that go beyond the hypermasculine, which reveal something beneath the leather jacket or the armour-plated car? At first, both men appear locked into a form of masculinity that celebrates autonomy while leaving little space 'for dependency, relationship or feeling'.[54] Belmondo cried on screen for the first time in *Itinéraire d'un enfant gâté*, in 1988, thirty years after his screen debut! Delon appears fixated on trials of strength, and has been equated with the enclosed 'autistic masculinity' of his hit-man character in *Le Samouraï*.[55] As he himself has acknowledged, 'Le Samouraï *c'est moi*'.[56] Both on screen and off, fatherhood may seem the only alibi for the expression of these stars' feelings. However, this reduced vision of masculinity is 'a false conception'; it can be challenged by star images that 'displace false polarities', and present themselves as 'both dependent and independent, emotional as well as rational, tender as well as strong'.[57] This appears to be the case with Jean Gabin or Gérard Depardieu.[58] It is also, perhaps surprisingly, true of Belmondo and Delon.

The theatricality of Belmondo's gestures and the warmth of his voice soften his tough image. His entrances and exits are exaggeratedly theatrical. In *Le Professionnel* he casts himself as Harlequin and tiptoes out of a hotel room leaving the 'stage' to a prostitute and her client, whom he christens Columbine and Caro.[59] *Flic ou voyou* (1979) sees him driving an open-top sports car straight into a living room before calmly interrogating the owner of the house. His off-screen appearances can be equally flamboyant. Whereas for Delon the 1980s was a time of posing in leather jackets with large vicious dogs,[60] in the same

---

53• O'Shaughnessy, op. cit., p.230.

54• Seidler, op. cit., p.298.

55• See G. Vincendeau, '"Autistic Masculinity" in Jean-Pierre Melville's Crime Thrillers', in A. Hughes and J. Williams (eds), *Gender and French Cinema*, Oxford and New York, Berg, 2001, pp.139–158.

56• 'I am The Samourai' – Jousse and Toubiana, op. cit., p.24.

57• Seidler, op. cit., p.298. Seidler is not talking about stars specifically here, but about fathering.

58• See Vincendeau, *Stars and Stardom*, pp.59–81 and 215–240, as well as Chapter 7, below.

59• The allusions here are to the stock characters from the *commedia dell arte*.

60• See M. Guichoux, 'Au nom du père', *Libération*, 15/16 February 1997, p.52.

period and into the nineties, a tiny Yorkshire terrier accompanied Belmondo in numerous photos, rendering his image at once more feminine and more middle class, since this '*boule de poils*' belonged '*sur le tapis persan d'un salon bourgeois*' rather than '*nichée dans des bras athlétiques*'.[61] As Commissaire Borowitz in *Flic ou voyou*, Belmondo pushes his characteristic clowning and flamboyance to excess. The macho violence of the narrative is repeatedly offset by humour (his appealing grin, his one-liners) and by the extravagance of his costume and mannerisms. He wears a long silk scarf and old-fashioned pilot's helmet, thus superimposing several of his well-known personae (the adventurer of *L'Homme de Rio* or *L'As des as*, the thirties tycoon of *Stavisky*) onto the role of a modern detective. The effect is to foreground the theatricality and artificiality of the performance. Every gesture – lighting a match, picking up the phone, or pulling out his gun – is excessive and self-conscious. Thus his tough guy act – the scenes where he blows up a casino or torches a bar – seems as theatrical as the clowning. The athletic masculinity celebrated in the car chases and stunts is comically undercut by the sequence in which Borowitz, dressed in a pink silk dressing-gown, is rejected by his lover and his daughter, and is pushed off the spare bed by a large hound. To the feminisation of the action hero in such scenes, one might add the warm and lisping tone of his voice throughout the film. As his most recent biographers have stressed, it is above all Bébel's voice – his cheeky accent, his everyday tone – that allows him to remain a man of the masses, a millionaire superstar '*en qui chacun, de l'ouvrier au bourgeois de province, peut se reconnaître*'.[62] That well-loved voice is, in contrast to the neutral tones and frequent silences of Delon, a demonstrative instrument. It gives something away: feeling, humour, warmth.

Not all of Belmondo's performances were as popular as *Flic ou voyou*, which attracted four million spectators. Those films which appear to have contradicted his star persona and disappointed his fans seem to have done so because they undermined his macho image, not with flamboyance and showmanship, but with passivity and impotence. In both *La Sirène du Mississippi* (1969) and *Stavisky* (1974), Belmondo plays characters who attempt to project an active, extravagant form of masculine authority. In the former, Louis Mahé is a successful entrepreneur who travels across the world from from Réunion to France, who drives fast cars, scales the facade of a hotel, and eludes capture by the police after committing a murder. In the latter, Serge Alexandre is a charming tycoon given to astounding displays of wealth, declaring that '*La seule façon d'attirer l'argent, c'est de le montrer*'.[63] But neither man is secure in his apparent identity. Mahé is, in fact, a puppet, manipulated by Marion (Catherine Deneuve), the femme fatale whom he has married. His is the flawed, masochistic masculinity of the film noir hero, whose '[e]xtreme romantic idealisation' leads him to abandon 'his active position as masculine subject by willingly setting himself in thrall to the loved object. He allows himself to become engulfed by the

---

61. 'bundle of fur [belonged] on the Persian carpet of a bourgeois living room [rather than] in the arms of an athlete', Strazzula and Leduc, op. cit., p.156.

62. 'in which everyone, from the workers to the provincial middle classes, can recognise themselves', ibid., p.12.

63. 'The only way to attract money is to make a show of it.'

woman.'[64] This is made explicit in Mahé's nightmare vision of huge women towering over him. Twice in the film he is bedridden, first in the clinic (scene of the nightmare) and then in the finale when he discovers that Marion is poisoning him, but continues to let this happen. Such 'self-abnegation and passivity [...] run[s] counter to his "responsibilities as a man",[65] and hence to Belmondo's star image. He is no longer the *voyou* – she is: '*pour moi, Catherine était un garçon, un voyou [...] et Jean-Paul, une petite fille [...] vierge*'.[66]

Stavisky, if not quite as explicit a reversal of gendered power as *La Sirène du Mississippi*, does nonetheless present a very similar disempowering of the Belmondo character. Although not feminised like Louis, Stavisky is increasingly passive. His first incarnation, as the conspicuously wealthy Serge Alexandre, is revealed as a false identity. Behind the facade of riches and ease is a rather desperate outsider, a Russian Jew with a criminal past. In the France of the thirties, with fascism on the rise, he is a useful scapegoat for financial scandals, and he ends the film in snowy isolation, lying on a bed like Louis in the Swiss cabin at the end of *La Sirène du Mississippi*. Like Louis too, Stavisky is fixated by the image of his wife. Waiting passively for the police to come for him, he lies in bed cutting out photos of her from the newspaper. He dies off screen, without a struggle. Throughout the film, Stavisky's flamboyance is financial rather than physical, and his stunts are merely impetuous forms of consumption, like the abundance of flowers that he orders for his wife. By contrast, Louis does at least attempt to behave like an action hero. But there is no place for external action in a psychological drama, where the action is inside the characters. In both films, the props of masculinity, like Louis's revolver and Stavisky's false moustache, are not enough. Divested of them, incapable of escape, the hero is a frozen failure.

Jean-Luc Godard, who had directed Belmondo in *A bout de souffle* (1959), felt that *Stavisky* should have starred Delon instead.[67] Despite Belmondo's excellent, vulnerable performance, he had a point. For Delon has frequently played characters, like Stavisky, who are divided or doubled: in *Plein soleil* (1960), *Histoires extraordinaires* (1967), *Monsieur Klein* (1976), and Godard's own *Nouvelle vague* (1990), among others. If masculine authority is predicated on the 'the Kantian idea that autonomy consists in the denial of the other',[68] then Delon seems often to have accepted or even become the other. *Plein soleil* includes a sequence in which Delon's Ripley famously dresses up as Philip and then kisses himself in the mirror, murmuring to himself in Philip's voice. As Yves Boisset noted in his review, Delon is '*Un héros double, courant toujours après la moitié de lui-même*'.[69] More recently, both *Positif*

64• F. Krutnik, *In a Lonely Street: Film noir, genre and masculinity*, London, Routledge, 1991, p.84.

65• Ibid., p.84.

66• 'for me, Catherine was a boy, a yob, and Jean-Paul was a young girl, a virgin', Truffaut, the film's director, cited in A. Gillain, *François Truffaut: le secret perdu*, Paris, Hatier, 1992, p.199.

67• See Strazzula and Leduc, op. cit., p.148. For Belmondo's reaction, see ibid., p.149.

68• Seidler, op. cit., p.286.

69• 'The hero as double, always running after the other half of himself', cited in Violet, op. cit., p.98.

and *Cahiers du cinéma* have commented on the duality of Delon's star image.[70] It is the traumatised inner self of many of Delon's protagonists that qualifies their otherwise unremittingly macho authority. Hard on the outside, his performances at times reveal something else on the inside: the melancholy fatalism of Jef Costello welcoming death in *Le Samouraï*; the weary passivity (or is it a noble solidarity?) that informs Monsieur Klein's final decision to accept deportation. In contrast with the assured, vengeful war veteran played by Belmondo in *Le Professionnel*, Delon's lost soldiers in *L'Insoumis* and *Lost Command* are divided souls. Hence alongside, or rather, inside '*l'homme d'action [. . .] un idéal imaginaire de virilité*', there exists '*l'homme fragile [. . .] tourné vers son intériorité*'.[71]

The mirror scenes from *Plein soleil*, *Le Samouraï* and *Monsieur Klein* suggest that this dualism and interiority is narcissistic. Delon's star image is more eroticised than Belmondo's, and is valued more by female fans, but it remains literally self-regarding. More consistently than Belmondo – for whom the role is an exception, as in *La Sirène du Mississippi* – Delon evokes the masochistic film noir hero who, no matter how professional, is doomed to failure by a flaw in his masculine efficiency, a gloomy fatalism:

> the defeatist and self-pitying 'tough' hero suggests a masculinity that has turned narcissistically in upon itself. [. . .] Rejecting external attachments and value systems, the loner-heroes can cling to their own secluded [. . .] sense of perfection.[72]

One can apply this comment not just to Delon's performances, but to his isolated and increasingly bitter position with regard to French cinema. Behind the intimidating beauty, the ferocious reputation, the links with the underworld and, more recently, with police organisations, behind the leather jacket and the expressionless face, there is a hidden sadness that allows the romanticising of Delon's image. This subtext of sadness is most apparent in the slightly lost air of Jef Costello in *Le Samouraï*, or in the interviews where Delon speaks of his childhood, combining familiar tropes, but in a poignant tone, to declare '*J'étais seul comme un animal*'.[73] It is above all present in Delon's eyes, the most revealing part of his often mask-like face. A 1997 feature from *Le Point* magazine shows Delon on stage, applauding the audience with tears in his eyes, and accompanies the photo with Pascal Jardin's description of the star's gaze: '*il promène sur le monde un regard d'acier où semblent briller des larmes venues de la petite enfance*'.[74] Delon's machismo is ultimately qualified by pathos, just as Belmondo's is by comedy.

70· See P. Rouyer, 'Le petit théâtre de Jean-Pierre Melville', *Positif*, December 1995, p.101, and J-F. Rauger, 'Alain Delon, l'unique et son double', *Cahiers du cinéma*, 501 (April 1996), pp.32–3.

71· 'the man of action, an imaginary masculine ideal'; 'the fragile man, turned inwards on himself', J-P. Gorce, 'Delon-Tonkin', *Cahiers de la Cinémathèque*, 57 (October 1992), p.113.

72· Krutnik, op. cit., p.90.

73· 'I was alone like an animal', cited in Guichoux, op. cit., p.52.

74· 'he looks at the world with a steely gaze in which the tears of a young child seem to sparkle', cited in P. Billard, 'L'énigme Delon', *Le Point*, 1272 (1 February, 1997), p.75.

CHAPTER 6

Focus on the face in soft porn: Sylvia Kristel on the set of *Emmanuelle* (1974).

A star is porn: Sylvia Kristel and Joe Dallesandro

GENDER IN PORN STARDOM

If one measures film stardom by the popularity of an actor's films, then the biggest female star in French cinema is not Catherine Deneuve, Isabelle Adjani or Brigitte Bardot. It is in fact the Dutch actress Sylvia Kristel who, 'thanks to her success in the erotic *Emmanuelle* series, turns out to be the highest ranking female star at the French box office.'[1] But, as Ginette Vincendeau points out (shortly before dropping Kristel from her own account), star encyclopaedias like *Les Acteurs français* and the *Dictionnaire du cinéma* 'leave Kristel out completely.'[2] Most versions of French film stardom tend to ignore the porn film, and therefore neglect the importance of Kristel and other stars of the genre. And yet throughout the 1970s, pornography, both soft-core and hard-core, was a significant feature of French cinema. In 1974, the year that porn broke into the mainstream in France, the two most successful films at the box office were the soft-core fantasies *Emmanuelle* and *Contes immoraux*. Even after government measures launched in late 1975 to combat, or at least control, the industry (including the new, highly-taxed X rating) pornography remained a force in French film production and consumption. By 1978 almost half of all French films were rated X, and the following year these hard-core movies accounted for 6 per cent of cinema spectators.[3] The status enjoyed by pornographic cinema at this time (before its demise with the development of the straight-to-video market) had implications for representations of gender in stardom.

In France, male stars have always generated higher box-office receipts and commanded bigger fees than their female counterparts. This is partly due to the fact that male rather than female stars tend to work consistently within comedy, the most popular genre.[4] But this trend was bucked in the mid-seventies, when the female stardom celebrated by porn was briefly a bigger box-office draw than the male stardom celebrated by comedy. Hence, Sylvia Kristel in *Emmanuelle* was watched by nine million spectators in France, more than the pre-eminent male star of the period, Louis de

---

1. G. Vincendeau, *Stars and Stardom in French Cinema*, London and New York, Continuum, 2000, p.28.

2. Ibid., p.29.

3. See R. Prédal, *Le Cinéma français depuis 1945*, Paris: Nathan, 1991, pp.344–5.

4. See Vincendeau, op. cit., p.28. As Vincendeau explains, one exception to this would be the comedy actress Josiane Balasko, star and director of the comic hit *Gazon Maudit* (1995).

64

Funès, in any of his seventies comedies.[5] Not only is Kristel the most popular female star in French cinema, she is also the most popular porn star in France, male or female. This is because heterosexual porn stardom is, in gender terms, an inversion of mainstream stardom. Porn cinema is an 'industry of feminine display' where '"Actresses have the power"'.[6] The women are the stars:

> Porn, at least porn produced for a heterosexual audience, is one of the few contemporary occupations where the pay gap operates in women's favor; the average actress makes 50 to 100 per cent more money than her male counterpart. But then, she is the object of desire; he merely her appendage, the object of the object.[7]

However, it should be noted that porn is the cheapest and most exploitative sector of the film industry. Low budgets meant that most French porn stars of the seventies were far from highly paid: '*les films porno se tournent en 8 ou 15 jours maximum avec en moyenne 100,000 francs et même souvent moins; Claudine Beccarie, vedette d'*Exhibition*, a été payée moins de 1000 francs la journée'.*[8] Kristel herself was paid 'peanuts' for her role in *Emmanuelle*, although the subsequent success of the franchise meant that in 1994 she was presented with 'an offer I couldn't refuse' to take part in *Emmanuelle Forever*.[9] The expansion of French porn cinema in the nineties has not seen any change in this situation. Current star Coralie reveals that although actresses are the 'most important thing' in X-rated films' they are woefully paid:

> *La plupart des filles commencent à 1500 F par jour de tournage, ce qui n'est même pas le tarif syndical d'un petit role dans un film traditionnel. [. . .] On a l'impression de s'être fait doublement baiser. Je déconseillerais à une fille de faire du X si l'argent est sa seule motivation.*[10]

Even if star status increases earning power and gives the star a certain authority to specify what she will and won't do on screen, it can also dissolve the distance between actor and spectator/fan. This also applies to mainstream film stars, but with porn actresses, sex is the

---

5• See Prédal, op. cit., p.404. *Emmanuelle* (1974) with 8.9 million spectators, is well ahead of *Les Aventures de Rabbi Jacob* (1973) with 7.4 million, and *Le Gendarme et les extra-terrestres* (1979) with 6.2 million. Admittedly, de Funès was an ageing star by the seventies, but several hit films from his heyday (*Le Gendarme de Saint-Tropez, Les Grandes Vacances*) and similarly from that of Gérard Depardieu (*La Chèvre, Jean de Florette*) have been outperformed at the box office by *Emmanuelle*.

6• S. Faludi, *Stiffed: The Betrayal of the Modern Man*, London, Vintage, 2000, pp.534–5. Faludi is quoting a male would-be porn actor in the second phrase here.

7• Ibid., p.535.

8• 'porn films were shot in one or two weeks maximum, for on average 100 000 francs, and often less; Claudine Beccarie, star of *Exhibition*, was paid less than a thousand francs per day', Prédal, op. cit., p.345.

9• Kristel cited in T. Hibbert, 'Sylvia Kristel: 70s Icon', *Empire* 58 (April 1994), p.50.

10• 'Most girls start on 1500 francs per day, which is less than the union rate for a minor role in a mainstream film. You feel as if you've been screwed twice over. I would discourage any girl from getting involved in porn for the money.', F. Dordor, 'X Fille', *Les Inrockuptibles*, Numéro special été: Génération X, 29 July 1998, p.32.

defining quality of their stardom and hence of the assumptions (about nymphomania and prostitution) that their predominantly male fans make. When a fan recognises Coralie, '*En un instant, toute la fausse intimité que ses performances à l'écran ont supposé établir avec le spectateur lui revient en pleine figure*'.[11]

Male stars are generated by gay porn and, on rare occasions, within heterosexual porn too. Rocco Siffredi, star of dozens of hard-core porn videos made in the United States during the nineties, has recently become a key porn star in France.[12] Siffredi is, however, the exception, as a male porn star of at least equal celebrity to his female peers. In the seventies, Sylvia Kristel had no male competitors at a time when she personified the arrival of porn in mainstream French cinema. She can nonetheless be compared with the 'underground' star Joe Dallesandro, her co-star from *La Marge* (1976), in order to explore gender distinctions in the construction of heterosexual porn stardom.

SYLVIA KRISTEL: THE PORN STAR AS MAINSTREAM

If sexual liberation in Britain is associated with the mid-sixties, in France it is positioned slightly later, in the aftermath of the anti-establishment struggles of May 1968. In the protests, campaigns, and graffiti of the late sixties and early seventies, '*le sexe, le désir et le plaisir [étaient] au coeur de toutes les métaphores*'.[13] Popular forms such as BD (comics) took delight in portraying the body in all its intimate glory: in 1973, the adult comic *L'Echo des savanes* featured the 'genital adventures' of a walking penis exploring the female body.[14] The year 1973–74 was also a watershed for the representation of sex in French cinema. Numerous sexually explicit films were released, including huge commercial successes *Les Valseueses, Contes immoraux* and *Emmanuelle*. Viewing habits changed rapidly, so that the estimated size of the audience for erotic cinema in Paris, for instance, increased from 50,000 spectators in 1972 to over 250,000 two years later.[15] In 1975, *Paris Match* reported on '*La France porno*', finding that porn accounted for 12 per cent of the domestic film market and predicting that 25 per cent of the film-going public would watch a porn film that year.[16] The low budgets for most porn films meant that only 30,000 spectators might be required for a film to break even, and that risk margins were much smaller than for other genres or for art cinema.[17] The representation of nudity and eroticism was no novelty, and had already informed the star images of Brigitte Bardot and Jeanne Moreau. However, the sexual

---

11• 'In the space of a second, all the fake intimacy with the spectator that her on-screen performances are meant to establish is thrown back in her face', ibid., p.31.

12• See Chapter 11.

13• 'sex, desire and pleasure were at the heart of every metaphor', D. Fischer, *L'Histoire des étudiants en France, de 1945 à nos jours*, Paris, Flammarion, 2000, p.395.

14• See *L'Echo des savanes*, 4, pp.3–7. Many thanks to Wendy Michallat for showing me this.

15• Prédal, op. cit., p.344.

16• See *Paris Match*, 20 September 1975, p.38.

17• See ibid., p.38.

politics of the early 1970s and the sensational success of *Emmanuelle* (the biggest box-office attraction of the decade) ensured that soft-core porn and even, for a brief time, hard-core, became mainstream. This was facilitated when major companies became involved in the distribution of porn films, which now played alongside mainstream films at commercial (as opposed to specialist) cinemas: *Les Jouissances* was distributed by Gaumont and *Exhibition* by UGC. Both films starred Claudine Beccarie and were hard-core porn, in that they showed actual sex acts rather than simulations. Where hard-core pornography is characterised by 'the principle of *maximum visibility*', soft porn is characterised by 'indirection' and 'masquerade'.[18] This is significant with regard to Sylvia Kristel since her image, unlike that of Beccarie or the even more extreme Sylvia Bourdon,[19] is not defined by visibly real sexual performances, but by elements of 'masquerade' such as non-sexual performance, costume and the fetishising of the star body and face.

Kristel had an early career as a fashion model and was named Miss TV Europe in 1973. The resulting publicity tour brought her to the attention of Just Jaeckin, a fashion photographer and former art director of *Marie Claire*, who was hoping to film Emmanuelle Arsan's erotic novel *Emmanuelle*. Kristel took the lead role, 'a part that had been turned down by every eligible French actress,' and the film's huge international success (it was to be seen by over 250 million spectators worldwide) meant that she 'came to typify the world's idea of a sexy, liberated French girl.'[20] Thus her Dutch nationality did not prevent her global star image from being firmly identified as French, while in France itself she was termed a kind of Parisian landmark, 'aussi célèbre que les "Folies Bergère" ou la Tour Eiffel'.[21] Alongside this artificial and erotic Frenchness, her star image was, perhaps surprisingly, characterised by innocence. Jaeckin describes her as 'this very innocent-looking girl'[22] and Kristel recalls him asking her to cultivate '*le regard vague de quelqu'un qui ne sait pas très bien où il en est. [. . .] Je devais avoir le visage d'un enfant de Marie*'.[23] The director of *Emmanuelle 2* (aka *Emmanuelle l'anti-vierge*, 1976) called her a cross between Katharine Hepburn and Minnie Mouse,[24] while *Paris Match* introduced her in July 1974 as '*l'heroïne aux yeux de myosotis et au regard ingénu de petite fille bien sage*'[25]. Kristel was featured twice more in 1974 by the magazine, first looking in a mirror and contemplating motherhood, then

---

18• L. Williams, *Hard Core: Power, Pleasure and the 'Frenzy of the Visible'*, Berkeley, Los Angeles and London, University of California Press, 1999, expanded paperback edition, pp.48 and 49.

19• Star of *Exhibition 2* and other extreme hard-core films, Bourdon's performances included zoophilia. See C. Tohill and P. Tombs, *Immoral Tales: Sex and Horror Cinema in Europe 1956–1984*, London: Titan Books, 1995, p.248.

20• Ibid., p.255.

21• 'as famous as the "Folies Bergère" or the Eiffel Tower', Anon., 'Une comédienne: Sylvia Kristel', *Cinéma français* 11 (1977), p.37.

22• Cited in B. Farrow, 'Emmanuelle exposed', *Hot Dog*, October 2000, p.74.

23• 'the vague look of someone who doesn't really know what they're up to. [. . .] I had to have the face of a convent school girl', J.-L. Lechat, 'Sylvia Kristel', *Stars & Cinéma* 3: 7 (September 1975), p.15.

24• See *Cinéma français* 11 (1977), p.39.

25• 'the heroine with the forget-me-not eyes and the innocent look of a good little girl', Anon., 'Peut-on aller voir *Emmanuelle*?', *Paris Match*, 20 July 1974, p.17.

later heavily pregnant in fur coat and hat.[26] These features emphasise a maternal, domesticated and thus largely desexualised image, with the mirror photo placed in a feature on stars and their children. Each time, the focal point is the star's face rather than her body. In fact, the only photograph in *Paris Match* of 1974 that presents Kristel's body is the one showing her heavily pregnant late in the year. Even the still from the end of *Emmanuelle*, used in July 1974, is demure, revealing only Kristel's head and shoulders, while her breasts appear deliberately obscured. This contrasts strongly with the triumphant display of Bardot's body in a contemporaneous issue of *Paris Match*, which sees the forty-year-old star posing nude on the beach while we are informed that: '*le photographe vous la montre toute nue devant son destin de femme et de star*'.[27] It also serves to demarcate Kristel's 'innocent' eroticism from the explicit sexuality of hard-core porn stars, who she later revealed often laughed at her performance and compared her to a refrigerator.[28]

The balance between star face and star body is caught in the famous publicity still for *Emmanuelle*, showing Kristel sitting topless in a cane chair and staring at the camera.[29] Her body is on display, the legs fetishised by long socks and boots, her breasts and shoulders naked, but attention is also drawn, via a string of pearls she is holding, upwards to her face. Her expression is thoughtful, her mouth slightly open as she holds the pearls towards it, her gaze intent and straight at the camera. Her hair is short and boyish, again in a marked contrast to Bardot's star image of the time.[30] In other publicity photos from the period, emphasis is placed on Kristel's face, rather than her body, by the use of various framing garments such as scarves and hats, and most obviously by close-ups,[31] which hold out a promise of sexual pleasure that is somehow both innocent and daring: 'Small-breasted, tall and lithe, Kristel was no buxom bombshell, her winsome, open face promising a form of sex that was natural.'[32] While much of this is at odds with Bardot's star image (where the emphasis is much more on the body than the face), it has something in common with Juliette Binoche, whose stardom is encapsulated not by her body but by her 'erotic face', the emphasis

---

26• See *Paris Match*, 28 September 1974, p.7, and 2 November 1974, p.7.

27• 'the photographer shows her to you completely naked before her destiny as a woman and as a star', F. Caviglioli, 'Etre Brigitte à 40 ans', *Paris Match*, 28 September 1974, p.48. One might argue that age is the crucial difference here, that Bardot is asserting her physical beauty 'even' at the age of forty, while Kristel, in her twenties, has no need to. However, Kristel's star image is always more demure than Bardot's. Hence, when interviewed by *Empire* at age 41 about her role in *Emmanuelle Forever*, although we are told she looks 'jolly attractive' there is no photo of Kristel, let alone nude. See Hibbert, op. cit., p.50.

28• See Kristel interviewed in *Cinéma français* 11 (1977), p.38.

29• Reproduced in L. R. Williams, 'The oldest swinger in town', *Sight and Sound*, August 2000, p.24, and Hibbert, op. cit., 51, among others. This shot does not actually appear in the film.

30• Compare the Bardot photo in Caviglioli, op. cit., p.48.

31• See, for example, the facial close-up publicising *Emmanuelle 2* reproduced in A. Cox, 'My Kind of Woman', *The Guardian (Review)*, 15 December 2000, p.8. Kristel's hair (longer in the sequel than in the original) is completely covered by a scarf and the entire focus is on her eyes and mouth.

32• L. R. Williams, op. cit., p.24.

on which 'has led to an erasure of her body'.[33] The case of Kristel is not as extreme or etherealised; she is still a porn star, whose body is fetishised throughout her films (and to a certain extent in her publicity photos). *Emmanuelle* includes several scenes in which another character or the camera itself focuses on Kristel's long legs, for example as she lounges on couches and beds, fixes her stockings, lies back in a carriage while a man pulls off her underwear. A feature in *Paris Match* from 1982 (during the period when Kristel had left the *Emmanuelle* series) again exhibits her legs to the camera, this time in photos of her stretched along a wall, or lying on her back pedalling her feet in the air.[34] But her face remains the site of pleasure in Kristel's performances as in her publicity.

The female face is important in erotic cinema, since it is the crucial index of a pleasure that would remain otherwise inaccessible to the camera. Because 'female orgasm takes place [. . .] in an "invisible place" that cannot easily be seen',[35] the sight (and sound) of female pleasure is often relocated to the face, and in particular the mouth. In hard-core pornography, of course, women's genitals are represented in a repeated search for verification of sexual pleasure, which has been termed 'the frenzy of the visible'[36] and 'the will to know'.[37] The 'slogan of pornography – "everything shown, everything seen" ' – requires the close-up as its 'basic element',[38] but where the close-up is genital in hard-core, it is often facial in soft porn. In *Emmanuelle* and *Emmanuelle 2* the frequent sexual 'numbers' tend to be introduced by a lush musical theme and a close-up on Kristel's face, often in soft focus. During sex, the camera again focuses on her face, particularly her partially open mouth and her closed eyes. As well as such facial close-ups, there are images of Kristel's body, at times in medium shot, often fragmented as the camera focuses on her breasts or legs, but rarely displayed entirely naked and never showing genitalia in close-up. This accords with the conventions of soft porn, according to which 'the medium shot of the body [. . .] closes down on to the sex' but is 'always blocked off by a piece of lingerie, by a thigh movement, by the angle of the framing, etc'.[39] Thus, when Emmanuelle masturbates in the first film, the site of pleasure is quickly elided by her thigh and then by her gown as the camera pans up to show her face, the mouth half open, gasping, the eyes shut, in Kristel's characteristic and much repeated articulation of orgasm. Similarly in the sequel, when Emmanuelle masturbates while undergoing acupuncture the upper half of

---

33· G. Vincendeau, 'Binoche the erotic face', *Sight and Sound*, June 2000, p.16. Vincendeau notes in ibid., p.15, that many of Binoche's films, including *Les Enfants du siècle* and *La Veuve de Saint-Pierre*, 'end on a close-up of her face looking straight into the camera.' This is also true of Kristel in the first two *Emmanuelle* films, most particularly in the second; see below.

34· See *Paris Match*, 31 December 1982. This is an exception; most photos concentrate on her face.

35· L. Williams, op. cit., p.49.

36· Ibid., p.7. Williams takes the term from Jean-Louis Comolli.

37· Y. Lardeau, 'Cold Sex (on pornography and beyond)', in D. Wilson (ed.), *Cahiers du cinéma, Volume Four, 1973–1978: History, Ideology, Cultural Struggle*, London and New York, Routledge, p.205.

38· Ibid., pp.207, 205.

39· Ibid., p.209.

her body is naked but the lower half remains covered by the folds of her dress. Both films end with an image not of Kristel's body, but of her face, held in a freeze-frame. *Emmanuelle 2* in particular focuses on her eyes, as the camera zooms in to isolate the gaze, which is addressing the audience one last time in the controlled, almost thoughtful soft porn 'come-on'.

In the late 1970s, Kristel made the premature farewell *Goodbye Emmanuelle* (1977), and attempted to reposition her image by taking roles in non-erotic drama and in comedies. The resulting films were not successful, however, and there was no significant renegotiation of her star image. In 1977, both *Alice ou la dernière fugue* and *René la Canne* flopped, despite genuinely novel performances from Kristel (pensive and determined in the first, feisty and comical in the second). Distinct as these films are from the *Emmanuelle* series, they both include allusions to the soft-porn stardom that Kristel was unable to break out of. As Alice, Kristel is trapped inside a mysterious house, just as the actress is trapped inside erotic cinema, and is spied on by largely unseen male voyeurs. Emmanuelle's 'come-on' smile is replaced by frowns of concentration and then, in the final scene, by a dying grimace as the camera shows Alice in facial close-up, dead in a car accident. While *Alice* reinterprets Kristel's porn stardom ironically, so that her existence is a form of imprisonment and her smile a rictus, *René la Canne* presents it farcically, so that the star body becomes literally so much meat: reunited with her husband (who has been sent to Germany as 'voluntary' labour in the war) Kristel pulls a huge leg of ham from her bag, then two strings of sausages from her overcoat, before she herself undresses and gets into bed.[40] Publicity interviews with Kristel in this period tended to downplay these roles, and concentrated on questions about eroticism, pornography and the *Emmanuelle* films.[41] During the 1980s, press reports on her private life (marriage and divorce) still referred to her as 'Emmanuelle' rather than Sylvia.[42] By 1984 and *Emmanuelle 4*, the actress had returned to the franchise that her star image had never left. In the early 1990s, she was still playing Emmanuelle, but in the later sequels 'her ageing body is traded in for younger models, leaving her to narrate rather than perform her erotic adventures, like a kind of sexual Scheherezade.'[43] By means of a 'special perfume', Kristel as 'old Emmanuelle' can experience sex via another woman's body, a narrative twist that prolongs the franchise and uses the 'ageing porn star [. . .] without challenging the boundaries of the erotic to include older bodies.'[44] Kristel will, it seems, remain forever enclosed within the body of films that is the *Emmanuelle* series.

---

40. This is authorised by the film's wartime setting, and by reference to the classic French comedy *La Traversée de Paris* (1956), which concerns the transport of black-market meat across occupied Paris. *René la Canne* also seems to predict Kristel's later move from 'young Emmanuelle' to 'old Emmanuelle', as her prostitute character becomes a high-class madam after the war.

41. See, for example, the interviews in *Cinéma français* 11 (1977), pp.37–40 and *Ciné-Revue* 58: 13 (30 March 1978), pp.6–11.

42. See, for example, *Paris Match*, 31 December 1982 and 11 July 1986.

43. L. R. Williams op. cit., p.24.

44. Ibid., p.25.

JOE DALLESANDRO: A BODY WITHOUT A VOICE

Like Kristel, the Italian-American Joe Dallesandro was a foreign actor who became associated with French erotic cinema in the mid-seventies. His five French films were all made between 1975 and 1979, and include a performance alongside Kristel in *La Marge*. Dallesandro was an underground star in the United States during the sixties, first in nude 'beefcake' photography, then as one of the so-called 'Superstars' of Andy Warhol's Factory film studio. Although Dallesandro himself is straight, his star body and hustler persona in the Warhol/Paul Morrissey films *Flesh* (1968), *Trash* (1970) and *Heat* (1972) made him a gay icon. The hustler is a 'representative figure of the gay underground' who appropriates some of the glamour of mainstream American stars, aping 'the sullen hunkiness of Brando, Dean, Presley and co.'[45] The business transaction whereby a star – whether underground like Dallesandro, or mainstream like James Dean – trades on their image, is made explicit in the figure of the hustler: he literally sells his body. As Dyer points out, stars are commodities: 'they are both labour and the thing that labour produces.' Hence certain stars' sense of betrayal at having been 'turned into something they didn't control is particularly acute because the commodity they produced is fashioned in and out of their own bodies and psychologies'.[46] This seems to be the case with Dallesandro, who has complained that at the Factory he was treated simply as a tradable resource to make money for Warhol and Morrissey's productions.[47] Celebrated by American *Vogue* in 1971 as 'the first really big star to come of the New York film underground',[48] Dallesandro hoped to profit himself from his star image by making it in Hollywood. He almost secured a role in *The Godfather,* but when he did leave the Factory to go 'overground' it was not in Hollywood but in Europe, thanks to the French and Italian films he made during the seventies.

At Warhol's Factory, androgyny and sexual ambivalence had been part of Dallesandro's star image. *Vogue* had described him as exhibiting 'a new uni-sexed glamour'.[49] This sense of crossing sexual boundaries was to continue in his French films, notably the first two, Louis Malle's *Black Moon* and Serge Gainsbourg's *Je t'aime, moi non plus* (both 1975). In the former, Dallesandro and Alexandra Stewart play twins, both called Lily. Cast for his resemblance to Stewart, Dallesandro represents a kind of male ideal in the film, androgynous in appearance and, at least initially, harmoniously identified with his sister. (This harmony between brother and sister is in direct contrast to the literal battle between the sexes that gives the film its violent context.) Although Dallesandro's physical appearance is emphasised (again, largely via the identification with Stewart), his voice is

---

45• R. Dyer, *Now you see it: Studies in lesbian and gay film*, London and New York: Routledge, 1990, p.153.

46• R. Dyer, *Heavenly Bodies: Film Stars and Society*, London, BFI/Macmillan, 1986, pp.5 and 6.

47• See M. Ferguson, *Little Joe Superstar: The Films of Joe Dallesandro*, Laguna Hills, Ca: Companion Press, 1998, pp.24–6.

48• Cited in ibid., p.24.

49• Cited in ibid., p.24.

not part of his star image. In *Black Moon* he never speaks, and communicates telepathically. The singing he indulges in is clearly dubbed, just as his dialogue is throughout *Je t'aime, moi non plus*. These seem to have been aesthetic as much as linguistic decisions. Malle chooses not to show Dallesandro moving his mouth at all, so that we only hear his song from afar, while Gainsbourg told him that 'when you speak French, your whole face contorts and you don't look like who you are.'[50] In contrast with Gérard Depardieu, whose tender voice successfully balances a strong physique, Dallesandro's star image, at least in his French films, appears contradicted or jeopardised by his (French-speaking) voice and is therefore entirely visual.

If *Black Moon* crystallises Dallesandro's androgynous appearance, *Je t'aime, moi non plus* reiterates his earlier, Warholian association with ambivalent sexuality. He plays Krassky, a butch refuse collector who is having a gay affair with his queenish buddy Padovan (Hugues Quester), but who falls in love with Johnny (Jane Birkin), an extremely androgynous barmaid. The homosexual overtones of Krassky's affair with Johnny are explicit: she has a boy's name and appearance (both in costume and body), and the sex between them is always anal. In fact, Krassky is associated with anality throughout the film: hence his job, his nick-name (Krass, i.e. 'crasse', meaning filth), and the repeated shots of him from the rear, whether clothed or, more often, nude. His appearance is a display of butch masculinity, complete with the props of the macho man: tattoo, vest, tight jeans, muscles. In Richard Dyer's terminology, he is the gay man as 'powerful [. . .] masculine [. . .] fucker', while Padovan (like his female replacement, Johnny) is the 'powerless [. . .] feminine [. . .] fuckee'.[51] But there is a vulnerability associated with Dallesandro here, which recalls his role as an impotent junkie in Morrissey's *Trash*. Hence Krassky's impotence when confronted with the prospect of vaginal intercourse with Johnny, and his fear of female sexuality. When he and Johnny do have sex, it is associated with pain for her and desperation for him. Gainsbourg's film is a celebration of complicated sexuality, and Dallesandro's role in it is to suggest a collision of opposites within the character of Krassky: Is he gay or straight? Tough or sensitive? Clean or dirty? (He poses on piles of old clothes and eulogises the rubbish dump as 'a mountain of shit', yet we also see him in a pristine white t-shirt brushing his teeth carefully.) He is all of these, and above all an object of desire for Padovan and Johnny, memorably seen from Johhny's point of view in a soft-focus mirror sequence where the camera slowly moves across his star torso. The 'uni-sexed glamour' of Dallesandro's star image is thus expressed in his early French films either as a visible androgyny (*Black Moon*) or, in *Je t'aime, moi non plus*, as a cross-gender sex appeal that enacts in Padovan's and Johnny's reaction. Vincent Canby's description of the star: 'His physique is so magnificently shaped that men as well as women become disconnected at the sight of him'.[52]

50· Cited in ibid., p.154.

51· See Dyer, op. cit., p.92. These terms are taken from Dyer's discussion of gay sex in *Querelle*.

52· Cited in Ferguson, op. cit., p.157.

CONCLUSION: *LA MARGE* AND THE PERFORMANCE OF THE ORGASM

In hard-core porn there is an essential difference between male and female stars: the visibility of the orgasm. This entails visual proof of orgasm for the male star, whereas the female star, even if engaging in actual sex acts, still has, in a sense, to perform her orgasm, to enact the unseen. In soft porn this distinction no longer holds. The sex is not real but performed, and so are the orgasms. *La Marge* is relatively unusual for a soft-porn film in that it teams a major female porn star with a male star of some calibre (although by no means equal), whose star image is explicitly sexual. So how are the star images of Kristel and Dallesandro represented in tandem and what does this tell us about gender and the performance of the orgasm?

La Marge was made in 1976 by Walerian Borowczyk, two years after his vast commercial success with the soft-core fantasy *Contes immoraux*. The characterisation is simple and traditional, following a pattern familiar from melodrama and myth: loving husband (Dallesandro) is tempted away from wife, family and countryside by the corruption of the big city, personified in the figure of the vamp or seductress. Kristel plays the latter role, a prostitute called Diana, her name highlighting the suggestions of predatory female sexuality that run throughout the film.[53] As Diana, Kristel is the embodiment of both sexualised Paris and commodified sexuality, namely prostitution. There is an irony here since the Dutch actress had already become a kind of Parisian sexual landmark, thanks to her role in *Emmanuelle*.[54] The importance of the city and the body together is expressed in the film's title, which has been variously translated as *The Margin* and *The Streetwalker*, and which relates to both the pavement where the prostitutes ply their trade and the eroticised margin of the female body (between lower and upper garments). The midriff area is, in effect, fetishised throughout the film, with waist-high camera angles used frequently for both stars, particularly in the scenes where they undress before sex. Kristel's body is repeatedly framed to show her pubis and stomach, most notably when she rolls a hard-boiled egg from her navel to her pubis. This sequence is sound-tracked by the song '*Une femme*' by Charles Drumont, and in effect the camera presents a kind of catalogue of Kristel's body (neck, breasts, navel, pudenda), concluding with an extreme close-up of her mouth as she slips the egg in, then out. This shot gives a clear indication that in soft porn not all of the star's body is available to the camera: hence the displacement upwards, in which the mouth becomes a sexual symbol to suggest the vagina (eminently representable in hard core).

The question of the star body as a commodity is raised in the scenes when Dallesandro, as the client, literally buys Kristel's body, paying her first for removing her skirt and then giving her a second payment to remove her top. In their second transaction, by paying

---

53. Diana was the goddess of the hunt. Carlos Fuentes associates her with the sexual appetite of the star Jean Seberg in his novel *Diana, The Goddess Who Hunts Alone*. See Chapter 8.

54. See above, note 21.

500 francs up front, he (and the spectator) is presented with Kristel in full frontal nudity for the first time in the film. The theme of buying the sexualised body is emphasised throughout the film by the iterative shots of money changing hands, and during the first sexual 'number' between Kristel and Dallesandro, the client's money is deliberately visible in Diana's hand. Kristel's role here is removed from the 'pornutopia' of the *Emmanuelle* series, in that it concentrates on the exchange of money for sex, and only features the expression of female pleasure in one of the three sex scenes between the film's stars. There are relatively few facial close-ups on Kristel in *La Marge*, and her performance is largely devoid of the sounds of pleasure that fill the soundtracks of the *Emmanuelle* series. Linda Williams notes that 'the allure of the sounds of pleasure resides at least partly in the fact that they come from inside the body and [. . .] speak, almost preverbally, of primitive pleasures.'[55] Such sounds are often anchored, at least in soft porn, by repeated shots of the mouth, as evident in Kristel's performances throughout the *Emmanuelle* films, for example the magic lantern scene in *Emmanuelle 2*. However, in *La Marge* the spontaneity of the orgasmic groan is jeopardised by the unspontaneous nature of sex as a business transaction. Only once, in the shared orgasm of her second number with Dallesandro, do we hear sounds of pleasure coming from Kristel, and even here they are partially obscured by the pop soundtrack.

If the mouth, and hence the gasping voice,[56] function as indices of female pleasure in pornography and erotica, this is, as we have seen, because of the invisibility of the female orgasm. The male orgasm, by contrast, is not only visible in hard-core porn, but often fundamental to it: known in the trade as the 'money shot', it traditionally structures the hard-core film by providing the literal climax to any sexual number.[57] But in soft porn this option is no longer available, so that an actor like Dallesandro has to perform his orgasm, visually with his body and audibly with his voice. We might therefore expect Dallesandro's performance of sexual pleasure to share some characteristics with Kristel's, for example in the prominence of facial close-ups to synchronise the sight and sounds of orgasm, or in the use of fragmented images of the eroticised star body. The latter is certainly apparent, with Dallesandro's body presented as an object of desire for Diana (seen from her point of view when they first meet), and frequently shot in close-up at crotch level or framed in an erotic pose (for example, the compositions early in the film displaying his muscular torso after he has cut his arm on some thorns). The first sexual number in particular seems to reinforce the two stars' respective images, with long takes showing a naked rear view of his body (as in *Je t'aime, moi non plus*) behind which her face is glimpsed. However, the performance of the male orgasm that concludes the numbers is problematised in the film. This is partly because of the general qualification of sexual

---

55· L. Williams, op. cit., p.126.

56· See also the female vocalising of sexual pleasure in erotic songs, especially Gainsbourg's *Je t'aime, moi non plus* (recorded first with Bardot and later, for the film of the same name, with Jane Birkin).

57· See L. Williams, op. cit., p.73. She describes the 'money shot' as 'the ultimate confessional moment of "truth"' and also 'the very limit of the visual representation of sexual pleasure', ibid., p.101.

pleasure in *La Marge*: the narrative equates sexual pleasure with guilt for Dallesandro's character (his wife and child both die while he is in Paris with Diana) and with business for Kristel's (albeit leavened with sentiment).[58] Hence, even in Kristel's performance the sounds of sexual pleasure in *La Marge* are muted, far from the exuberance of the *Emmanuelle* series, where her orgasmic articulations provide the 'allure' of 'primitive pleasures' in sophisticated surroundings. But the problematising of pleasure is most specifically identified with Dallesandro's performance of the orgasm.

The articulation of the orgasm already poses a problem for a star who has no strong vocal identity, and whose European work is often dubbed. The vocalising of pleasure is not a feature of Dallesandro's star image, we know. Furthermore, the pop soundtrack used throughout *La Marge* tends to articulate his feelings in lieu of a monologue or other vocalised performance. Even though Dallesandro's own voice is heard in the film, dialogue is extremely sparse, and his character's existential crisis is expressed not vocally but visually (by shots of his face in mirrors, or of his family in flashback) as well as musically: the hushed romantic rush of 10cc's *I'm Not in Love* accompanies the first sexual number with Kristel; the freezing, intergalactic strains of Pink Floyd's *Wish You Were Here* express his isolation after the third number when he searches for Diana in a deserted Paris.[59] Of their three sexual numbers together, only the second ends in a shared orgasm, with audible sounds of pleasure from both actors (albeit muffled, and competing with the music track) and with two brief glimpses of Kristel's face to anchor the sounds of female pleasure (there are no similar facial close-ups of Dallesandro here). The first number illustrates a gulf between his pleasure and her business-like detachment, although it does include the sounds of his orgasm (again, overlaid with music). The third number concentrates exclusively on Dallesandro's character, as Diana undresses him, kisses his muscular body and performs fellatio on him. The focus is on his naked torso and head, shot in medium close-up, while her head is just visible at the bottom of the screen. The lighting picks out his face and, as the scene progresses, he begins to cry out, grimace and move his head backwards and forwards. The sound of his cries is audible above the guitar solo on the backing track, but his performance also involves the tensing of his body, so that at the moment of orgasm his eyes are shut, the tendons in his neck are straining, and a grimace is on his face. The performance, both bodily and vocally, is long, intense and increasingly anguished. His orgasm is performed and received (by a horrified Diana) as an expression of pain as much as pleasure. This is Dallesandro's most sustained performance of orgasm in the film and also the crucial point in the male protagonist's journey (it is followed by Diana's flight and his suicide). The narrative context suggests that sexual pleasure here is not competing with physical pain (Jane Birkin as Johnny in *Je t'aime, moi non plus*), but with existential pain, and that it may even be the expression of the guilt, loneliness and despair that the protagonist feels. Dallesandro is left gasping, as if

---

58• Diana's feelings are signalled when she buys lingerie to please him, for which display of sentiment she is attacked by her pimp.

59• It is notable that the segment used here is purely instrumental, further emphasising the sense of loneliness and distance, as well as the voicelessness of Dallesandro's star image.

wounded, while a repulsed Kristel retreats in horror to the bathroom and then flees from the apartment, shouting '*Adieu!*'. The intensity of the (unshared) orgasm and the anguish visible and audible in Dallesandro's performance has, in effect, driven her away.

As in his earlier years at Warhol's Factory, Dallesandro's star image here is both sexualised and wounded. The allure of his body as an object of desire is qualified by the narrative associations of his roles (prostitution, drugs, impotence, despair) and the tendency towards voicelessness that is at times literal (the dubbed European films) and at others figurative. In *La Marge*, the sexual exuberance and the face of female pleasure associated with Kristel are superceded by the melancholy sexuality of Dallesandro's image. This is particularly true of the use of facial close-ups in the film: those of Kristel are extremely rare, and are mainly limited to a couple of erotic sequences. The facial close-ups of Dallesandro, however, are more frequent yet identified not with sexual pleasure but with angst, hence the repeated shots of him looking at his face in the mirror, particularly in the scenes leading up to his suicide. Even his orgasm is performed as pain rather than simple pleasure – the latter is only found in the uneroticised flashbacks to his son, where the face of male pleasure is associated with family life and game-playing rather than with sex.[60] *La Marge* narrativises and problematises Dallesandro's character rather than Kristel's; it places his sexual adventures in the kind of moralistic context that is lacking from the *Emmanuelle* series. Even though Kristel is the face of the film (pictured on the posters, on the video box and in most publicity stills), in terms of performance she is not the star of the film. Far from being the female porn star's 'appendage', 'the object of the object',[61] the male porn star is, here, an object of desire in his own right and at least as regards performance and narrative (if not marketing), it is *she* who is *his* appendage.

60· We see Dallesandro's face in close-up as he blows his cheeks out and kisses his son. Kissing is notably absent from the sexual encounters between Dallesandro and Kristel (client and prostitute).

61· See note 7, above.

CHAPTER 7

Metaphorical brothers: Patrick Dewaere and Gérard Depardieu on the set of *Préparez vos mouchoirs* (1978).

Threat or reassurance? Gérard Depardieu and Patrick Dewaere

BROTHERS AND EQUALS

Gérard Depardieu's star image has become so ubiquitous and so familiar that it has ossified into a myth. He dominated the French film industry for over two decades, and at the turn of the millennium remained its highest paid actor. However, for a number of years in the 1970s, the name of Depardieu, now synonymous with French cinema,[1] was most strongly associated with that of his contemporary and friend Patrick Dewaere. In their early careers the two were linked, both as metaphorical brothers and as professional equals, to an extent which now seems surprising. Although long submerged by Depardieu's mature stardom, the link between the pair is still evoked at times by the French press, as when Frédéric Mitterrand, writing in June 2000, declared:

> *Patrick Dewaere est tout simplement inoubliable. Disparu à 35 ans, il a pronfondément marqué le cinéma français, à l'égal de Depardieu dont il fut à la fois le partenaire et le faux jumeau dans notre imaginaire.*[2]

Furthermore, in the mid-seventies it was Depardieu's image that was the more troubling and hence the less popular. The film producer Daniel Toscan du Plantier has commented that, '*Au début, Dewaere était beaucoup plus vedette que Depardieu. Les gens du cinéma [. . .] disaient que Patrick Dewaere est rassurant pour le public bien-pensant et Gérard Depardieu est inquiétant.*'[3] Gradually, however, the roles became reversed. Dewaere's image disintegrated at the turn of the eighties and his suicide in 1982 suggested that in fact, '*c'était lui le plus marginal des*

1· See, for instance, G. Vincendeau, 'Gérard Depardieu: the axiom of contemporary French cinema', *Screen*, 34:3 (Winter 1993), pp.343–361. This view is further elaborated in Vincendeau, *Stars and Stardom in French Cinema* (London and New York, Continuum, 2000), pp.215–240.

2· 'Patrick Dewaere is quite simply unforgettable. Dead at 35, he had a profound impact on French cinema, equal to that of Depardieu, who, in our imaginations, was his comrade and his fake twin', F. Mitterrand, 'Portrait d'un star', *TéléPoche*, 17–23 June 2000.

3· 'At the start, Dewaere was much more of a star than Depardieu. Cinema people [. . .] said that Patrick Dewaere is reassuring for the right-thinking public and Gérard Depardieu is unsettling', Toscan du Plantier interviewed on TV5, *Spécial Cinéma*.

deux.[4] Moreover, Dewaere's demise and death coincided almost exactly with the renegotiation of Depardieu's star image from the threatening working-class yob of the seventies to the popular 'everyman' of the twenty years since. Dewaere is no longer twinned with Depardieu's supremely powerful, global star image, but he remains the ghost at the feast.

Both actors became rising stars when paired in a crucial film of the early 1970s, Bertrand Blier's *Les Valseuses* (1974). Their performances embodied contemporary socio-political themes, notably of urban alienation and sexual liberation, but they also brought to the screen an utterly new kind of acting. They exhibited '*Un humour désespéré, une violence apparamment difficile à controller, une tendresse qui faisait éclater le syndrome du jeune premier*'.[5] This was a veritable revolution in film acting to match the revolution in film form launched fifteen years earlier by the French new wave. The film-makers of the new wave had privileged *mise en scène* over performance, and had favoured actors who, with few exceptions (such as Jean-Paul Belmondo), had no theatrical training. Meanwhile, there remained a very strong tradition of French film comedy, which prospered in the fifties and sixties but did not share its stars with those of the new wave.[6] The directors of the 1970s, Blier in particular, began to break down these distinctions and did so in part by employing young theatrically trained actors from the comic, marginal genre known as *café-théâtre*.[7] The three leads from *Les Valseuses* – Depardieu, Dewaere, and Miou-Miou – all came from the *Café de la Gare*, as did the clown Coluche, a star of stage comedy who was to start his film career later. Their performance style was both stylised and naturalistic, with the emphasis on body language and slang, on expressive gestures and social types rather than psychological inwardness. (It is, thus, far removed from the American 'Method', where the stress is on theory and on psychological research into the characters.) So much did Depardieu and Dewaere seem to embody the everyday French language of the 1970s, that *Positif* magazine suggested the sociologists and linguists of the future should consult their films as a record of the slang, speech rhythms, gestures and attitudes of a generation.[8] Above all, after *Les Valseuses*, 'for the first time in French cinema, it became possible to exploit the resources of the body'.[9] This was crucial to the star appeal of both Depardieu and Dewaere, since neither had traditional good looks (Depardieu has large, heavy features, while Dewaere has a rather lost, hang-dog face), but both had a great ease of

---

4• 'he was the most marginal of the two', ibid.

5• 'a desperate humour, a barely-controlled violence and a tenderness that blew apart the syndrome of the romantic lead', A. Corneau, 'A Patrick Dewaere', *Positif* 300 (February 1986), p.38. For an account of the theatrical origins of acting types, such as the 'jeune premier', see Vincendeau, *Stars and Stardom*, pp.7–8.

6• For analysis of Louis de Funès, the major star of French comedy, see ibid., pp.136–157.

7• See I. Jordan and H. Niogret, 'Serrault, Piéplu, Galabru ... et les autres', *Positif* 300 (February 1986), pp.46–7, although their stress is more on Tavernier and Miller than on Blier. For more on *café-théâtre*, see J. Forbes, *The Cinema in France After the New Wave*, London, BFI/Macmillan, 1992, pp.173–9.

8• See I. Jordan and H. Niogret, 'Depardieu/Dewaere', *Positif* 300 (February 1986), pp.45–6.

9• Forbes, op. cit., p.179.

bodily expression. Throughout *Les Valseuses* they form a double act, with the exuberant Depardieu a protective older brother to the more melancholy Dewaere. The pastoral sequences towards the end of the film accentuate this with visual twinning by means of costume and gesture. The twosome were paired visually again – wearing the same sweaters and performing in unison – in Blier's *Préparez vos mouchoirs* (1978), and in the 1980s, *Positif* magazine used a still from the latter film in a homage to 'Depardieu/Dewaere' as a great acting duo. However, although as actors Depardieu and Dewaere shared theatrical origins and performance styles, their star images were distinct.

Depardieu entered French cinema as a threat, and he tended to live up to this image throughout the seventies. In his first major screen role, for Marguerite Duras's *Nathalie Granger* (1973), he plays a washing-machine salesman. But he is no ordinary salesman: he is an impostor of sorts, and may even be (on first appearance) a murderer. The film's context and atmosphere are ones of violence: two women in a house hear radio reports that detail the killing spree undertaken by two young men in the nearby woods; one of the daughters of the house has been expelled from school for violent actions. When Depardieu enters the domestic, feminised realm of the house (occupied in the film by women and girls only) his looming physical presence is mysterious and menacing. Indeed, he was cast because of his intimidating physique.[10] Characteristically, in Depardieu's performance the threat is undercut by vulnerability, signalled by the tenderness and hesitancy of his voice. (This has become a regular trait of his acting: see *Danton* among many other examples.) The ambivalence that results might be considered a mixture of 'masculine' strength and 'feminine' vulnerability, and Depardieu has often been described in these terms. He himself has stressed the sexual ambivalence of his character's confrontation with the two women in *Nathalie Granger*: '*Moi, je me suis senti dans* Nathalie Granger *autant femme que les deux hommes qui m'interrogeaient*'.[11] Such ambivalence makes it harder to answer the mystery surrounding Depardieu's salesman: Is he part of 'la classe de la violence'?[12]

This question mark hangs over Depardieu's star image throughout the seventies, and although Duras means by her phrase, violence as a class that transcends social divisions (she defines it as '*la nature même de l'enfance, de la jeunesse, confrontée avec la société moderne*'),[13] in the construction of Depardieu's early image, the traditional, conservative identification is made between violence and the working classes. This particular myth of Depardieu (and of the working class) ignored the tenderness and saw only the threat. It underpins his roles throughout the seventies, playing delinquents (*loubards*) in films such as *Les Valseuses*,

---

10· See Depardieu quoted in P. Chutkow, *Depardieu: The Biography,* London, HarperCollins, 1994, p.177: 'It was winter, and I was wearing a big coat and my motorcycle helmet. [...] "Come toward me!" she [Duras] demanded. [...] I just kept coming at this tiny woman until I was right up against her, towering over her. Finally she cried out, "Stop! It's good; you scare me. You can have the part."'

11· 'I felt in *Nathalie Granger* just as much a woman as the two men who were questioning me', Depardieu interviewed in the 1984 TV documentary, *La Classe de la violence*. Compare Depardieu's famous comment that Catherine Deneuve is the man he always wanted to be.

12· 'the violent class'. This is how Duras describes the subject of the film in ibid.

13· 'the very nature of childhood, of youth, confronted with modern society', Duras interviewed in ibid.

Maîtresse, Buffet froid and *Loulou*. It provides the repeated image of breaking and entering, which one can interpret as both a social and a sexual threat against the bourgeois order, and which is perpetrated by Depardieu's characters in *Nathalie Granger, Les Valseuses, Maîtresse, Dîtes-lui que je l'aime, Buffet froid,* and *Tenue de soirée*.[14] Above all, it fuels the legend of Depardieu's own origins: the drunken father and unhappy mother, the brutal childhood, the drinking, the prostitutes, the fights, and finally the arrival, penniless, in Paris to study acting (a scene replicated at the start of *Maîtresse,* which also includes several scenes of parodic violence that play on Depardieu's 'bad boy' image). The legend was well established by 1978, when it was first expounded in the American film press,[15] but when revisited in the 1990s, it no longer fitted Depardieu's mature image. The result was the *Time* affair of 1991, in which the wild man of the seventies returned to haunt the global star.[16]

By contrast, although Dewaere also played delinquents on screen, he was rarely characterised as one in the press. This may be due in part to his origins, as a child star in a family of actors rather than an authentic working-class lad. Where Depardieu seemed threatening, Dewaere's star image remained romantic, even tragic. He was the *loubard* as a dreamer, a lover, a loser. He was, in the obituary headline from *Le Monde* that greeted his death, '*Le Loubard romantique*'.[17] Even in life his image was reassuring, and his genuinely tragic demise and suicide only seemed to confirm the star image of a fragile and suffering soul. On the one occasion that the image was broken and a threat emerged, his public profile was almost destroyed: in 1980, he threatened to assault a journalist and was consequently ostracised by the French film press for the last two years of his life. But for the most part, the reassurance associated with Dewaere was expressed in both films and the press as a vulnerability which, unlike Depardieu's, was rarely obscured by violence or menace.

Even in *Les Valseuses,* which is essentially the story of two louts looking for sexual kicks, Dewaere's Pierrot is rendered less threatening than Depardieu's Jean-Claude in a number of ways. Not only is he younger, more passive and less physically intimidating, he is emasculated temporarily (by being shot in the testicles) and is repeatedly infantilised (as when Jean-Claude bathes him and washes his hair, and again when he sucks the breasts of the nursing mother). Finally, Pierrot is raped (off screen) by Jean-Claude. Dewaere the loser is, in a sense, the victim of Depardieu the burglar (the rape scene takes place in a chalet that they have broken into). In his subsequent career, Dewaere plays characters who are literally injured (*La Meilleure façon de marcher*), psychologically damaged (*Série Noire, Beau-Père, Un mauvais fils, Hôtel des Amériques, Paradis pour tous*), or killed (*Le Juge Fayard, dit*

14· In reference to *Nathalie Granger*, Depardieu has called the role of the door-to-door salesman a 'violation' and a 'penetration'. See G. Braucourt, 'Gérard Depardieu ou le genie de l'excès', *Ecran* 44 (February 1976), p.29.

15· See H.Stein, 'Depardieu: French Primitive', *Film Comment* XVI: 2 (1978), pp.19–24.

16· The controversy centred on the disputed translation of a comment Depardieu made in the 1978 interview about having witnessed or participated in a rape when he was a boy. It was felt by some that the affair cost Depardieu an Oscar for *Cyrano*. For full details, see Chutkow, op.cit., pp.253–287.

17· J. Siclier, 'L'acteur Patrick Dewaere, Le Loubard romantique', *Le Monde*, 18 July 1982, p.7.

'le Shérif'). His star image also depicts a victim. While Depardieu represented the brute force of the 'French primitive' as a kind of peasant Tarzan,[18] Dewaere was 'the fragile hero',[19] the star as romantic loser.[20] This was, of course, exaggerated by his suicide, after which his image was painted even darker, with obituaries picking out the performances that hinted at vulnerability or death, and that seemed therefore to have predicted his own fate.[21] It should also be noted that Dewaere is in some ways closer than Depardieu to the iconic French male star of the thirties, Jean Gabin. Depardieu has often been compared to Gabin, particularly via the importance of the land, work and 'feminised' masculinity in their star mythologies.[22] Although this is certainly true of their mature images, in the 1970s and early 1980s it was actually Dewaere who came closer to Gabin's pre-war status as the romantic, doomed hero. One could easily substitute Dewaere for Gabin in this assessment of the latter:

He was at once an ordinary bloke-next-door and a tragic hero [...]. He was a romantic figure, an *homme fatal*, though mostly fatal to himself. [...] The trajectory of many of Gabin's characters positioned him as victim: of the past, of events, of bad luck, occasionally of women – hence the development of the idea of his characters as victims of 'fate'.[23]

As the director Alain Corneau has pointed out, in the 1930s '*Gabin a été une espèce d'amoureux éperdu, sentimental, et constamment malheureux; pas Gérard.*'[24]

Stars incarnate values and concepts, in particular those surrounding issues of identity. It is 'this visualising of identity which makes the bodies of stars and the actions performed by those bodies into such a key element of a star's meaning.'[25] The bodies of Dewaere and Depardieu tend to signify contrasting things. Dewaere's vulnerability and his apparent

---

18· See Stein, op. cit., p.19, and M. Haskell, 'You Gérard, Me Jane', in ibid., p.23.

19· See, for example, the cover of *Paris Match*, 30 July 1982, which reported Dewaere's suicide as '*la mort du héros fragile*', and also J. Nacache, 'Patrick Dewaere: L'homme fragile', *La Revue du cinéma*, 484 (July–August 1992), pp.32–3.

20· See Corneau, op.cit., p.38, where Dewaere is described as '*toujours du côté des "désastrés"* '. Although the term *astre* (star) is not used in French to mean a film star, it does lend itself to a pun here: Dewaere is an ill-starred star, the star as disaster.

21· See, for example, P. Labro, 'Ses derniers rôles ressemblent à sa mort', *Paris Match*, 30 July 1982, pp.46, 51, and M. Amiel, 'Patrick Dewaere: "Son étonnement d'être là"', *Cinéma 82*, 285 (September 1982), p.16. A frequent reference is to Dewaere's line in *Préparez vos mouchoirs* when he laments Mozart's death at thirty five (Dewaere was to shoot himself at the same age). See, for example, Chutkow, op. cit., p.223.

22· See, for example, Vincendeau, *Stars and Stardom*, pp.71–2.

23· Ibid., pp.62, 63.

24· 'Gabin was a kind of wild lover, sentimental and always unhappy. Gérard is not like that.' Quoted in J. Zimmer et al, 'Gérard Depardieu: Le chromosome supplémentaire', *La Revue du cinéma*, 482 (May 1992), p.56. See also Braucourt, op. cit., p.24, for a critique of those who compared the young Depardieu to the young Gabin.

25· P. McDonald, 'Supplementary Chapter: Reconceptualising Stardom', in R. Dyer, *Stars*, new edition, London, BFI, 1998, p.180.

reluctance to be part of the star system are hidden by the confident and even glamorous display of his star body throughout the 1970s. Richard Dyer notes that if stars are seen as members of the 'leisure class', then 'a man's athletic body may be much admired, but only on condition that it has been acquired through sports not labour.'[26] Dewaere often adheres to this model: he is displayed as a sportsman in *Lily, aime-moi* (boxing), *La Meilleure façon de marcher* (running, swimming, etc.) and *Coup de tête* (football). In his last film he was to have played a French boxing champion, and his muscular, hairy torso is also on display in many others, even when the subject matter does not appear to lend itself. For example, *Le Juge Fayard*, a conspiracy thriller about a real-life political scandal, shows Dewaere, playing the crusading judge, in a semi-naked love scene after only ten minutes, while a later sequence places him in swimming trunks by a lake in the sun.[27] Hence, although in the film his character personifies justice and the battle against corruption, the display of Dewaere's body connotes romance, leisure and sex appeal (an appeal that is explicitly enacted when a middle-aged female archivist lets Fayard see secret files because she is in love with him). Romance, leisure and sex appeal are, of course, associated with stardom itself, particularly in classical cinema.[28] These values are, in a sense, symbolised by the element of Dewaere's star body that links him most explicitly to the classical Hollywood film star – his moustache.[29] On display throughout the seventies, Dewaere's moustache is a display of romantic bravado that conceals the insecurities of his characters (and of the actor himself). As Claude Sautet reported when he cast Dewaere for *Un mauvais fils* in late 1979:

> *Je pensais à cette sacrée petite moustache qu'il arborait depuis quelques années comme un drapeau, une superstition, une parade contre sa fragilité. [. . .] l'idée de ce 'machin-à-la-Clark-Gable' sur la lèvre me bloquait complètement.*[30]

Miraculously, Dewaere shaved off his moustache before meeting Sautet and the film went ahead, but the modification of Dewaere's star image enacted by the loss of his moustache and by his role in Sautet's film was to prove damaging, as we shall see shortly. The meaning of Dewaere's star body was beginning to change, for the worse.

In his early career, and despite the great impact his physical performances were to have in blowing aside conventions of screen acting in France, Depardieu was actually much

---

26• Dyer, op. cit., p.39.

27• Although other characters are present, including Aurore Clément as the judge's fiancée, the focus is literally on Dewaere's star body.

28• For more on the importance of leisure in the lifestyle of classical stars, see Dyer op. cit., pp.38–9.

29• On the role of the moustache in the male star body, see *Paris Match*, 26 November 1960, pp.126–7, where a photographic tribute to Clark Gable's career is headlined 'L'histoire de ses succès c'est aussi l'histoire d'une moustache', and where we are told how crucial the growing of the moustache in 1933 was to his subsequent star image. Dewaere's moustache operates in the same way, but in reverse.

30• 'I thought of that damned little moustache that he had been parading for years like a flag, a superstition, a defence against his fragility. I just couldn't handle the idea of filming him with that "Clark-Gable-thing" on his lip', C. Sautet, 'A Patrick Dewaere', *Positif* 300 (February 1986), p.39.

less at ease with his body than Dewaere. He himself has commented on his lack of physical ease compared with his co-stars in *Les Valseuses*.[31] In the improvised hitch-hiking sequence, for example, Dewaere and Miou-Miou are much more active and gestural than Depardieu, who ends up sitting on the ground while Dewaere continues to try to thumb a lift in a variety of poses. Depardieu's star body in the 1970s was, in fact, a contradiction which, rather like Dewaere's but in a different way, combined power with vulnerability. With Dewaere, the power tended to be romantic, glamorous even, while the vulnerability was hidden behind the moustache. With Depardieu, the power is again visually displayed, but is a matter of strength rather than glamour. It is qualified, however, by the fragility of his voice, which is naturally weak, with a chronic stammer that had to be overcome before he could act. If the voice signifies inner fragility, the body signifies brute force. This physical strength is not always associated with the *loubard* roles, where tenderness usually shines through (in *Les Valseuses, Maîtresse* and *Loulou*), but is terrifyingly present in *Dites-lui que je l'aime* (1977) where, in one of his most deliberate physical performances, Depardieu plays a repressed office worker whose sexual obsession is expressed by sudden acts of violence, most notably by picking people up and throwing them. As with *Nathalie Granger*, the brutish body is clothed in an apparently sober, correct appearance, which fails to hide the threat; Depardieu's character is told at one point that he repels his former girlfriend: '*Physiquement tu la dégoûtes. Elle ne te supporte pas. Tu lui fais peur*'.[32] This threat informs Depardieu's sex appeal as a 'bit of rough' or, in Molly Haskells' words, 'the genuine article, sexism and brutishness intact [...] sexy [...] in a slobbish, overblown way'.[33] But despite his naked appearances in *Les Valseuses, Loulou* and others, Depardieu tends to replace the star body as display, sports and leisure with the star body as work. And this means not working out and the muscled, gym-toned body that results, but working without any thought to one's body image. It means filming, even when one is a star, as 'Everyday labor.'[34] Depardieu has criticised the cinema of the 1960s and 1970s for its dependence on overdeveloped macho heroes.[35] His attitude towards the star body – a rejection of the pampered leisure of the traditional movie star and the muscular fitness of the action hero – is reflected not just in his own ungroomed, untrained physique, but also in his infamously workaholic approach to cinema. This constant need to work means that Depardieu has tended to average more than three films per year throughout his career. In the twelve years between *Les Valseuses* and Dewaere's suicide, the latter – himself no slouch – appeared in twenty-four films; Depardieu appeared in thirty-four.

31· See G. Depardieu, 'C'est le manque de confiance en lui qui l'a tué', *Paris Match* 30 July 1982, p.44.

32· 'Physically, you disgust her. She cannot bear you. You scare her.'

33· Haskell, op. cit., p.23.

34· Sylvester Stallone cited in S. Faludi, *Stiffed: The Betrayal of Modern Man*, London, Vintage, 2000, p.584.

35· See O. Dazat and Goldschmidt, 'Gérard Depardieu' [interview], *Cinématographe*, September 1985, p.6.

THE END OF THE SEVENTIES

In 1979, Depardieu and Dewaere were among the ten highest-paid stars in French cinema, but the turn of the decade was to prove a watershed in the careers of both men. While Depardieu gradually freed himself from the constraints imposed by the myth of the working-class brute, Dewaere's image slipped rapidly from romantic rogue to loser, from *loubard romantique* to *paumé*. Essentially, it was now Dewaere rather than Depardieu who found that his star image (both on and off screen) began to match his real-life problems. In this case, the problems came not from a troubled past but from a troubled present, and the result was a figure not of strength but of doomed weakness. This collision of life and screen was not immediately noted by the press, and tended to be constructed retrospectively after Dewaere's death. With hindsight, the watershed was often identified with Dewaere's performance as a psychotic in *Série Noire* (1979), but it was certainly exacerbated by his growing heroin addiction and the ill-advised attack on a journalist in 1980. It was to culminate in his suicide two years later.

At the same time, Depardieu found a wider acceptance by the public in response to his maturing and less threatening roles in five diverse films shot in 1979–80, including the Resistance drama *Le Dernier Métro* and the comedy *Inspecteur La Bavure*. Speaking in 1981, he declared, '*ça a vraiment commence pour moi il ya deux ans; c'est à ce moment que j'ai été accepté par le public [. . .] ici j'ai jamais été tellement estimé ni reconnu comme acteur*'.[36] He explained this statement by reference to the unsympathetic roles he took in the seventies, such as the self-mutilating Gérard in *La Dernière Femme* (1976) and the repressed fantasist David in *Dites-lui que je l'aime* (1977). By contrast, his new roles were lighter and more tender than his early image had generally allowed.[37] Moreover, the success of *Préparez vos mouchoirs* (1978) in the United States, where it was awarded an Oscar, pointed to two key areas for the future of Depardieu's star image: the comedy genre and Hollywood. It is perhaps no coincidence that in *Préparez vos mouchoirs* Depardieu plays a bourgeois character rather than a working-class lout. The gradual softening of his image during the eighties and nineties was to be accompanied by a shift away from the (often negatively portrayed) values of the working class and towards roles where he incarnates either middle-class or, more often, historical and even mythical values. In this regard, *Loulou* (1980) is a kind of leave-taking, one of his last serious *loubard* roles[38] and one that manages to combine the positive and negative elements of working-class life that are united in Depardieu's seventies star image (camaraderie, insouciance and warmth, but also violence, inarticulacy and alienation).

36• 'it really began for me two years ago; that's when I was accepted by the public. Here in France I've never been that highly rated or recognised as an actor', cited in S. Daney and D. Dubrout, 'Entretien avec Gérard Depardieu', *Cahiers du cinéma* 323/4 (May 1981), p.111. The five films Depardieu refers to are (in order of release in France): *Loulou, Mon Oncle d'Amérique, Le Dernier Métro, Je vous aime*, and *Inspecteur La Bavure*.

37• See ibid., 112.

38• See below for a consideration of Depardieu as a comic *loubard*.

Where *Loulou* at least balances these elements, *Série Noire* accentuates the negative in its portrayal of poverty on the edge of Paris, and in a crucial change to Dewaere's star image, his performance no longer bears any but the thinnest relation to a romantic hero. Underneath the facade of the Gable moustache, the elegant gestures and the long mac, Dewaere plays a tortured loser, driven to murder to escape from his situation. The film is a summation of his physical acting style, full of tics, mannerisms, slang and spoonerisms, a barrage of salutes, thumbs-up, slaps and assaults. It is also a violent exploration of the theme of victimhood which, as we have seen, dominates Dewaere's star image. He plays Franck Poupard, a door-to-door salesman, who is at once a victim of coincidence and a serial killer. His nickname *Poupée* (based on 'Dolly' from the original novel) infantilises him, and thereby links him to the 'little brother' roles Dewaere played alongside Depardieu in *Les Valseuses* and *Préparez vos mouchoirs,* and to the vulnerability of the lost child that was part of his star image in the French press,[39] but this time the victim is not reassuring or romantic, because he simply retaliates in a frenzy. As Poupard, Dewaere is by turns anguished, pathetic and terrifying. This exhausting virtuoso performance turned the film into *'un reportage sur les comédiens',*[40] in which the director abandoned traditional filming practices to chase after Dewaere, with handheld cameras and direct sound recording, as the actor tore round the mean streets of Créteil. The result, although hailed as Dewaere's greatest performance, also irremediably darkened his star image. After *Série Noire*, a genuinely flawed Dewaere rather than the more resilient Depardieu became synonymous with the alienated modern male:

> *Admirable en paumé, en 'perdant', [. . .] Patrick Dewaere a été le symbole d'une sensibilité, d'une fragilité modernes des hommes qui se heurtent aux implacables contraintes des sociétés déshumanisées.*[41]

The degradation of Dewaere's image intensified with roles as an ex-convict heroin addict in *Un mauvais fils* (1980), a failed suicide in *Paradis pour tous* (1982) and a despairing, self-hating 'zombie' in *Hôtel des Amériques* (1981). After his own suicide, *Paris Match* was to use the same term to describe *'Ce veritable "zombie" que j'aperçus, un soir, il y a deux ans, à la sortie d'une projection du Festival de Deauville'.*[42] For the last two years of his life, Dewaere was a shadow of his former self, ostracised by the film press, his presence in films seeming to bring only bad luck.[43] Ironically, in his last few weeks, he had been preparing to play a

---

39. See, for example, Amiel, op. cit., p.16.

40. 'a report on the actors', Y. Alion, 'Entretien avec Alain Corneau', *Avant-scène cinéma*, 233 (October 1979), p.6. Corneau is the film's director.

41. 'Exemplary as a misfit, a loser, Patrick Dewaere was a symbol of the modern sensitivity and fragility of men when they come up against the implacable constraints of a dehumanised society', Siclier, op. cit., p.7. The French here literalises the image of collision (*se heurter*) from *Série Noire*, where Dewaere repeatedly bashes his head against the side of his car.

42. 'That complete "zombie" I saw one evening two years ago, coming out of a screening at the Deauville festival', Labro, op.cit., p.51.

43. *'on a l'impression que Dewaere "porte la poisse" '*, ('You get the impression that Dewaere "brings bad luck"'), ibid.

winner, boxing champion Marcel Cerdan, in a role that might have recuperated his damaged star image.[44] The final photograph of Dewaere alive is a promotional shot for *Edith et Marcel* – he looks relaxed and in shape, laughing as he lies on the grass bare chested, in boxing shorts and boots. Despite this display, in the reporting of his suicide only hours later, Dewaere's demise was represented as a process of physical destruction, as the gradual unmaking, via drugs and despair, of a previously glamorous star body. By the end of the seventies, a process of attenuation had already been visible: gone was the moustache, and along with it the wild, physical vitality of his acting, which had reached a crescendo in *Série Noire*. In the 1980s, Dewaere's performances are increasingly restrained, passive, and bleak: he walks instead of running, mumbles instead of shouting. His characters lack will-power, strength, at times (as in *Hôtel des Amériques*) even charisma. The thinning hair gets shorter, the star body seems to shrink so that the muscular torso displayed so deliberately in *Le Juge Fayard* is seen less often, and there is less of it to see. This process of etiolation is summarised by *Paris Match*:

Que lui est-il arrivé? Les épaules se sont affaisées, les jambes flageolent, la moustache s'est faite rare, comme le cheveu qui semble foutre le camp. [. . .] Le teint est pâle, aussi, ce garçon flotte dans ses vêtements, [. . .] l'homme s'est profondément modifié, et son "image" va en pâtir.[45]

Ultimately, the reduction is complete: from star body to star corpse.[46]

So, what does Dewaere's stardom mean socially and culturally? And does he manage to reconcile contraries in the way that Richard Dyer suggests all genuine stars do?[47] These two questions have a single answer: Dewaere's stardom signifies pessimism, loss, failure and death, and it does so by failing to reconcile opposites. Thus, where it has become a commonplace to describe Depardieu as embodying a mythical synthesis (of masculinity and femininity, violence and tenderness, popular cinema and art cinema, and so on), Dewaere tends to represent a gradual intensification (of vulnerability) and a precise historical malaise experienced in France after 1968. *Paris Match* called him the incarnation of '*le désenchantement et les turbulences des années 70*'.[48] He embodies both the celebratory, freewheeling origins of the decade (a child of May '68 and the *café-théâtre* genre)[49] and, in his gradual decline from a romantic youth to an increasingly despairing maturity, the

---

44· See *Paris Match*, 30 July 1982, p.31, where we are told that his was going to be 'the' role of his life.

45· 'What happened to him? His shoulders dropped, his legs went weak at the knees, his moustache practically disappeared, like his hair, which seemed to desert him. A pale-faced lad, floating in oversized clothes, the man had completely changed, and his "image" would suffer as a result', Labro, op. cit., p.51.

46· See the photograph of Dewaere's body being carried away by police after his suicide: only the bare feet are visible, *Paris Match*, 30 July 1982, p.33.

47· See Dyer, op. cit., pp.26 and 82.

48· 'the disillusionment and unrest of the seventies', *Paris Match*, 30 July 1982, p.45.

49· See Mitterrand, op. cit.: '*Un enfant de la balle, de Mai 68, incarnant la révolte avec Coluche et Miou-Miou, au "Café de la Gare"*'.

social shift that followed, in which the battle ground shifted from the revolutionary and the ideological to the material and sexual, and in which it seemed to some that all struggles were doomed to failure. Reviewing the documentary on Dewaere released in 1992, Jacqueline Nacache described the film as '*le chant nostalgique des années 70, époque [. . .] où tant de gens de vingt ans ont trainé des révoltes usées et des espoirs informes*'.[50] She singles out *Les Valseuses* as epitomising this malaise, '*parce qu'il parle remarquablement de ce grand vide du coeur et de la tête, alors qu'il n'y avait plus que la libération sexuelle, mince compensation pour remplacer les idéaux perdus et les rêves des jours meilleurs*'.[51] Dewaere's subsequent films are a further index of this 'emptiness' – a despairing and almost accidental assault on sexual taboos in *Beau-Père* (1981), sexual confusion and self-destruction in *Hôtel des Amériques* – as is the representation of his star persona over the years, the romantic glamour gradually eclipsed by drugs and death. Dewaere's filmography also coincides strongly with the presidency of Valéry Giscard d'Estaing (1974–81), and reflects pessimistically on that period; hence the corruption in *Le Juge Fayard* and *Coup de tête*, and the brutal attempt in *Série Noire* to exit urban poverty and buy into the modern materialist dream. Even when purer ideals remain, in *Le Juge Fayard*, the battle against political corruption ends with the hero's death (just as in the real-life scandal that inspired the film). As with the death four years later of the clown Coluche – a colleague in the *Café de la Gare* and another star born out of the spirit of '68 – Dewaere's suicide seems, in retrospect, to confirm the end of a generation.[52]

DEPARDIEU AFTER DEWAERE

Dewaere's death left '*un immense boulevard que le génie de Gérard Depardieu a su occuper*'.[53] His star persona rapidly matured into the ubiquitous 'everyman' of French cinema and then the global star he is today. The 1980s began with a farewell to the 'mad dog' *loubard* and concluded with the award of a *super César* as the 'actor of the decade'. Depardieu's box-office appeal exploded, with *Jean de Florette* (1986) attracting over seven million spectators, and Francis Veber's *La Chèvre* (1981), *Les Compères* (1983) and *Les Fugitifs* attracting 6.9, 4.8 and 4.5 million respectively. During the 1970s, Depardieu's performances had been far less popular, with only *Les Valseuses* (3.8 million) coming close, and only four other appearances attracting more than a million spectators.[54] By the time of *Cyrano de Bergerac*

50• 'a nostalgic lament for the seventies, a time when so many young people hung onto vague hopes and threadbare dreams of revolution', Nacache, op. cit., p.33.

51• 'because it speaks in a remarkable way of the great emptiness in people's hearts and minds when the only thing left was sexual liberation, a poor replacement for the lost ideals and dreams of better days', ibid.

52• Coluche was much more politically involved than Dewaere, and stood as a candidate in the 1981 presidential election. None the less, although the domain was rather different, the effect of his loss was the same. See Mitterrand, op. cit.

53• 'a huge gap which Gérard Depardieu was able to fill with his genius', Toscan du Plantier interviewed on TV5, *Spécial Cinéma*.

54• The other four are *Vincent, François, Paul et les autres* (1974, 2.8 million *entrées*), *1900* (1976, 1.6 million), *Préparez vos mouchoirs* (1978, 1.3 million) and *Sept morts sur ordonnance* (1975, 1.1 million). Figures taken from http://www.ecrannoir.fr

(1990), he was being described as '*le pivot du cinéma français*' by *Cahiers du cinéma*,[55] while *La Revue du cinéma* declared that he personified the call for French film to become one, uniting Belmondo (the popular thriller, action comedy) and Duras (intellectual, low-budget art cinema).[56] He became synonymous with the popular but cultural appeal of the heritage genre, from *Danton* and *Le Retour de Martin Guerre* (both 1982) via the hugely successful *Jean de Florette* to its latest incarnation, as producer and star of the television mini-series *Balzac* (1998) and *Le Comte de Monte-Cristo* (1999). The working-class marginal of the 1970s was repositioned as a comic figure, no longer a threat but a source of amusement. While comedy and menace are balanced in Depardieu's performances for Blier in *Les Valseuses* and *Buffet froid* (1979), the comic *loubard* comes into his own in Veber's eighties trilogy.[57] Where Dewaere's star persona had centred on the tragic victim, Depardieu's now included the comic victim, wounded for laughs in *Inspecteur La Bavure* and *Les Fugitifs*.[58]

Depardieu was also increasingly cast not only as fictional characters, but also as historical figures – the title role in *Danton* (1982), Rodin in *Camille Claudel* (1988), Columbus in *1492* (1992) – and as embodiments of national values – resistance against the German Occupation in *Le Dernier Métro* (1980), resistance against the Roman Occupation in *Astérix et Obélix contre César* (1999), imperial honour in *Fort Saganne* (1984) and *Le Colonel Chabert* (1994), and the very personification of stereotypical French *joie de vivre* in his first Hollywood hit, *Green Card* (1990). If Dewaere had become a prime candidate for the role of martyred film star, Depardieu was eventually to become French cinema's life force. In a letter to his dead friend, published in 1988, Depardieu wrote: '*j'ai toujours senti la mort en toi. [. . .] la mort connais pas. Je suis la vie, la vie jusque dans sa monstruosité*'.[59] A decade later, Carole Bouquet could declare of Depardieu that, '*Lorsqu'il entre dans une pièce, c'est la vie qui entre avec lui*'.[60] While Dewaere had in certain interpretations been consumed by stardom, Depardieu still consumes everything in his path, his legendary appetite celebrated as '*sa boulimie de vivre*'.[61]

The success of Depardieu's star image also entailed a re-eroticisation of his star body, so that 'since the mid-1980s [he] has occupied the place of the simultaneously nurturing and erotic father figure'.[62] His weight and appearance have fluctuated wildly, for example

---

55• 'the fulcrum of French cinema', I. Katsahnias and S. Toubiana, 'Entretien avec Gérard Depardieu: L'exercice de la passion', *Cahiers du cinéma* 419/420 (May 1989), p.25.

56• Zimmer et al, op.cit., p.51.

57• For more on Depardieu as a comic *loubard*, see Vincendeau, *Stars and Stardom*, pp.220–21.

58• See ibid., p.222.

59• 'I always saw death in you, [while, by contrast, I] don't know what death means. I'm life, warts and all', G. Depardieu, *Lettres volées*, Paris, Editions J.C. Lattès, 1988.

60• 'When he enters a room, life enters with him', cited in C. Pigozzi, 'Depardieu-Bouquet: Le triomphe de l'amour', *Paris Match*, 17 September 1998, p.46.

61• 'devouring life', ibid., p.47.

62• Vincendeau, *Stars and Stardom*, p.229.

between the slimmer, moustachioed hero of *Fort Saganne* (filmed in late 1983) and the huge, lumbering cop of *Police* (filmed fourteen months later). But despite this, certain eighties films – notably *Fort Saganne, La Lune dans le caniveau* (1983) and *Trop belle pour toi* (1989) – portray Depardieu as an object of female desire, even though this had not been a central part of his star persona.[63] In each film he is desired by two women, at least one of whom is a star actress of world-renowned beauty (Catherine Deneuve, Nastassia Kinski and Carole Bouquet respectively). Bouquet's role in *Trop belle pour toi* generated rumours about a romance with Depardieu, and the two began living together in the late nineties. When *Paris Match* reported on their romance, Depardieu's intimidating physique remained central to his star image,[64] balanced by an inner tenderness (previously signified by his voice, but here by his supposedly private, inner nature): '*Elle l'aime parce que, derrière son corps bâti comme une forteresse, il reste fragile et doux*'.[65]

It has become banal to assert, as Bouquet does here, that Depardieu reconciles opposites (strength and weakness, the macho and the feminine, art and entertainment, the global and the local), but it is worth noting that his star persona did not always function in this mythical and uniting way. In the 1970s, for all the sexual and social ambivalence of some of his performances, his working-class origins and physical appearance meant that the 'masculine' dominated the 'feminine' in his image, that the threat he embodied tended to submerge the tenderness. In 1976 Guy Braucourt described Depardieu as always excessive,[66] while six years later Robert Chazal characterised him solely in terms of violence (albeit increasingly harnessed and eventually transcended).[67] At that point, marginality remained part of his persona, but that is no longer the case. As *Paris Match* notes, '*son look de camionneur au grand cœur incarne à la fois la force rassurante et la sensibilité pacifique*'.[68] The marginal is now central, a reassuring presence. And Dewaere is long absent.

63· An exception to this is the portrait of Depardieu in Haskell op. cit.

64· As it did when, in October 1996, a two-metre tall bronze statue of his body was unveiled in Paris, entitled 'La Force aveugle' (Blind Force).

65· 'she loves him because, underneath that body built like a fortress, he is fragile and gentle', Pigozzi, op. cit., p.46.

66· See Braucourt, op. cit., p.24.

67· See R. Chazal, *Gérard Depardieu – l'autodidacte inspiré*, Paris, Hatier, 1982, cited in D. Sauvaget, 'La raison et la déraison', *La Revue du cinéma* 482 (May 1992), p.54.

68· 'his big-hearted lorry-driver look embodies both reassuring strength and peaceful sensitivity', Pigozzi, op. cit., p.47.

CHAPTER 8

The face of North Africa? Isabelle Adjani as Arab revolutionary in *Ishtar* (1987).

Foreign bodies: Jean Seberg and Isabelle Adjani

ETHNICITY AND FRENCH CINEMA

This chapter will explore issues of race and stardom, whiteness and female sexuality, via an American actress who worked and died in France, and a French actress of German and Algerian parentage. Their star images illuminate the representation of ethnicity in French cinema. Of course, it is true to assert, as Ginette Vincendeau does, that 'French cinema has been slow to acknowledge the ethnic diversity of the population'.[1] But this is not to say that ethnicity is not at stake in the images of French film stars. Whiteness is, of course, a form of ethnicity, albeit an unmarked, culturally normalised one and, as Richard Dyer has observed, the 'white woman' is idealised in western culture as the 'light of the world', the guarantor of whiteness, 'the most highly prized possession of the white man and the envy of all other races.'[2] This idealisation of whiteness resonates in the images of numerous female stars in Western society, from Marilyn Monroe and Brigitte Bardot to Princess Diana. What is particularly instructive about the cases of Jean Seberg and Isabelle Adjani, as we shall see, is that because of their prominence as female stars and the racial questions their stardom has raised, both have been construed as foreign bodies, as threats to separatist concepts of whiteness, and yet both have also been ultimately recuperated as white stars in French film.

SEBERG: RACE AND THE WHITE WOMAN

As an American actress, Jean Seberg is clearly a foreign body in French cinema. Blonde and Nordic in appearance, she spoke French with an obvious accent and wore her nationality on her body (in the form of a *New York Herald Tribune* t-shirt) in her first and most celebrated French film, *A bout de souffle* (1959). In later parts she still played foreigners, as in *La Ligne de demarcation* (1966) where, although her French accent is much improved, her character is English. But her function as a foreign body in French film is not limited to these Anglophone identities. Through her stardom, and especially in the traumatic later stages of her life, Seberg forced a confrontation with issues of race in France, as she had done in America.

Unusually for a film actor, Seberg's public image was almost entirely independent of her on-screen roles. After her debut films in the late 1950s – *Saint Joan* and *Bonjour Tristesse* in

---

1· G. Vincendeau, *Stars and Stardom in French Cinema*, London and New York, Continuum, 2000, p.41, n.40. For more on ethnicity and current French stardom, see Chapter 11.

2· R. Dyer, *Heavenly Bodies: Film Stars and Society*, London, BFI, 1986, p.43.

Hollywood, *A bout de souffle* in France – her subsequent performances were dismissed as 'charming but banal'.[3] Seberg's career has been described as 'a two decades long joke', beginning with a 'publicity stunt' and ending with her suicide, having 'never shook the joke'.[4] Certainly her stardom was always defined by struggles off camera – originally by her struggle to win the lead in *Saint Joan*,[5] later by her struggles to maintain her career in the face of slander, depression, drink and drugs, and above all by her struggles to fight racism via her stardom, despite efforts by the FBI to 'neutralise' her. While her performances in the French films raise rather straightforward questions about nationality (she became a kind of American token or mascot,[6] through whom the French new wave both celebrated and attacked the USA), her star persona is galvanised by a much more difficult and ultimately dangerous question about gender and race: What happens when a white female star is identified with blackness? The answer, because Seberg's case is so extreme, sheds light on issues of gender and race within stardom, and in particular on the more recent but equally vitriolic controversy surrounding Adjani.

As Richard Dyer notes, 'The white woman is not only the most prized possession of white patriarchy, she is also part of the symbolism [. . .] of light and chastity.'[7] As a star, the white woman becomes 'a light source', 'shining', 'golden', 'glittering' with a 'stellar luminescence'.[8] Such luminous whiteness is the foundation of Seberg's stardom. She is in many ways a white dream-girl, 'the fair, blond star with blue [. . .] eyes',[9] '*une actrice radieuse*', '*le rêve féminin d'une génération*'.[10] Her blondeness encodes Seberg, like Marilyn Monroe, as 'the most unambiguously white you can get'.[11] Like Monroe and countless other white actresses, Seberg is also lit in her publicity shots in order to emphasise radiance and whiteness. In Dyer's words, 'Glow remains a key quality in idealised representations of white women',[12] and this glow – a visual indication of abstract qualities such as innocence,

---

3· See J. Siclier, 'Le rêve féminin d'une génération' [obituary], *Le Monde*, 11 September 1979, p.17. The main exception is *Lilith* (USA, 1964) in which Seberg plays a schizophrenic. Seberg describes this as the one film in which she is not 'always the same', J. Seberg, 'Lilith and I', *Cahiers du cinéma in English*, 7, January 1967, p.36. (The original French version is in *Cahiers* 177, April 1966.)

4· K. Lewis, 'Jean Seberg of Iowa and Paris', *Films in Review*, 31 (4), 1980, p.225. Lewis contends that both American audiences and French new wave film-makers constructed this 'joke' at the expense of Seberg's genuine, 'unmanufactured personality'.

5· As an unknown teenager, Seberg was chosen from eighteen thousand hopefuls to play Joan. This is the 'publicity stunt' referred to by Lewis in ibid., p.225.

6· '*la yankee fétiche de la nouvelle vague*', G. Monréal, 'Jean Seberg: La pasionara de l'impossible', *Voici* 248 (10–16 August 1992), p.58.

7· Dyer, *Heavenly Bodies*, p.44.

8· All terms taken from media descriptions of Princess Diana. See N. Segal, 'The Common Touch', in M. Merck (ed.), *After Diana: Irreverent Elegies*, London and New York, Verso, 1998, p.132.

9· C. Fuentes, *Diana, The Goddess who hunts alone*, London, Bloomsbury, 1995, p.191. This novel is a fictionalised version of Fuentes' affair with Seberg in 1970.

10· 'a radiant actress', 'the dream-woman for a generation', Siclier, op. cit., p.17.

11· Dyer, *Heavenly Bodies*, p.139.

12· Ibid., p.132.

goodness, and truth – informs Seberg's star image even in the difficult later years of her career. Witness the cover of *Films Illustrated* for August 1974, which celebrates her 'secret of survival' with a facial close up, the lighting 'high' and lending a luminous quality to her pale skin and golden hair. Lighting plays a similar role in filmic images of white actresses. In *White*, Dyer describes how the iconography of cinema creates 'connotations of dark desire for the light',[13] where the latter is embodied by the white heterosexual heroine. This can be seen in *A bout de souffle*, where Seberg plays the Nordic American Patricia to Jean-Paul Belmondo's Franco-Italian Michel. (Belmondo's Italian father was born in Algeria before moving to Paris as a young man. Michel, although not identified in the film as Italian, has Italian friends and is obsessed with escaping to Italy.) Not only is Seberg blonde while Belmondo is dark, in most stills showing them together she is lit so that her face is illuminated while his remains in shadow. This is true, for example, of the famous image of the couple walking down the Champs Elysées, reproduced as a film poster and in numerous books and magazines.[14] The stills from *Lilith* used by *Cahiers du cinéma* in a 1966 interview and again in a 1979 tribute, show Seberg as a source of light, illuminating her co-star Warren Beatty who is alternately behind her in the shadows or peering down at her luminous face and bright hair.[15]

Decor and costume add to the effect of such lighting. Hence, throughout *La Ligne de demarcation* Seberg is both literally and figuratively a source of light surrounded by darkness. She plays an idealised white woman, an almost virginal angel of salvation – actually named Mary – who works for the Resistance in occupied France and whose shining deeds are matched by her pale clothes and glowing blonde hair, while those around her (German soldiers, weak husband, passive friend) are dark in appearance, clothing and motivation. The idealisation of Mary as a sister of mercy is underlined by her apparent chastity: she refuses to kiss her defeatist husband and turns her back on him to listen to Resistance broadcasts in bed.[16] Indeed, the film suggests that there is a link within Mary/Seberg between the sexual and the political, as when the camera zooms in on her face in a kind of post-coital repose once she hears a secret message on the radio. Thus, even with a character as idealised as Mary, there remains a sexualisation of the political that connects with the demonising of Seberg's radical activities, as we shall see below. The tensions resulting from the 'white woman' convention – and the violent reactions when this convention is transcended – can be seen as factors in the decline of Seberg's career and indeed her life.

13• R. Dyer, *White*, London and New York, Routledge, 1997, p.139.

14• Reproduced in Vincendeau, op. cit., p.113, *Paris Match*, 21 September 1979, p.30 and *Sight and Sound*, 6 (8), August 1996, p.36. See also the two-shot from the bedroom scene on the cover of *Cinémathèque* 13 (May/June 1975). One could add that Godard uses the convention of light woman/dark man ironically since the film confounds the expected matching between literal and figurative values (pale Patricia acts like a dark *femme fatale* in the conclusion by betraying Michel).

15• See Seberg, op. cit., p.33 and *Cahiers du cinéma* 304 (October 1979), p.70. In both photos the lighting picks out her blonde hair and pale face, contrasting them with his dark hair and shadowed face.

16• For more on the metaphorical associations between virginity and the 'white woman' archetype, see K. Theweleit, *Male Fantasies I: Women, Floods, Bodies, History*, Cambridge, Polity Press, 1987.

In a glaring contrast with her white, mid-Western, small-town origins and the idealised whiteness her screen image was supposed to project, Seberg rapidly became associated with the civil rights movement and other racial causes. At the age of fourteen she had joined the NAACP (National Association for the Advancement of Colored People), and as a star she consistently spoke out against the treatment of blacks in America and of immigrants in France. Seberg's name 'was on every petition against racism, in favor of civil rights, against the OAS and the fascist generals in Algeria, in favor of animal rights'.[17] In the late sixties this was perceived as a form of 'radical chic' associated with other Hollywood stars such as Jane Fonda, but Seberg differed from Fonda: she was a lesser star (in terms of box-office power and iconic status) and she did not have the resources (famous parentage, celebrated acting skills, sexy straight image) that served to make Fonda's politics 'seem more ordinary and normal'.[18] Seberg's activism was never perceived in this way; rather it was seen as something threatening and strange. It therefore elicited an extreme reaction. This came in August 1970, when an anonymous item, apparently prepared by FBI chief J. Edgar Hoover himself, appeared in *Newsweek*, claiming that Seberg and her second husband Romain Gary (on the verge of divorce) 'are reportedly to remarry even though the baby that Jean expects in October is by another man – a black activist she met in California'.[19] Amidst the controversy and the libel suit that followed, Seberg's baby daughter Nina was born prematurely and died. Seberg returned to her home town of Marshalltown, Iowa, to bury Nina, and also to display to the public that the dead baby was white, not black.[20] Each year thereafter, Seberg tried to kill herself on the anniversary of her daughter's death. In 1979 she succeeded, and immediately after the suicide Gary held a Parisian press conference in which he blamed the FBI for her death, showing official documents which stated that '*Jean Seberg a financièrement soutenu le parti des Black Panthers et elle doit être neutralisée*'.[21] A year later, the FBI 'admitted it had slandered her in 1970 as part of a counter-intelligence program'.[22]

It was Seberg's identity as a woman that had been exploited to 'neutralise' her. Not only was her pregnancy used as a means of slander, her political activism in general was redefined in sexual terms. As Gary declared, '*Il fallait à tout prix expliquer son horreur du racisme par des penchants sexuels*'.[23] Seberg herself wrote that 'There's always a sexual aspect to these

---

17• Fuentes, op. cit., pp.38–9. The OAS (Organisation de l'armée secrète) was a terrorist faction within the French armed forces which fought against the granting of Algerian independence.

18• R. Dyer, *Stars*, new edition, London, BFI, 1998, p.81.

19• Anon., 'Newsmakers', *Newseek*, 24 August 1970, p.31.

20• Much has been made of the apparently glass coffin and the 180 photos taken of the dead baby. This very public display and the successful lawsuit for libel have been interpreted by some as evidence of Seberg's collusion in racist assumptions. For the counter case, see Fuentes, op. cit., 192–3 and 197.

21• 'Jean Seberg has financially supported the Black Panther movement and she must be neutralised', cited in R. Chateauneu, 'Une femme que l'on a acculée au désespoir', *Paris Match*, 21 September 1979, p.41.

22• Fuentes op. cit., p.218.

23• 'At all costs they had to explain her horror of racism as sexual desire', Chateauneu, op. cit., p.41.

so-called political vendettas'.[24] Hence, apparently, her decision to sue for libel: '[Seberg's] anger was directed against the political manipulation of her sex. The FBI had reduced her to a sex object. It had presented her as a white woman hungry for a black man.'[25] Even after her death, Seberg's political position was reduced to a sexual one, that of a nymphomaniac 'turned on' by certain causes, particularly those involving black men. This tendency applied in France as much as in the United States, although the specifics were different: American fears raged around black power and Seberg's Black Panther lover, while French fears surrounded 'the Arab cause' and her fourth husband, Ahmed Hasni. After her death she was described by *Paris Match* as having finished her days '*dans de sombres intrigues sentimentalo-politiques avec des terroristes noirs et arabes*'.[26] A vituperative account of her life given by *Voici* in 1992 stated that Seberg offered radical causes not just her fame and her time (a commitment that, we recall, was normalised when it came from Jane Fonda), but '*surtout son corps car, désormais, le moteur de son action politique est tout bêtement le sexe*'.[27] *Voici* concluded:

> *Le sexe est toujours curieusement mêlé chez elle à la politique, qui doit lui être une aphrodisiaque, puisqu'après les Panthères noires, démodées, elle s'enflamme pour la cause arabe [Hasni] parce qu'il est beau comme un dieu oriental et doté sans doute du glaive qui va avec, elle l'installe dans son lit.*[28]

The image of the 'white woman hungry for a black man' threatens Western conceptions of race, gender and desire. Underlying the representation of Seberg in sources such as *Voici* is a suspicion of (female) desire that crosses racial boundaries, and a fear of racial mixing, in *Voici*'s own terms '*Que Jeanne d'Arc, la pucelle blanche, couche avec un terroriste black sex-machine*',[29] or in Fuentes' words, 'that the fair, blond star [. . .] that this favorite of the white God would descend to the depths of miscegenation'.[30] As Dyer explains, 'Inter-racial heterosexuality threatens the power of whiteness because it breaks the legitimation of

---

24· Seberg's journal, cited in M. Rappaport, 'I, Jean Seberg', *Film Quarterly*, 55: 1 (Fall 2001), p.7. See also Rappaport's film, *From the Journals of Jean Seberg*.

25· Fuentes op. cit., p.197. See also pp.192–3.

26· 'in dark politico-sexual intrigues with black and Arab terrorists', Anon., 'La Chute d'une star', *Paris Match*, 23 April 1982, p.5, my emphasis.

27· 'above all her body, because the driving force behind her political actions was quite simply sex', Monréal, op. cit., p.58.

28· 'For her, sex was always strangely mixed up with politics, which must have been an aphrodisiac for her, since after the Black Panthers became old hat, she got all excited about the Arab cause. Because [Hasni] was as handsome as an eastern god, and no doubt endowed with a sword to match, she took him to her bed', ibid., p.59. The term 's'enflammer' (to get excited about something) is also used of Seberg, again in the context of the Black Panthers, in the *Le Monde* obituary – see Siclier, op. cit., p.17.

29· 'that Joan of Arc, the white virgin, should be sleeping with a black terrorist sex-machine', Monréal, op. cit., p.58.

30· Fuentes, op. cit., p.191.

whiteness with reference to the white body'.[31] Seberg's pale, blonde, blue-eyed appearance may have embodied whiteness in an apparently unambiguous way, but her actions and desires were beyond the pale.

Seberg is a white star who came to identify herself with black causes, and who was identified by certain sections of the press (*Time* and *Newsweek* in the United States, *Voici* in France) as a threat because she mixed whiteness with blackness. In Fuentes's fictionalised account, she speaks on the phone to her Black Panther lover, 'acting a part she'd never be given in a film', the part of a black woman. She calls herself Aretha, assumes a deeper tone of voice, and is told 'Know how you can make yourself black, Aretha? [. . .] make yourself into a black victim [. . .]. Be a victim as a black so nobody feels sorry for you'.[32] Fuentes's text is full of racial assumptions about black identity (including blackness as victimhood and black masculinity as sexually threatening), but nonetheless Seberg can be construed as a genuine victim of her support for black and immigrant rights. Certainly this is the gloss on her career given by the largely sympathetic *Paris Match* tribute that followed her suicide. But while describing her death as 'a crime',[33] *Paris Match* does not cast Seberg as a black victim. Rather, it restates in positive terms her whiteness. For *Paris Match* Seberg is a tragic white star whose associations with 'the black cause' were in no way sexually motivated.[34] This is because she has somehow become an iconic white woman, metaphorically as well as literally white, associated (like Mary in *La Ligne de démarcation*) with good deeds and a chaste form of martyrdom. While 'nobody feels sorry' for the 'black victim' in Fuentes' model, *Paris Match* certainly feels sorry for Seberg the white star, and it does so to the extent of representing her as a virginal, white French icon: Joan of Arc. Her first role, in *Saint Joan*, is reinterpreted as revealing Seberg's own soul, while with her suicide Joan of Arc dies for a second time.[35] Seberg the foreign body thus becomes a very French martyr, her struggle with stardom is integrated into 'the history of freedom',[36] and she becomes in death the very archetype of the spotless 'white maiden'.[37]

ADJANI AS WHITER THAN WHITE

Like Seberg's, Isabelle Adjani's whiteness is crucial to her star image. Because she is dark haired rather than blonde, her whiteness is symbolised principally by her pale, 'porcelain'

31• Dyer, *White*, p.25.

32• Fuentes, op. cit., pp.149 and 153.

33• Chateauneu, op. cit., p.41. For a less sympathetic view from *Paris Match*, see note 26, above.

34• See ibid., p.41.

35• Ibid., pp.40, 41. The vocabulary of tragedy and courage is common in star tributes and was much used on the death of Romy Schneider in 1982. See the *Paris Match* tribute issues from 11, 18 and 25 June 1982. Schneider is even described as 'a little soldier' who 'died in battle', *Paris Match*, 11 June 1982, p.34. But there is no explicit mobilisation of the Joan of Arc myth in her case.

36• See Chateauneu, op. cit., p.41.

37• Dyer, *Heavenly Bodies*, p.44. For a less charitable view of Joan of Arc as a paradigm of the star-as-political-activist, see Dyer, *Stars*, p.79, where Henry Fonda is quoted as saying of his daughter Jane: 'She's the instant cause girl, working for the right causes for what I think are the wrong reasons. She won't be satisfied until they burn her, like Joan of Arc'.

skin, the 'radiance' of her face and her blue eyes.[38] These elements of her star image are emphasised verbally in articles and visually in posters, film stills and magazine photos. The monochrome cover of a 1995 issue of *Time Out*, for example, publicising the British release of *La Reine Margot*, shows Adjani's face in extreme close-up as perfectly white. The only colour in the photo is the tinted blue of her eyes, which only exaggerates further her status as visibly white. The photos inside, although in colour, still emphasise the whiteness of Adjani's face by contrast with her black hair, red lips and blue eyes.[39] Adjani's appearance in a publicity still of the same period, used as the poster for *La Reine Margot*, is chosen by Dyer to illustrate the cinematic and photographic 'glow' valued in images of white women:

> The sense of the man being illuminated by the woman is a widespread convention, established in classic Hollywood cinema [. . .] but still current today, from Isabelle Adjani and Vincent Perez (*La Reine Margot* (1994)) to the covers of romantic fiction.[40]

In the compositions targeted by Dyer, 'the light constructs the relationship' within the straight romantic couple.[41] *La Reine Margot* is only one of several films starring Adjani in which this convention is evident. In what we may term her 'whiter than white' roles, Adjani's pale, radiant characters are contrasted with dark male co-stars who are often in need of salvation through her (in plot terms, by means of her help, love or forgiveness, but also symbolically by means of the abstract ideals that her whiteness embodies: innocence, goodness, charity, virtue). Adjani's performance in *La Reine Margot* may at first sight seem a strange candidate for this category, since she plays a predatory vamp, a queen who goes out at night to search for lovers. But significantly she wears a black mask during this sequence, while in the romantic finale of the film (alluded to in Dyer's still) she is unmasked, and radiantly pale. Both scenes concern her desire for La Môle (Perez), but the first is encoded as dark, dirty sex and the second as glowing true love.[42] Margot's moral salvation takes place between these two scenes and is effectively signalled by visual contrasts between her and those she helps throughout the film (her weather-beaten husband, her dark lover). The St Bartholomew's Day Massacre is the turning point, during which Margot is recast as an angel of mercy, a white woman who is as luminous in appearance as in actions, like Seberg as Mary in *La Ligne de démarcation*. Margot, too, is

---

38• See, for example, G. Andrew, 'Isabelle époque', *Time Out*, 11–18 January 1995, p.23; A. Cojean, 'Les Protestations contre le projet Debré', *Le Monde*, 22 February 1997, p.8; and J-C. Loiseau and M-E. Rouchy, 'Adjani: questions d'image', *Télérama*, 2468, 30 April 1997, p.26. See below for an account of how these tropes are used in the *Paris Match* special on Adjani from 30 January 1987.

39• See *Time Out*, 11–18 January, 1995, cover and pp.23, 25.

40• Dyer, *White*, pp.134–5.

41• Ibid., p.134.

42• Compare the representation of gay sex (nocturnal, dark) and straight romance (diurnal, bright) in Cyril Collard's *Les Nuits fauves* (1992).

paler and seemingly better than everyone she meets, her white face and costumes marking her out from the blood-streaked mob that surrounds her. She thus turns from darkness to light, and personifies the rejection of the Medicis' bloodlust in favour of the idealised values of tolerance, compassion, and romance.[43]

Adjani's most luminous roles are, however, from the first decade of her career, before her star image underwent a hysterical modification in the mid-1980s. *Barocco* (1976), a seminal precursor of the *cinéma du look*, is perhaps the most ravishingly photographed of Adjani's films, and like the *cinéma du look* makes great use of colour symbolism. In a labyrinthine plot, it is the cinematography that expresses the essence of the characters. Adjani plays Laure, a teenager whose blonde boyfriend Samson (Gérard Depardieu) is murdered by his double (also played by Depardieu). What follows is the recuperation of Samson's dark double thanks to Adjani's radiant young woman. The film is, in a sense, a remake of Hitchcock's *Vertigo*, but with the genders (and the outcome) inverted, so that here a dark-haired man is dyed blonde by a woman in order to save him through love.[44] Passing the killer off as the real Samson, Laure redeems him and also finds a hope of romance, however macabre, for herself. Although Adjani is as ever dark haired and not blonde, as Laure she is incessantly associated with pale colours and, above all, with yellow, linking her not only to the blonde dye of the plot but also to the positive symbolism of gold and light. She wears a pale mac for much of the film, and is described at one point as being 'yellow from head to foot'. Her face is often shot close up, in a soft yellow light, and in the finale a freeze-frame isolates her, all in yellow, among a dark crowd of dancers. Her pale appearance contrasts with that of Samson's dark killer (whom she literally enlightens during the film) and with her friend Nelly, a red-headed prostitute who is, of course, in another literalisation of colour symbolism, a scarlet woman.[45] Laure is not simply illuminating and valuable, but another example of the 'white maiden', in contradistinction from the sexualised red woman with her red lipstick, red hair, and red-lit window. Nelly has sex with the killer (she gives him her 'special'); Laure saves him.

Adjani plays the 'white maiden' again as Lucy Harker in the German horror film *Nosferatu the Vampyre* (1979). Once more the themes of chastity, purity and love are expressed through her appearance – in this case, her exaggeratedly pale make-up (contrasting with her black hair and the kohl round her eyes), the iris effects of the lighting, and the white nightgowns she wears.[46] The early scenes between Lucy and her husband Jonathan (Bruno Ganz) conform to the romantic paradigm of light woman/dark man and also offer,

---

43• It is significant that the family whom Margot has to betray in order to save her husband and her lover is Italian. This relates not only to the light/dark dichotomy (where Adjani inhabits one side but turns to the other) but also to the Mafia-like tensions which are unusually strong in this violent heritage film.

44• In *Vertigo*, a brunette is (twice) dyed blonde by a man and subsequently (twice) falls to her death.

45• For more on the symbolism of the sexualised red woman and the chaste white woman, see Chapter 4.

46• The first two effects are deliberate allusions to silent cinema and to Murnau's *Nosferatu* (1922), of which Herzog's film is a remake. It is noticeable that several of the shots of Adjani illuminated at night are 'impossible' in terms of realism: light appears to shine on her from outside, i.e. from the dark.

in the visual contrast between her glow and his gloom, a suggestion that his future is overshadowed by darkness. He will become the vampire's victim; she his destroyer. This is Adjani the vampire slayer, the apogee of the white woman, the devoted wife, embodying goodness and purity, resisting the plague (the *Black* Death which decimates her hometown but spares her) and fighting the forces of evil as the 'woman of pure heart'[47] who alone can destroy Count Dracula. She is the light and Dracula the darkness; she sacrifices herself to kill him, asking him into her bed and keeping him there until daybreak. As she waits on the white bed, dressed in white, with a white vase of white flowers above her, she is purity incarnate, whiter than white and confident of triumph.

ADJANI AS 'BEUR STAR' AND DARK OTHER

And yet … is it only with hindsight that Adjani's early stardom gives the impression of something else, something more difficult, more resistant, than simply idealised whiteness? Certainly *Barocco* has been considered '*un corps étranger dans la filmographie de l'auteur, dans l'époque et plus généralement dans le cinéma français*'.[48] Already in December 1974, when she was first featured on the cover of *Paris Match*, the eighteen-year-old Adjani had been presented as both sweet and sour, winning the Prix Citron 'despite her smile'.[49] Ambiguity informed her performances in *The Driver* (1978) and *Les Soeurs Brontë* (1979), in both of which her characters' typically white appearance was dirtied by their excessive behaviour. In the former, the dirt is metaphorical and secret: as The Player, Adjani exchanges 'dirty money for clean' and is told by a detective, 'You're clean, no problem. Course there was that little scrape, you remember, that kind of nasty one that got swept under the rug … '. In the latter, the dirt is literal and plain to see: as Emily Brontë, Adjani is chastised for muddying her clothes (and also for wearing male dress when out on the moors). These suggestions of excess, ambiguity and resistance were to become central to Adjani's star image, and crystallised around the vexed question of racial identity.

Adjani was *the* French female star of the 1980s. The decade began with her winning her first César and being voted favourite actress (ahead of Deneuve and Schneider) by the readers of *Paris Match*.[50] It ended with another César, an Oscar nomination, and the confirmation that she was a global star.[51] But the major development in her stardom during this time was much more unexpected and controversial. In 1974, her first *Paris Match* feature had noted in passing that although born in the working-class Parisian district

---

47· This epithet is stressed throughout the film in readings from a book on how to kill vampires.

48· 'a foreign body in the work of the director, in the period, and more generally in French cinema as a whole', R. Prédal, *Le Cinéma français depuis 1945*, Paris, Nathan, 1991, p.297, my italics. The director in question is André Téchiné.

49· F. Caviglioli, 'Isabelle: Prix Citron malgré son sourire', *Paris Match*, 7 December 1974, p.102. The Prix Citron is given to the star who is most unpleasant to journalists and interviewers.

50· See *Paris Match*, 5 March 1982. The César was for *Possession* (1981).

51· See *Voici*, 104, 6–12 November 1989, pp.4–9, for a report on the global success of *Camille Claudel* (1988) and Adjani's 'international career'. The César and the Oscar nomination were also for this film.

of Gennevilliers, Adjani bore '*le nom d'une princesse des "Mille et Une Nuits"*'.[52] More than ten years later, the racial origins of Isabelle Yasmine Adjani became the catalyst for a hysterical renegotiaton of her star image. In the mid-1980s she declared her ethnicity, becoming, in the words of *Paris Match*, France's first *beur* star,[53] and was subsequently reported to have died of AIDS. Adjani's image may have seemed white, but in fact she was a foreigner, half German and half Algerian. She was both light and dark, and like Jean Seberg, she had to pay a price for representing racial ambiguity through her stardom.

In October 1986, Adjani spoke in an interview with Harlem Désir, the president of SOS-Racisme, about her own racial identity, declaring that 'I always felt like a *Beur*'.[54] Adjani's revelation was provoked by her father's own struggle with his ethnic identity in the time before his death:

I'd felt a need to help [my father] in his reconciliation with himself, so I decided to speak out about his being Algerian. I'd always been seen as such a French product, and there was I saying, 'My blood is mixed, my father is Algerian, my mother's German.'[55]

The writer Philippe Sollers noted in an open letter to Adjani that there were 'two hidden powder kegs in France: the Occupation and the Algerian War. By some unlikely chance, you were born at the exact juncture of these two secrets.' The French public's favourite actress had in one stroke become 'a foreigner in their midst'.[56] Moreover, she was not just foreign but Algerian (this line of descent proved to be much more problematic than her German roots). Her ethnic identity, therefore, suddenly brought into play a host of tensions deriving from the Algerian War (1954–62), the most crucial national event since 1945,[57] and the source during the 1980s of demonstrations and debates on issues such as war crimes, torture and rights for Algerian immigrants.[58] As the *Revue française de sciences politiques* reported in 1987, as far as image was concerned, Algerians occupied the lowest rung of the social ladder.[59] In the eyes of French public opinion, Adjani had joined the lowest of the low.

52• 'the name of a princess from *The Arabian Nights*', Caviglioli, op. cit., p.102. Gennevilliers housed a largely immigrant community, but this was not picked up on by *Paris Match*.

53• 'Première grande star "beur"', *Paris Match*, 30 January 1987. *Beur* is French slang for 'Arab'. For an analysis of the current *beur* star Jamel Debbouze, see Chapter 11.

54• Cited in M. Rosen, 'Isabelle Adjani: The Actress as Political Activist', *Cinéaste*, 17: 4, 1990, p.24.

55• Adjani cited in Andrew, op. cit., p.25. See below for a consideration of how paternal identity informs some of Adjani's film roles.

56• Cited in Rosen, op. cit., p.24.

57• According to a 1990 *Paris Match* poll cited in B. Stora, *La gangrène et l'oubli: La mémoire de la guerre d'Algérie*, Paris, La Découvertre/Poche, 1998, p.363.

58• These included a '*Beur* march' of 30,000 people demanding equal rights in Paris on 2 December 1984 and accusations (followed by law suits) in *Le Canard enchaîné* and *Libération* in 1984/5 that the Front National leader Jean-Marie Le Pen had taken part in torture during the Algerian War.

59• See Stora, op. cit., p.356.

According to subsequent rumours, apparently spread by the Front National, Adjani became a diseased foreign body, infected with AIDS: 'the French have long regarded foreigners as an infectious body within the nation, and of course that's like AIDS. So to the right-wingers like Le Pen I became a good target'.[60] In late 1986 it was reported that Adjani had died of an AIDS-related illness. Her star image took on a life of its own, and she became 'an itinerant cadaver, transported from one city to another, [...] especially in the southern part of France, where the extreme right wing is strong'.[61] Finally, on 18 January 1987, in a startling *coup de théâtre*, Adjani appeared on the TF1 evening news to prove that she was alive and well. In a gesture comparable to Seberg's display of her dead baby, Adjani literally presented her star body to the public for their scrutiny; hence the significance of the moment, commented on in a *Paris Match* exclusive, when she moved her left hand away from her cheek to reveal 'smooth' (i.e. healthy) skin underneath.[62] As with their tribute to the dead Seberg, *Paris Match* celebrated Adjani's public return to life by reanimating the symbols of her whiteness. The first indication that all is well is her 'radiant smile'; the magazine also comments on her 'blue eyes' (twice), her 'dazzling look' and her 'radiant beauty'. It concludes that Adjani is 'shining with brilliant health', contrasting these luminous qualities with the darkness of the rumours, which are repeatedly characterised as 'shadows'.[63] The darkness has, in effect, been defeated by her stellar luminescence.

Not all accounts of the AIDS affair managed to reinscribe Adjani so successfully into the imagery of whiteness. In an open letter to Adjani from his 1988 book *Lettres volées*, Gérard Depardieu described the controversy in terms that unwittingly reaffirmed an association between AIDS and ethnicity, thus mobilising without realising it (the letter was one of support) racist tropes about the 'dark continent' as a source of disease:

> In certain African tribes, when Evil is at the gates of the villages, they sacrifice the most beautiful young woman in the tribe, to appease the anger of the demons. To quiet the fear of an epidemic, public opinion demanded a sacrifice. ...[64]

Adjani's own response to the hysteria of 1986 has often been located in *Camille Claudel* (1988), the heritage project for which she set up her own production company[65] and persuaded her former partner Bruno Nuytten to direct his first film. *Camille Claudel* does mobilise themes of health and decay, of the lone artist rejected by society, of survival in the face of slander. As in *L'Histoire d'Adèle H.* (1975) and *L'Eté meurtrier* (1983), Adjani's

---

60• Adjani cited in Rosen, op. cit., p.25.

61• Adjani cited in M. Goldin, 'The Story of Isabelle A.', *Interview* 20 (1), January 1990, p.42.

62• See *Paris Match*, 30 January 1987.

63• See ibid. For an account of the 'shadowy' dark side of Seberg's career, see *Paris Match*, 23 April 1982, p.8.

64• Cited in Goldin, op. cit., p.42.

65• Named 'Lilith', possibly as a tribute to Seberg's performance in the film of that name.

performance is almost melodramatically excessive, combining extremes of violence and tenderness, vulnerability and strength, but nothing in the film engages with the issue of Adjani's racial identity. That had already been addressed in the unlikely form of a Hollywood comedy, but in the storm of vitriol that greeted *Ishtar* (1987) and has dogged it ever since, the resonance of Adjani's performance was largely ignored.[66]

In 1988 Adjani visited Algeria for the first time, in order to '*lutter contre le complot du silence*'[67] surrounding human rights abuses and to support the student movement. She did so in response to the 'Black October' of 1988 when government troops shot dead hundreds of demonstrators. *Ishtar*, made a year previously in Morocco, has to be seen in this political context even if it was not received as such; in fact, all the more so, since the unremittingly negative press the film received may in part be attributable to its political ambitions. Despite being a rather poor comedy, *Ishtar* did try to satirise American foreign policy and to present something (slightly) beyond racist stereotyping in its portrayal of North Africa, while Adjani's appearance in the film fits between her assumption of her father's Algerian heritage and her interventions regarding French policy in Algeria. Adjani plays Shirra Assel, a revolutionary fighter in the 'people's movement' of Ishtar (a fictitious North African state for which one might read Algeria). Shirra is pitted in armed anti-imperialist struggle against the corrupt Emir, who is backed by the CIA (a situation which has some parallels with French support for the regime in Algeria). Because the film is a comedy, with two big Hollywood stars (Warren Beatty and Dustin Hoffman) playing inept singers Rogers and Clarke, the political narrative and Adjani's performance have both been marginalized. But far from being just the 'love interest' in the film, Adjani is in fact an embodiment of various racial, political and gender ambiguities that relate to her star image.

The least convincing of these is the gender confusion, which seems to derive from an American stereotype about homosexuality and North Africa, and which results in several attempts at comedy when Adjani, disguised as a man, has to prove to Beatty and Hoffman that she is a woman.[68] More intriguing is the relation between the United States (and the West in general) on one hand and Ishtar/Africa on the other. At first the film seems to be trading in conventional Western archetypes, as when Adjani tells Hoffman, 'This is an ancient, devious world, and you come from a young country'. This is in itself remarkable for the fact that Adjani is being used to personify Africa and not Europe or France. It is followed by an account of American foreign policy that portrays the CIA as blunderingly manipulative and the West as far from innocent. Adjani's role as Shirra is thus clarified as more freedom fighter than terrorist (although this is in turn eased by her disagreement

---

66• There remained rumours, however, that Adjani wore scarves in the film in order to hide signs of ill-health (i.e. AIDS) on the 'infamous left cheek' that had been covered by her hand during the TV appearance in January 1987. See, for example, *Le Nouveau VSD*, 537 (17–23 December 1987), p.102.

67• 'struggle against the wall of silence', Adjani cited in Cojean, op. cit., p.8.

68• Although present to an extent in *Les Soeurs Brontë*, gender ambiguity is not part of Adjani's star image. One could instead relate the display required to prove her gender (showing her breasts) to Adjani's display on French TV to prove she was alive and well in January 1987.

with more militant rebels). The action plot sees Adjani, Beatty and Hoffman stranded in the desert, using bazookas to fight off CIA helicopters. Their victory assures 'social reforms in Ishtar as dictated by Shirra Assel' (plus a live album and worldwide promotion for Rogers and Clarke). It is only in the final sequence, the live concert, that Adjani is seen in Western clothes, and hence 'dressed like a girl' as Beatty puts it. Previously she has always worn a disguise, a headscarf, or combat fatigues. But although the gender ambiguity is therefore resolved, the political tensions remain, and are celebrated when, in the presence of the American military, Hoffman dedicates a song to Shirra, 'a very lovely lady of the Left'. As for Adjani's ethnic identity, notwithstanding her change of costume, she remains strongly identified with Ishtar/Algeria, while on a more personal level the hysteria surrounding her star image in 1986 is encapsulated by the title of the theme song dedicated to Shirra: 'Telling the truth can be a dangerous business'. This Adjani knew to her cost.

The association forged in 1986 between Adjani's star image and AIDS has been sporadically revived in the 1990s and beyond, but as a conscious theme chosen by the star rather than as a rumour. Adjani has thus renegotiated the meaning of the association in a positive way, to grant her performances a certain resonance in the indirect representation of AIDS. *La Reine Margot* (1994) considers an entangled network of blood, sex, poison and death, and includes a scene in which Adjani as Margot embraces the dying king, his poisoned blood soaking her white dress.[69] In 2000, her stage role as *La Dame aux camélias* was interpreted as being about AIDS rather than consumption, because '*Isabelle Adjani a voulu en faire une pièce moderne sur une maladie actuelle*'.[70] More intriguingly, Adjani seems to have viewed the play as a conflation of disease and identity, so that the protagonist, Marguerite, '*est doublement exclue à cause de ce qu'elle est: malade et mal née*'.[71] The link with Adjani's own experience in the late 1980s is clear: she too was excluded (to the extent of being killed off) because of what she was (in terms of ethnic identity). As in *La Reine Margot* where Adjani, although playing a queen, declares '*Je suis du côté des opprimés*',[72] here she again identifies herself with the marginal and the excluded:

> *L'ennemie, c'est 'la malade'. Et il est encore et toujours rassurant pour la société que la maladie frappe celles et ceux qui vivent à la marge, désignés et exclus par l'ordre social et l'ordre moral: Marguerite et les prostituées, les homosexuels, les usagers de drogue, les Noirs, les artistes, les femmes ...*[73]

69• Jean-Hugues Anglade, playing the king, had just starred as a man infected with HIV in *Killing Zoe* (1994). This scene perhaps also recalls the famous embracing of an AIDS victim by Princess Diana.

70• 'Isabelle Adjani wanted to make this into a modern play about a present-day disease', F. Joucla, 'Isabelle Adjani: "Vivre avec la mort aux trousses"', *Le Nouvel Observateur* 1881 (23 November 2000), p.52.

71• 'is doubly excluded because of what she is: sick and lowborn', Adjani cited in ibid., p.54.

72• 'I am on the side of the oppressed'.

73• 'The enemy [in the play] is the "sick woman". And it's still always reassuring for society that disease should strike those living at the margins, labelled and excluded by the social and moral order: Marguerite, prostitutes, homosexuals, drug users, blacks, artists, women ... ', cited in ibid., p.53.

Adjani, of course, fits into two or three of these categories. As a star, she has paid a certain price for occupying these positions, but although not perceived as essentially 'ordinary and normal' like Jane Fonda, she has developed a star image of fierce independence which is far removed from the self-destruction associated (however unfairly) with Seberg. This is partly because of Adjani's jealous guarding of her privacy (including a lawsuit victory against *Voici* in 1995), but also because her political involvement has been very selective and focused, as in her statements on Algeria or, more recently, her signing of the petition against the *loi Debré*,[74] and it has never been belittled through sexualisation in the way that Seberg's politics were.[75]

CONCLUSION: ORIGINS AND AMBIGUITIES

Despite the hysteria of the mid-1980s, her performance in *Ishtar*, and her public comments on foreign policy and immigration, ethnicity has not become an explicit part of Adjani's star image.[76] Or rather, her star ethnicity remains of the unmarked kind: visible whiteness, stellar luminescence. The controversy surrounding her racial origins seems not to have left a mark. (It seems to have been replaced to some extent during the nineties by gossip regarding her relationship with Daniel Day-Lewis.) In 1995 she won a César for *La Reine Margot* and in 1997 became the youngest ever President of the Jury at the fiftieth Cannes festival;[77] but her image is resolutely unsettling – 'I am here to disturb, to destabilize, to disarm the invincible,'[78] – and issues of identity, alienation and origins have always been central to it. Adjani has said that in *La Dame aux camélias* the sick Marguerite is excluded from her lover's family because of '*peur de l'opprobe public, mais, bien plus profondément, refus de remettre en cause la lignée, la continuité du nom*'.[79] This links with the crises of identity and genealogy which, in retrospect, seem to characterise many of Adjani's roles and, indeed, her career as a whole, with the relation to her father and his racial identity as the crux. The melodramatic roles for which Adjani is famous, and in which her characters often regress to a state of childhood or suffer neurosis and breakdown, repeatedly dramatise the transfer of identity from father to daughter. In the film that made her a star, *L'Histoire d'Adèle H.* (1975), Adjani's volatile performance has at its heart Adèle's attempt to deny her identity as the daughter of Victor Hugo, the most famous man alive. Unable to pronounce his name, she can only write it in the dust of a mirror before hastily erasing it again. In

---

74• A petition signed in 1997 by film-makers and actors protesting against proposals to encourage French citizens to inform on illegal immigrants or those suspected of harbouring them. For more on this campaign, and in particular the leading role played by Emmanuelle Béart, see Chapter 10.

75• Hence, while Seberg was '*la pasionara de l'impossible*', Adjani has always 'vigorously refused the role of *pasionara*'. See Monréal, op. cit., and Cojean, op. cit. respectively.

76• *La Repentie* (2002) is the only ethnically-marked role she seems to have taken since *Ishtar*.

77• Although her film appearances were scarce during the late 1990s, this is attributable to Adjani's own decision to reduce her workload and bring up her second son, who was born in 1995.

78• Adjani cited in Rosen, op. cit., p.24.

79• 'fear of public disgrace, but more deeply because of a refusal to jeopardise the line of descent, the continuity of the family name', Adjani cited in Joucla, op. cit., p.53.

the subsequent scene she fantasizes that she is born of an unknown father, a desire that is inverted in *L'Eté meurtier* (1983) when Eliane discovers that she is the child of a rape and that she is thus '*de père inconnu*' (of an unknown father). The film details her anguished efforts to erase these origins and ends with her regression to a childhood state before her father's paternal identity was revealed as false. As in *L'Histoire d'Adèle H.*, the father is for the most part physically absent, but his vast psychological importance is the key to the protagonist's alienation. While Adèle fought to deny her father's existence, Eliane's entire motivation is to honour her father and rescue both of their identities. The two films could thus be said to dramatise and even predict Adjani's own shift from maintaining silence about her origins during early stardom (rendering her parentage unknown) to reconciliation with her father and through him with Algerian identity in the eighties.[80]

Adjani's performances in these films also appear significant in articulating her divided origins, her mixed racial identity, to put it most crudely, her light and dark sides. This dichotomy is strangely more explicit in Seberg's star image, according to which she is a divided self, 'half light, half shadow, perfectly cut in two', as if there were 'two people inside her'.[81] The point is emphasised by a photo taken shortly before her death, showing Seberg in close-up, one side of her face in the light, the other in complete shadow. The darkness, we are told, won.[82] There is nothing so obvious in Adjani's star image, although one could perhaps say that in her battle, the light won; but signs of ambivalence remain. In *L'Eté meurtrier*, for example, despite Eliane's idolising of Marilyn Monroe and assumption of her wiggle, there is no simple display of Monroe's 'ultimate' and unambiguous whiteness.[83] Eliane is dark (shot no lighter than her male co-star), troubling, schizoid. If she is white, it is in a nuanced, ambiguous way. And as the rumours aimed at both Adjani and Seberg showed, there is a 'hysteria surrounding ambiguity'[84] in matters of stardom and race. Both Adjani and Seberg have been perceived hysterically because both, one literally and one figuratively, have lived out in their star bodies 'the racial confusions of a society'.[85] Only one – the true star – has transcended the hysteria and the ambiguity. She has done so in a manner which seems to reiterate whiteness but which also, as we have seen, manages to accommodate the foreign body.

---

80. Adjani's films and statements concern the father much more than the mother. But it is perhaps significant that Eliane's mother in *L'Eté meurtrier* is German, as is Adjani's.

81. Fuentes, op. cit., p.174 and *Paris Match*, 21 September 1979, p.39.

82. See ibid., 39: 'Deux personnes en elle: la Maudite a gagné'. In one possible translation it is evil that has triumphed, since *Le Maudit* means the 'Evil one'.

83. Dyer, *Heavenly Bodies*, p.43.

84. Ibid., p.139.

85. Ibid., p.138.

CHAPTER 9

Romantic male struggles with hysterical female: Jean-Hugues Anglade and Béatrice Dalle in *Betty Blue* (1986).

Desire on display: Béatrice Dalle and Jean-Hugues Anglade

STARDOM AND THE *CINÉMA DU LOOK*

It might seem unusual that during the 1980s and early 1990s the films of Jean-Jacques Beineix, Luc Besson and Léos Carax should reveal a number of new stars. After all, in their work the images appeared to have the starring roles. Known in French as *le cinéma du look* or *le visuel*, the film style which became associated with these directors was deemed by critics to emphasise spectacle above all else, and was often attacked for a perceived similarity to visual forms such as music video and comic strips. Beneath the glossy images there remained, however, in films like *Subway, Betty Blue, Nikita* and *Les Amants du Pont-Neuf*, narratives about young people attempting to find romance or happiness in an alienating environment. And these young people were played by several actors who went on to become stars: Christophe Lambert (*Subway*), Juliette Binoche (*Mauvais Sang, Les Amants du Pont-Neuf*), Jean Reno (*Subway, Le Grand Bleu, Nikita*), Béatrice Dalle (*Betty Blue*) and Jean-Hugues Anglade (*Subway, Betty Blue, Nikita*).

With the exception of Reno, whose powerful physique and monosyllabic performances positioned him as a fairly traditional action hero (he was to be typecast as such in later films like *Léon* and *Ronin*), the male stars coming out of the *cinéma du look* tended to privilege emotion over action, and could be classed as 'sensitive'. In 1986, commenting on Anglade's break-through role in Beineix's *Betty Blue*, the magazine *Télérama* declared that '*Après la génération des acteurs "à flingue", les Berry, les Lanvin, et même les Giraudeau, voilà donc les comédiens "à coeur": [. . .] Christophe Lambert, Jean-Hugues Anglade.*'[1] A further contrast was made in the French press between Anglade's generation and the 1970s generation of Patrick Dewaere (to whom he had compared himself). Anglade was felt to be sufficiently distant from the uprising of May 1968 to have escaped the tropes of pessimism, disillusion and defeat that had followed, and which had defined Dewaere as an idealistic rebel turned pathetic loser: '*Ils n'ont pas fait Mai 68, mais en ont vu juste assez pour ne plus croire aux utopies,*

1· 'After the generation of "gun-toting" actors like Berry, Lanvin, and even Giraudeau, here are the "heart-felt" actors: Christophe Lambert, Jean-Hugues Anglade', F. Pascaud, 'Acteur "à coeur"', *Télérama* 1891 (9 April 1986), p.25.

aux espoirs collectives. Ils s'accrochent, simplement, à leur destin individuel.'[2] The *look* generation hoped for nothing and were simply interested in *'l'émotion, comme unique lien possible dans la société française éclatée des années 80'.*[3] For Beineix himself, Anglade was a lone representative of the classic romantic male star, again as distinct from the previous generation of actors:

> *Il y a eu l'école du naturalisme voyou des années soixante-dix et quatre-vingts: Patrick Dewaere, Gérard Depardieu, Gérard Lanvin, même Bernard Giraudeau, qui ont tous une espèce de virilité affirmée [. . .]. Des jeunes premiers plus sensibles, il n'y en a pas tellement. Il y a Jean-Hugues Anglade.*[4]

Hence, Anglade can be said to stand out from both his predecessors and his peers. While Lambert's originally sensitive, romantic star image underwent a gradual change to that of action hero,[5] Anglade's has persisted through the nineties, and he has become 'the quintessential romantic Frenchman'.[6]

The female stars discovered or revealed by the *cinéma du look* were Béatrice Dalle (who made her film debut in *Betty Blue*), Juliette Binoche (who was remodelled by Carax in *Mauvais Sang* and *Les Amants du Pont-Neuf*) and to a lesser extent Anne Parillaud (a former child star who made her adult break-through in Besson's *Nikita*). As Ginette Vincendeau has pointed out, in French cinema generally during the mid-eighties many new actresses came to the fore, including Sandrine Bonnaire, Emmanuelle Béart and Sophie Marceau, as well as Binoche and Dalle:

> fifteen years later, these actresses, except for the unpredictable (and sadly typecast) Dalle, are all active and successful. [. . .] While Dalle's 'in-your-face' sexuality seems to confine her to repeats of her *Betty Blue* persona, [. . .] Marceau and Béart managed the transition to international blockbusters [. . . and] Binoche succeeded in going international while remaining identified as an auteur cinema star.[7]

Vincendeau emphasises in particular the contrast between Dalle's 'pop sexual persona (a throwback to Bardot)' and Binoche's 'altogether more cerebral, more anguished and more

---

2• 'They didn't go through May '68, but they saw just enough of it to no longer believe in utopias, or in collective dreams. Instead, they just hang on to their individual destiny', P. Salanches, 'Jean-Hugues Anglade: "J'ai grandi. Le cinéma, c'est mon chemin" ', *Première* (Paris), 109 (April 1986), p.94. See Chapter 7 for more on Dewaere as a personification of the hopes and failures of May '68.

3• 'emotion, the only possible link in the fractured French society of the 80s', Pascaud, op. cit., p.25.

4• 'There was the naturalistic school of the 1970s and 1980s yobs: Patrick Dewaere, Gérard Depardieu, Gérard Lanvin, even Bernard Giraudeau, who have a kind of established virility. More sensitive leads are pretty rare. There's just Jean-Hugues Anglade', M. Moricini and C. d'Yvoire, 'Le Choix de Beineix', *Première* (Paris) 109 (April 1986), pp.93–4.

5• This is particularly due to his performances in the *Highlander* series. He has also Anglicised his name, changing it to Christopher.

6• M. Adams, 'Betty Blue Director's Cut', National Film Theatre Programme, September 1997, cited in P. Powrie, *Jean-Jacques Beineix*, Manchester and New York, Manchester University Press, 2001, p.2.

7• G. Vincendeau, *Stars and Stardom in French Cinema*, London and New York, Continuum, 2000, p.241. Vincendeau associates Binoche with 'neo-romanticism' rather than the *cinéma du look*.

fragile' image, which she compares to that of 'New Wave actresses'.[8] But this is a rather restrictive reading of Dalle's star image, as I hope to show. Moreover, the dismissal of Dalle's later career is premature. The year 2001 saw Dalle's re-emergence, thanks to her roles in *Trouble Every Day* and *H Story*, both of which were shown at the Cannes festival, and her allegedly disruptive performance at the festival itself. During the summer of 2001, she appeared on the covers of *Télérama* and *Repérages*, and was the subject of features in *Cahiers du cinéma* and *Paris Match*. Unlike Bardot, Dalle has made a comeback as a mature – although still controversial – film star.

Dalle had been discovered by Beineix on the cover of a photography magazine, and was cast alongside Anglade in *Betty Blue* (aka *37°2 le matin,* 1986*)*. Like many others subsequently, Beineix compared Dalle to Brigitte Bardot, and described her as a force of nature:

> *la nature, la bombe, le don à l'état pur: Béatrice Dalle. [. . .] Elle est le naturel d'une génération. Comme a pu l'être Brigitte Bardot en son temps, elle représente un certain compromis entre la sensualité et l'époque.*[9]

If Anglade's star image is, at least from *Betty Blue* onwards, that of the romantic hero, Dalle's is more extreme, associated with transgression, excess, and the explicitly erotic. She is by far the most sexualised actress of her generation (although this sexualised image becomes increasingly self-conscious and ironic in her later career, as we shall see). In a 1986 *Première* feature on *Betty Blue*, Anglade is photographed in a pensive, sensitive pose, frowning into the distance. Dalle, by contrast, is shown laughing, clutching a bottle of champagne and a cigarette, with her shirt unbuttoned to reveal part of her breasts. The headline next to Anglade suggests personal growth – '*J'ai grandi. Le cinéma, c'est mon chemin*'[10] – while the one next to Dalle celebrates excess: '*J'aime ce qui est trop.*'[11] And yet there are also key similarities in their star images, most of which derive from their performance together in *Betty Blue*.

HIS AND HERS: DESIRING BODIES IN *BETTY BLUE*

In the opening scene of the film, the camera slowly tracks forwards towards Betty (Dalle) and Zorg (Anglade), both naked, having sex. The first sounds are Betty's high-pitched groans of pleasure. Her face is clearly lit as she grimaces, and then bites Zorg's shoulder at the moment of orgasm. (Both the groaning and the biting will be revisited with hyperbolic intent in Dalle's performance from *Trouble Every Day*.) Despite the slight privileging of Dalle over Anglade in this sequence – she makes the most noise; her face is

---

8• Ibid., p.242.

9• 'a force of nature, a bombshell, a pure gift: Béatrice Dalle. She is the natural of her generation. Like Brigitte Bardot may have been in her day, she represents a certain compromise between sensuality and the times', Beineix cited in Moricini and d'Yvoire, op. cit., pp.94–5.

10• 'I've grown up. The cinema is my way forward', *Première* (Paris), 109 (April 1986), p.94.

11• 'I love things that are too much', ibid., p.96.

visible while his is hidden – the scene is essentially a shared instance of sexual pleasure, and as such sets the tone for the film, during which both Dalle and Anglade spend a lot of screen time naked and displaying their bodies to each other (and to the audience). One reviewer was prompted to write that '*pour la première fois au cinéma, nudité masculine et nudité féminine sont traitées également*'.[12] Beyond the film itself, although very strongly rooted in it, nudity has become a key part of both actors' star images. In this respect, Anglade and Dalle are comparable as sexualised stars associated with the display of the desiring body.

Betty's first appearance after this sex scene foregrounds the notion of display, as she swaggers up to Zorg's shack in a revealing dress and asks '*Alors, comment tu me trouves?*'.[13] Dalle is also introducing herself to the audience here, since this is her first film role. Her face is shot in a medium close-up as she beams, her wide mouth spread in a smile that shows her strong teeth. This shot establishes the iconic importance of Dalle's mouth, the focus for many of her film stills and publicity photos, and a symbol of her sexualised and potentially devouring star image. *Première* describes it as '*une bouche qui vous envoûte, gourmande et carnassière*'.[14] Their feature on *Betty Blue* includes an image of Dalle grinning as she suggestively bites the tip of a finger with her front teeth.[15] This eroticising of Dalle's mouth is replicated in the film when Betty sucks on an ice lolly while watching Zorg at work, and in the numerous facial close-ups which show her mouth accentuated by red lipstick. There are also several shots of Dalle fully nude, as there are of Anglade, and the film is punctuated by frequent sex scenes. As a result, *Betty Blue* has been celebrated as 'one of the ten great bonking movies of all time' and condemned as 'a male fantasy of the "supreme fuck"'.[16] But the frequent nudity that results in these overtly eroticised readings of the film was in fact challenged by Dalle during filming. As she told the press, she regularly protested to Beineix about the amount of nude scenes she was asked to do, and in some instances persuaded him to change his mind.[17] Nonetheless, excess and display are central to Dalle's performance and to the publicity surrounding *Betty Blue*.

The key to Dalle's performance and its reception is the pathologising of female sexual desire and bodily display as something violent, excessive, and ultimately destructive. In contrast to the nurturing trope of motherhood – an ideal to which Betty aspires but which she fails to achieve – the desiring but unproductive woman is represented as dangerous and violent. Hence the scenes in which Betty attacks other people and increasingly herself, including the tearing of the baby clothes to shreds when she learns that she is not pregnant.

12· 'for the first time in the history of cinema, male and female nudity are treated equally', D. Jamet, 'Chaud les passions chaud', *Quotidien de Paris*, 9 April 1986, cited in Powrie, op. cit., p.138.

13· 'Well, what do you think?'

14· 'a mouth that bewitches you, greedy and carnivorous', C. d'Yvoire, 'Béatrice Dalle: "J'aime ce qui est trop"', *Première* (Paris), 109 (April 1986), p.96.

15· See *Première* (Paris), 109, April 1986, p.99.

16· *Empire*, November 1992, cited in Fox Video souvenir booklet for *Betty Blue*, long version box-set, 1993, p.11; S. Hayward, *French National Cinema*, London and New York, Routledge, 1993, p.293.

17· See d'Yvoire, op. cit., pp.96–7.

She ends by punching her fist through a glass door and eventually by tearing out her own eye. And yet in interview, Dalle claimed that her own behaviour could be even more violent and hysterical than Betty's: '*Ses moments d'hystérie ou l'effet qu'elle provoque sur les gens, c'est complètement moi. [. . .] pour ce qui est de la violence, je suis encore pire*'.[18] The transgression of norms is expressed not just in Betty/Dalle's behaviour, but also in her body. Beineix has suggested that her appearance has a kind of 'monstruosité gracieuse'.[19] Throughout *Betty Blue*, this monstrosity is expressed via the repeated association between excess and the body. Bodily excess is a feature of what Linda Williams has called the 'body genres' of popular cinema: pornography, horror and melodrama.[20] *Betty Blue* combines the codes of these three genres, and represents Betty's excess in terms of bodily fluids such as tears and blood, be it menstrual (the period that proves she is not pregnant, figured metaphorically by her bleeding, mascara-streaked face and by Zorg's reaction)[21] or arterial (the blood-smeared walls of the bathroom where she rips out her eye). Dalle's performance is in essence corporeal, and not only embodies the desire and despair of her character, but also calls forth from the spectator a physical reaction (be it tears, sexual arousal, or screaming).[22]

Phil Powrie has compared Dalle's 'series of hysterical fits'[23] in *Betty Blue* to a similar performance by Bette Davis, in which 'the signs of her excessive desire are inscribed on her body in a hyperbolic manner'.[24] He also notes in reference to her performance that, according to Lapsely and Westlake, 'The hysteric is a woman asking [. . .] what it is to be a woman for a man.'[25] There is indeed, in Dalle's star image, and particularly in *Betty Blue*, an aggressive over-exaggeration of sexual display which we might interpret as a questioning of the importance attached to the sexualised female body. Powrie interprets the aggressive display of her pudenda in *Betty Blue* (complete with an invitation to have a good look) as demonstrating 'the female object's resistance to being made an object precisely by overemphasising her body as erotic attraction.'[26] This tendency becomes an essential, if subtle, component of Dalle's subsequent star image, finding its most explicit expression in the horror film *Trouble Every Day*, where the foregrounding of the sexualised body and of bodily fluids, and the association of 'excessive desire' with hysteria is reintroduced in an even more 'hyperbolic manner' that refers directly back to Dalle's role in *Betty Blue*.

18• 'Her hysterical outbursts and the effect she has on people, that's just like me. As for violence, I'm even worse', ibid., p.96.

19• 'graceful monstrosity', Moriconi and d'Yvoire, op. cit., pp.94–5.

20• See L. Williams, 'Film bodies: gender, genre and excess', *Film Quarterly*, 44: 4 (1991), pp.2–13.

21• In sympathy, he spreads red stew all over his face; this scene is later referenced by *Trouble Every Day*. The third code, porn, is audible rather than visible in Dalle's performance of sexual pleasure.

22• These are the spectator reactions that Williams identifies with the melodrama, the porn film and the horror film respectively. See ibid.

23• Powrie, op. cit., p.135.

24• M. A. Doane, *The Desire to Desire: The Woman's Film of the 1940s*, cited in ibid., p.135.

25• R. Lapsely and M. Westlake, 'From *Casablanca* to *Pretty Woman*: the politics of romance', cited in ibid., p.140.

26• Powrie, op. cit., p.138.

Hysteria or madness have long been used as means of pathologising and hence containing female desire, thanks to 'a cultural tradition that represents "woman" *as* madness, and that uses images of the female body [. . .] to stand for irrationality in general'.[27] Among the best-known female personifications of madness is Ophelia, whose 'death by drowning has associations with the feminine and the irrational, since water is the organic symbol of woman's fluidity: blood, milk, tears'.[28] Ophelia informs Dalle's performance as Betty (in the director's cut she jumps into the river and floats downstream in an echo of Millais's famous painting), and so does the figure of Lucy, the romanticised nineteenth-century madwoman who is both violent and yet 'an idealized, poetic form of pure femininity [. . .]: absolutely irrational, absolutely emotional, and, once the single act is accomplished, absolutely passive'.[29] For Betty, the endpoint is the enforced passivity of sedation and ultimately her 'mercy killing' by Zorg. Thus, while 'the beautiful woman['s] disordered mind and body are exposed' it is 'male control' that triumphs.[30] Of course, as we shall see, Anglade as Zorg does also expose his own desiring body, but his desire is always under control while Betty's seems always to be out of control, a distinction that applies equally to the star images of these two actors and to the cultural traditions in Western representations of sex.

If Dalle as Betty is represented in terms familiar from gender archetypes (the feminine as natural, emotional, passionate, sexualised, irrational, hysterical), so too is Anglade in the role of Zorg. Throughout the film, Anglade displays the fact that he is a man, mobilising 'the conventional signs of masculinity' such as muscles, hairiness and sweat.[31] The first establishing shot of Zorg alone shows him driving a pick-up truck, dressed in a baseball cap and a vest, his muscled arms and chest visible, his body and face slicked with sweat (as they are in the sex scene that precedes this). He is unshaven and whooping along to the sound of the truck's bell. This image condenses several facets of masculinity as it is conventionally represented, centring on the importance of work (the truck, the outfit, the muscles, the sweat), and on the virility of the male body (muscles, hairiness). The template established here is followed for much of the film. Like Tom Cruise in *Top Gun* (also 1986), Zorg gleams with sweat in almost every shot. He is almost always dressed in jeans and a vest, thus signifying his association with physical work.[32] He even wears a vest to go out for a Chinese meal, thus displaying his macho working man image in a social situation

---

27• E. Showalter, *The Female Malady: Women, Madness and English Culture, 1830–1980*, London, Virago, 1987, p.4, italics in original.

28• Ibid., p.11.

29• Ibid., p.17.

30• Ibid., p.3. For a reading of *Betty Blue* in terms of male narrative control, see G. Austin, *Contemporary French Cinema*, Manchester, MUP, 1996, pp.62–4.

31• R. Dyer, *Now you see it: Studies on lesbian and gay film*, London, Routledge, 1990, p.92.

32• The vest is shorthand for machismo in performances by Gérard Depardieu (*La Lune dans le caniveau*) and Bruce Willis (*The Fifth Element*) among others. For an account of macho workwear in gay fashion, see R. Meyer, 'Warhol's Clones', *The Yale Journal of Criticism*, 7 (1994), pp.79–109.

where it is incongruous. When not dressed in 'hypermasculine' workwear,[33] Zorg is often naked, with his muscled body on display. There are similarities here between his performance and that of Dalle as Betty. Where she asks Zorg (and the audience) 'How do I look?', so Zorg addresses both Betty and the spectator when showing off his muscles: he pauses while knocking down a wall to ask '*Tu trouves pas que je ressemble à Stallone dans* Rocky IV, *baby?*'.[34] Desire, as well as display, informs Anglade's performance too. As he states, '*il fallait qu'on sente le désir dans le corps de Zorg*'.[35] But where Betty's desiring body is increasingly 'disordered', Zorg's remains under control. He rejects sexual advances from Annie by citing his power of self-control over his desires: '*J'utilise mes forces pour ne penser à rien*'.[36] His strength is thus reiterated, but in a context of control that associates him with masculine order as distinct from feminine disorder.

The male desiring body is, in some of Anglade's performances, represented via a kind of hysteria as abject, a site of despair or decay, as in *L'Homme blessé* and *La Reine Margot* (see below). But in *Betty Blue* Zorg's desire is normalised and controlled, channelled through the structured body. Moreover, Zorg exerts control over the narrative as the writer of the story. Humour is another means of control in the film. Where Betty's hysterical fits are rooted in a (supposedly feminine) tendency to take things too seriously and too emotionally (hence her violent assaults on the publisher and the client at the pizzeria), Zorg can laugh at himself and at the constructed ideal of masculinity to which he aspires. This is made clear in the Stallone reference, and also in a similar scene where he wrestles, unsuccessfully, with a sofa bed, a task he describes as '*de la mécanique*' and hence suited only for '*un mec*'.[37] His comic failure to put up the bed transforms his nudity in this scene from a macho display to a moment of vulnerability, and the laughter he shares with Betty demonstrates that the hypermasculine ideal is not always appropriate.

One reason why hypermasculinity is referenced regularly throughout the film is to balance the elements of the narrative that run counter to accepted images of masculinity, for Zorg is in fact not a manual worker as he first appears, but a writer. His training as a plumber is invoked in one sequence, but he is on the whole a very domesticated figure, who stays at home to write and to prepare food (he cooks in the film much more than Betty does). The higher cultural associations of being a writer (and the voice-overs from Zorg's work that punctuate the film) are offset by a strand of macho language in Anglade's performance – in the homophobic jokes about 'pédés' (homosexuals), the use of 'baby' when addressing Betty, and the monosyllabic whooping in the establishing scene. But this macho tendency is balanced in turn by the scenes where Zorg dresses in drag, first to carry out a robbery (in the longer version only) and then to pass unnoticed into the hospital in

---

33· Ibid., p.98.

34· 'Don't I remind you of Stallone in *Rocky IV*, baby?'

35· 'You had to sense the desire in Zorg's body.' Cited in Salanches, op. cit., p.94.

36· 'I use my strength to think about nothing'.

37· 'mechanics' suited only for 'a bloke'.

order to kill Betty. In these sequences, the feminisation of Zorg hinted at in his association with the home becomes explicit and spectacular. The film concludes with Zorg no longer in drag but occupying the slightly ambiguous position of the romantic male: domesticated by his position in the home (sitting at the table writing, devoted to Betty's memory) but visibly masculine too (wearing vest and jeans again). This is the space of romantic masculinity that Anglade's image went on to occupy in his subsequent career.

JEAN-HUGUES ANGLADE AND ROMANTIC MASCULINITY

The hints of a tamed, domesticated, and hence romantically accessible masculinity that emerge from *Betty Blue* were to form a crucial part of Anglade's star image. They are reiterated most evidently in his role as Marco in *Nikita* (1990), where he is feminised first by his job – cashier at a supermarket – and later by identification with the domestic space – he stays at home, cooking and designing boats, while Nikita goes to work as an action hero(ine). It has been observed that the romantic hero (in film, as in literature) is a 'woman-made man', whose masculinity ultimately conforms to female standards and whose behaviour replaces brutal masculine values (aggression, strength) with the romantic values of gentleness, devotion and love.[38] If Anglade's star image is consistently that of the romantic hero, then it seems that the necessary modification of brute masculinity has already happened at some earlier, unseen point. Vestiges remain: the unshaven face, the muscular torso, the occasional flashes of passion. But we do not see a transformation within his performance from menace to tenderness – as we do for example in Jean Yanne's performance as the butcher Popaul in *Le Boucher* (1969). Nor are there tales of a wild, violent youth that predates the mature, reassuring image, as there are in Depardieu's case. Anglade is always already romantic. His website describes him as '*un romantique, un séducteur*' and '*le Chopin du cinéma français*'.[39] He is an idealised object of desire. The display of the star body is an important part of this process: in *Nuit d'été en ville* (1990), Anglade is nude for practically the entire film. Nude publicity stills are available for his performances not just in this film, but also in *Betty Blue* and *L'homme blessé*. More recently, in *Nelly et Monsieur Arnaud* (1996), Anglade remains clothed but appears as a 'confirmed bachelor' and romantic charmer. There are, however, two key performances that deviate from this romantic persona: as the homosexual adolescent Henri in *L'homme blessé* (1982) and as King Charles in *La Reine Margot* (1994).

Anglade's first starring role, in *L'homme blessé*, is in contradistinction from the idealised masculinity that informs his performance in *Betty Blue*, and that of his co-star in the former, Vittorio Mezzogiorno. Henri (Anglade) is a troubled, gay adolescent who is fixated by the macho and treacherous Jean (Mezzogiorno). Jean conforms to masculine conventions: he

---

38• See G. Studlar, 'Valentino, "Optic Intoxication" and Dance Madness', in S. Cohen and I. R. Hark (eds), *Screening the Male: Exploring Masculinities in Hollywood Cinema*, London and New York, Routledge, 1993, pp.23–45.

39• 'a romantic, a seducer, the Chopin of French cinema'.

is unshaven, hairy, muscled and strong; he wears a t-shirt, jeans and cowboy boots. Henri, by contrast, is pale, skinny, long-haired but clean-shaven, fragile and desperate; he wears slacks and long-sleeved shirts. Where Jean is casual about showing his naked body, Henri is insecure about such display and sleeps in his clothes. Anglade's performance as Henri suggest an adolescent searching not for sexual identity (his homosexuality is a given), but for the secure gender identity offered by the signs of masculinity. Henri only begins to assume a degree of agency in the narrative when he puts on Jean's clothes, and is only shown naked in the closing scene, where he is able to assert his dominance over Jean and to reveal his own muscled body.[40] In purely visual, iconic terms, Anglade as Henri appears to be striving for the masculine assurance of Zorg.

While the visible signs of masculinity are sought in *L'homme blessé* and celebrated (albeit at times ironically) in *Betty Blue*, they are also susceptible to a negative portrayal, as is the case in *La Reine Margot*. Playing the weak King Charles, Anglade embodies illness, decay and death, all represented via his hairy, sweaty and dirty appearance. Signifiers of conventional masculinity are here presented as excessive and unhealthy. This is a diseased masculinity, where muscles have wasted away, hair is long but thinning, dirt is linked with infection and poison, and sweat is not a sign of work but of illness, to be ultimately replaced by blood seeping from the pores. As the king's condition becomes more dangerous, he is associated with bodily fluids, that is to say with the 'feminine' principle of fluidity rather than 'masculine' qualities of hardness and control. He coughs, curses, cries and bleeds. He writhes in fits, exceeding the allotted space and leaving the frame of the shot (much as Henri does with his incessant darting to and fro in *L'homme blessé*). The feminisation of the king is paralleled by homoerotic moments with the page and with Henri of Navarre, but they are as fleeting and abortive as the sexual encounters in *L'homme blessé*. In both films, director Patrice Chéreau uses Anglade against his star image, as a figure of desperation, vulnerability and excess;[41] but both performances confirm the normative convention of romantic masculinity that Anglade, and the male star in general, usually inhabits.

BÉATRICE DALLE AND FEMALE SEXUALITY

If Anglade's star image is resolutely romantic, Dalle's is excessive. She has been nicknamed 'Béatrice scanDalle'[42] and has been arrested in France for drug offences, assaulting a traffic warden and shoplifting. Arrests for cocaine possession while filming *The Blackout* in the United States resulted in her classification as an 'undesirable immigrant', and a refusal to grant her a work permit when she was due to star in other American films. Her relationship with Joey Starr – from the controversial rap group

---

40· In an earlier scene where Anglade undresses, his outsize underpants make his body seem skinny. When nude in the final scene, it is revealed that he has a muscled physique not unlike Mezzogiorno's.

41· Any sexual vulnerability in Anglade's image was poignantly underlined by his revelation in 2002 that he had been raped at thirteen. See C. Rotman, 'Mortel travers', *Libération*, 22 July 2002, p.32.

42· See F. Strauss, 'Béatrice Dalle: actrice totale', *Télérama* 2687 (11 July 2001), p.36.

NTM, a star '*qui incarne la subversion et les excès*'[43] – has fed this transgressive image. During the Cannes film festival of 2001, Dalle and Starr were accused by the TF1 television show *Exclusif* of wrecking their hotel. But Dalle's excessive persona is primarily related not to drugs offences or antisocial behaviour but to her sexual display.

Dalle is represented most consistently as a sexualised and desiring female body. She is associated with passion, sex, bodily fluids (from the tears and blood of *Betty Blue* to the vampirism of *Trouble Every Day*) and, above all, the mouth. She is known, we are told, as 'La Grande Bouche'.[44] As we have seen, attention is drawn to her mouth during her performance in *Betty Blue* and in publicity stills from the film. A recent photo from *Télérama* shows her again biting the end of a finger while also holding a cigarette, her mouth outlined in lipstick and positioned in the centre of the image.[45] The mouth is not, however, an unproblematic symbol of female sexuality and desire. As Rosalind Coward notes,

> for women, the pursuit of oral pleasure runs up against prohibitions and controls [. . .] about women's appetite and women's duty to give out. The mouth for women is a site of drama, a drama between the desire to pursue active needs and the prohibitions levelled against women's behaviour.[46]

This drama is played out in Dalle's star image, and resolved in favour of appetite rather than maternal nurturing or submissive restraint. Coward asserts that 'the mouth appears to be the organ where the tightest controls are placed on women's behaviour, where women's sensual life is most closely policed', adding that the two key areas of control are on speaking – 'Men silence women's speech in public' – and on appetite – 'Women are expected to nourish, not to demand'.[47] For Dalle, these controls are broken: she is demanding, desiring and outspoken: one of the reviews of *Betty Blue* called her 'a foul-mouthed schoolgirl'.[48] Motherhood is not part of her star image, but appetite is; hence the attention drawn to her mouth and to 'the pursuit of oral pleasure' in the frequent images of her smoking, drinking, laughing, eating, sucking, kissing, grinning, and so on. Her 'sensual life' is celebrated in much the same way that male stars such as Depardieu are celebrated for their 'all-consuming' oral pleasure in living the good life. Hence Dalle transgresses the codes that structure gendered behaviour. This transgression is most explicit in her role as a flesh-eating vampire in Claire Denis's superb horror film, *Trouble Every Day* (2001).

43• 'who incarnates subversion and excess', P. Barbot and L. Rigoulet, 'La tchatche, pour dire quoi?', *Télérama* 2724 (30 March 2002), p.65.

44• 'Big Mouth'. See www.imdb.com

45• See *Télérama* 2687 (11 July 2001), p.34.

46• R. Coward, *Female Desire*, London, Paladin, 1984, p.22.

47• Ibid., pp.118, 119.

48• V. Ostria, review for *Cinématographe* 118 (1986), cited in Powrie, op. cit., p.123.

Vampirism intimately links sexual desire and the appetite for nourishment, alongside an equation between oral pleasures and blood, suffering and death, all figures for the prohibition of these pleasures. Unsurprisingly, publicity for the film mobilised these metaphors, concentrating above all on the mouth as what Coward calls 'a site for drama', in reference to Dalle's role as the vampire Coré. Hence *Télérama* declared that '*Béatrice Dalle y joue une "mangeuese d'hommes" au sens le plus littéral*'.[49] *Paris Match* added that Dalle, '*métamorphosée en ganstron'homme, disparaît derrière son impressionnante bouche carnassière*', and that in this display of '*une sexualité dévorante et dévoreuse [. . .] les pulsions sexuelles sont plus fortes que la retenue*'.[50] *Trouble Every Day*, of course, also mobilises these metaphors but in a self-conscious way that reflects ironically, not on the horror genre itself, but on Dalle's star image.

While '*la retenue*' (restraint) is embodied, as in *Betty Blue*, by the romantic but controlling male lover (Anglade as Zorg, Alex Decas as Coré's doctor husband),[51] sexual appetite is embodied by Dalle. By associating vampirism explicitly with sex, and dispensing with the metaphorical association of the two more usual in vampire stories, *Trouble Every Day* presents a literalised version of the elements already essential to Dalle's star image: the predatory female, the man-eater, a combination of sexual desire and excess that threatens to be dangerous. The key scene in the film unites sex and violence in the person of Coré/Dalle, and also reflects back on the origins of Dalle's public persona in *Betty Blue*. A youth breaks into the deserted house where Coré, after a series of vampire murders, has been incarcerated 'for her own good' by her husband. (She is contained thus to protect her from the consequences of her own desires, just as the uncontrollable Betty is, in effect, contained by Zorg's killing her 'for her own good'.) As the youth hovers on the threshold of the room where Coré – the madwoman in the attic – has been shut up, she lifts up her dress to show him her pudenda. This sexual display is the catalyst for what follows. It plays upon Dalle's sexualised star image, and in particular on the scene in *Betty Blue* where Betty defiantly displays herself to Zorg's boss. In that case, the man flees when confronted by overt female sexuality. In *Trouble Every Day*, the display is a form of entrapment or temptation, to which the youth willingly succumbs before becoming Coré's next victim. Most controversially, the ensuing sex scene culminates with Coré biting the flesh off his face and beginning to eat him alive. She rubs his blood and flesh over her face and body as she literally consumes him.

In another allusion to *Betty Blue*, her face drips with blood and gore just as Betty's runs with blood and tears of despair. But here the violence is directed outwards rather than at

---

49• 'Béatrice Dalle plays a "man-eater" in the most literal sense of the word', Strauss, op. cit., p.35.

50• 'transformed into a man-eater [there is a pun here on 'gastronome', meaning gourmet], disappears behind her strikingly carnivorous mouth'; in this display of 'voracious and devouring sexuality, sexual drives are stronger than restraint', A. Spira and C. S., 'Plus coupe-faim qu'excitant/Saisissant!', *Paris Match*, 19 July 2001, p.25.

51• Decas, who also plays Dalle's partner in Denis's *J'ai pas sommeil* (1994), is black, as is Dalle's real-life partner Joey Starr. Perceptions of inter-racial sex are not, however, explicit in her star image, as they were in that of Jean Seberg a generation earlier. See Chapter 8.

the self. This is the excessive and bloody apotheosis of the myth of the *vagina dentata* and of Dalle's star image as the voracious, desiring woman. Numerous film stills, poster images and magazine covers showed Dalle dripping with blood, while she herself emphasised the authenticity of this performance. Claiming that no other actress would have been able to portray the scene realistically, Dalle suggested that her own voracious appetite had to be held back at the last moment: '*Je ne sais pas ce qui se serait passé si nous avions poursuivi la scène plus longtemps. Je crois bien que nous aurions fini par faire vraiment l'amour.*'[52] This recalls her similar comments about *Betty Blue*. If that debut role already implied a certain exaggeration of female desire and of sexual display, *Trouble Every Day* marks the moment when Dalle's performance as the sexualised woman becomes utterly hyperbolic and hysterical.

Dalle's performances in *Trouble Every Day*, and in the more cerebral *H Story* (also 2001), provoked some hints at a change in her star image, at least as represented in the more intellectual French film press such as *Cahiers du cinéma*, which has praised her 'surprising rigour',[53] and *Télérama*, which has declared that '*la bombe est devenue actrice*'.[54] But Dalle's professionalism remains generally submerged under a tide of excess and of bodily imagery. Restraint is not part of her image. The *Cahiers* article on Dalle's resurgence (in two performances shown at the Cannes festival) also includes a reference to her throwing a fridge out of a hotel window, and is accompanied by a characteristic photo, showing Dalle looking directly at the camera, with her large red mouth exactly in the centre of the image, balanced above and below by the symmetrical, angular shapes of her face and her neck. A month later she was on the cover of *Télérama* and of *Repérages*, under the headings '*Le cinéma dans le sang*' and '*sang complexe*'.[55] As these headings suggest, Dalle is associated more than ever with the organic bodily fluids of the female body: it's in her blood.

CONCLUSION: GENDER AND PERFORMANCE

But are gender identities as inevitable and polarised as the representation of these stars, particularly in the press, implies? Recent theory suggests that gender identity is constructed and performed rather than a natural given. Judith Butler considers gender to be 'a set of repeated acts [...] that congeal over time to produce the appearance of substance, of a natural sort of being'.[56] Could one say that the images of Dalle and Anglade (and many other stars) have simply 'congealed over time' to give the impression

---

52. 'I don't know what would've happened if we'd carried on longer with that scene. I really think we'd have ended up by making love', H-J. Servat, 'Béatrice Dalle: tout ou rien', *Paris Match*, 26 July 2001, p.21.

53. J. L., 'Eloge de ... Béatrice Dalle', *Cahiers du cinéma*, 558 June 2001, p.36.

54. 'the bombshell has become an actress', Strauss, op. cit., p.36.

55. 'cinema in the blood' and 'no worries' (punning on *sang* (blood)/*sans* (without)), *Télérama* 2687 (11 July 2001); *Repérages* 21 (July/August 2001).

56. J. Butler, *Gender Trouble: Feminism and The Subversion of Identity*, London and New York, Routledge, 1990, p.33.

of the romantic (straight) man or the wild and passionate (straight) woman? Their performances seem, at times, to support Butler's view that 'gender is a kind of imitation for which there is no original',[57] an act of dressing up or drag. The myth of predatory female sexuality is almost parodied as horror by Dalle's performance in *Trouble Every Day*, calling into question its consistent use as a code to describe Dalle's image throughout her career (even if she herself buys into the myth, notably with her comments on the similarity between her own 'natural' off-screen self and the parts she plays onscreen). Anglade's performance in *L'homme blessé* explicitly presents macho male (bi-)sexuality as a suit of clothes to be worn (in this case, Jean's, as donned by Henri), while even his touchstone role as Zorg in *Betty Blue* (like Dalle's as Betty) hints at elements of masquerade and theatricality in the performance of one's gender (Zorg posing as Stallone, Betty displaying herself). One can even detect in Zorg's tendency to 'overindulge in macho signifiers to distance himself from codes of effeminacy' an example of what has been termed 'macho drag'.[58] These exaggerations and variations on the gendered body are not only key components of Dalle's and Anglade's meaning to their audience/s, they are also a crucial form of spectacle in the films that they inhabit. Despite the received wisdom that the *cinéma du look* privileges visual pleasures over acting, the two in fact combine in the spectacular display of gendered bodies that Dalle and Anglade provide.

57· J. Butler, 'Imitation and Gender Insubordination' in D. Fuss (ed.), *Inside Out: Lesbian Theories, Gay Theories*, London and New York, Routledge, 1991, p.21.

58· M. Healey, 'The mark of a man: masculine identities and the art of macho drag', *Critical Quarterly*, 36: 1 (Spring 1994), p.86.

CHAPTER 10

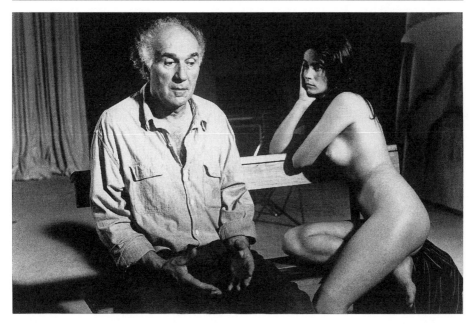

The star body as raw material: Emmanuelle Béart with Michel Piccoli in *La Belle Noiseuse* (1991).

The star in the 1990s: Emmanuelle Béart

THE STAR AS NATIONAL HERITAGE

Emmanuelle Béart crystallises several of the issues we have identified in modern French film stardom: glamour and iconicity, the star actress as national symbol, whiteness and gender, race and political activism, star labour and star leisure. Each of these strands can be identified in Béart's star image, but the most crucial is the clash (as with Adjani) between early configurations of the actress as a classic French star and later questions about politics, race and activism. And as in Adjani's case, it is instructive to see how Béart's star image is, in fact, recuperated as that of a classic star actress after the initially challenging renegotiation of her image in mid-career.

Béart began her career playing '*insipides personnages de comédie*'[1] in the early 1980s. With her breakthrough role in *Manon des sources* (1986), she became an embodiment of nationhood to the French, thanks to her performance as a wild goatherd who personifies the spirit of '*la France profonde*', the mythically strong sense of rural national identity. Her subsequent film roles, alongside theatrical performances, a heavily publicised relationship with star actor Daniel Auteuil, and a modelling contract as the face of Christian Dior, raised her to iconic status as an embodiment of both national and gender identity. Like Bardot and Deneuve before her (to whom she has often been compared),[2] Béart has been associated with Marianne, the French republican symbol. In Béart's case, the association has been implicit rather than explicit (she was not chosen as a model for the Marianne of the new millennium, to follow in Bardot and Deneuve's footsteps – that honour went to Laetitia Casta), but is traceable in her role as the painter's model Marianne in *La Belle Noiseuse* (1991). She has also given iconic performances in the lead role of the revealingly titled *Une femme française* (1995) and as Gilberte (daughter of Deneuve's Odette) in the adaptation of Proust's *Le Temps retrouvé* (1999). Meanwhile, her recurrent stage roles in classic French plays have further integrated Béart's image into traditions of French high culture (as with Adjani's early Molière roles for the *Comédie française*). In short,

Parce qu'elle a joué Musset et Marivaux, qu'elle s'est appelée Marianne chez Rivette, qu'elle sera 'Une femme française' dans le prochain Régis Wargnier, Emmanuelle Béart incarne quelque chose qui

---

1. 'insipid characters in comedies', D. Roth-Bettoni, 'Emmanuelle Béart: image donnée, visage volé', *La Revue du cinéma*, 477 (December 1991), pp.67–8.

2. See, for example, J. Mottram, 'Don't Look Now', *The Sunday Times: Culture*, 2 January 2000, p.8.

renvoie toujours à l'hexagone. Sa beauté lisse, ses choix professionnels (un cinéma public de qualité), son aisance dans le registre du cinéma des sentiments, prolongent et renouvellent à la fois une certaine tradition de vedettes françaises.[3]

The question of genre raised here – the 'popular quality cinema' Béart tends to star in – is crucial to her image. Béart's eroticised star body links her with Bardot (the body as national treasure), while her fashion status and her at times restrained but intense performances in emotional dramas (for example in *Un coeur en hiver*) link her to Deneuve. But it is above all her association with the heritage film that positions Béart as the key French female star of the 1990s.

The heritage film is essentially the official French genre of the eighties and nineties, and hence coincides exactly with Béart's rise to stardom. It is at once a return to the *tradition de qualité* (tradition of quality) that dominated post-war French film production before the new wave,[4] and a deliberate attempt, sponsored by the Socialist government, to develop blockbusters which could compete with Hollywood at the box office while maintaining French cultural specificity by reference to national literary sources (usually, but not exclusively, the nineteenth-century novel).[5] While the comedy genre – the *un*official popular cinema of the 1980s – brought to prominence its own stars in the form of Thierry Lhermitte, Josiane Balasko, Gérard Jugnot and Christian Clavier, the heritage film became closely associated with Béart, Daniel Auteil and the later career of Gérard Depardieu. It is also worth emphasising that film stars are heritage properties in the same way as the novels of Balzac or the chateaux of the Loire are. This obviously applies to the great stars of French film history, from Linder and Gabin to Bardot and Moreau, but it also applies to those more recent actors, from the mature Depardieu to the young Béart, who have successfully identified themselves with the heritage film as a genre. In this respect Béart's classic star image positioned her as part of French cultural heritage in at least three ways: as an actor in heritage films based on novels by Pagnol and Proust,[6] as an actor in stage plays by Molière, Marivaux and Musset, and as a star in the tradition of Bardot, Moreau and Deneuve.

---

3. 'Because she has starred in plays by Musset and Marivaux, because she's called Marianne in Rivette's film [*La Belle Noiseuse*], and she'll be *Une femme française* in Régis Wargnier's next film, Emmanuelle Béart embodies something that always relates back to France. Her smooth beauty, her choice of roles (popular quality cinema), her ease when starring in emotional dramas, all this both prolongs and renews a certain tradition of French stardom', J-M. Lalanne, 'Esquisses d'Emmanuelle Béart', *Le Mensuel du cinéma*, February 1994, p.21.

4. The terms of François Truffaut's famous repudiation of the *tradition de qualité* in his article 'Une certaine tendance du cinéma français' are echoed in Lalanne's description of Béart as belonging to '*une certaine tradition de vedettes françaises*' – see note 3, above.

5. For more on the genre, see G. Austin, *Contemporary French Cinema*, Manchester, MUP, 1996, pp.142–169, and G.Austin, 'Socialist Film Policy and the Heritage Film', in M. Maclean (ed.), *The Mitterrand Years: Legacy and Evaluation*, Basingstoke, Macmillan, 1998, pp.276–86.

6. One could also consider *Une femme française* as a heritage film, albeit one set in the post-war years of the twentieth century.

Béart's first starring role was in the second part of Claude Berri's major heritage project, *Manon des sources* (the first part being *Jean de Florette*). Her character, Manon, is mythical rather than realistic, incarnating innocence, hope and fertility via her associations with the wilderness, with the water source on which the villagers depend, and ultimately with childbirth and motherhood. As Manon, Béart is an embodiment of an idealised nature and an idealised femininity. These functions are local in the sense that they derive in part from the figure of the wood- or water-nymph, 'a completely mythical figure, the wild lass, barefoot and with flowing locks, who lives in the *garrigue* with her goats'.[7] But they are also representative of a broader tradition in Western culture, according to which the romantic heroine is a literal and figurative source of light. In cinematic terms, this is reflected in the convention of the white, blonde film actress photographed in a halo of light.[8] Béart's Manon adheres closely to this convention, with her fluffy golden hair lit up (ostensibly by the Provençal sunshine) in various scenes throughout the film. As for Béart's body, which is glimpsed nude in the film, this too is equated with innocence, a lack of inhibition and a oneness with nature, as in the sequence where Ugolin (Daniel Auteuil) spies on Manon bathing in a mountain pool. There was to be a radical shift in the meaning of Béart's naked body in *La Belle Noiseuse* five years later, but here its significance is unambiguous: she is a dream woman, the archetypal 'white maiden' of romantic convention, dreamt about by Ugolin and the schoolteacher, described by them as a ray of light and a saintly wild virgin.[9] At the climactic procession, Manon appears as a kind of local saint: she is asked to join the procession because she is 'innocent'; the water is apparently restored by her presence among the community; the survival of the village and its hope for the future are assured by the child that she and the schoolteacher will have at Christmas. Manon is thus a figure of elemental power but also of purity and continuity, who can unite the community and whose child will be born at Christmas. She is thus a folk version of the Virgin. (As we shall see, the archetype of the mother which became part of Béart's star image so early in her career was to be problematised in later performances and controversies.) Finally, via the film's literary source (the novelist and film-maker Marcel Pagnol), Béart's performance as Manon is inscribed into inherited representations of Provence, and in particular into the pattern of deference and influence which sustains that heritage, whereby Pagnol refers back to the writings of Daudet while, 'more recently, by a sort of cyclical repetition,' the films of Berri and Yves Robert refer back to Pagnol.[10]

---

7. F. de la Bretèque, 'Images of "Provence": Ethnotypes and stereotypes of the south in French cinema', in R. Dyer and G. Vincendeau (eds), *Popular European Cinema*, London and New York, Routledge, 1992, p.65. The *garrigue* is the scrubland or bush of southern France.

8. See Chapter 8 for an account of the role of lighting and hair colour in images of white actresses.

9. Compare the evocation of the 'dream woman' and the 'white maiden' in the early star image of Jean Seberg – see Chapter 8.

10. See de la Bretèque, op. cit., p.70.

THE STAR BODY AT WORK

Béart's role as *'une Manon pasteurisée'*[11] generated a star image that was blonde, innocent and reassuring. It was against this perception that several of her subsequent career choices were made, beginning with *Les enfants du désordre* (1988), where, her brown hair no longer dyed, she gives a far more expressive, aggressive performance. The shift away from Manon was taken a step further in *La Belle Noiseuse* (Rivette, 1991), a four-hour exploration of the working relationship between a painter (Michel Piccoli) and his model (Béart). The film has often been described as an account of the creative process, but it can also be read as a portrayal of the star labour that other films tend to hide. The painter's slow graduation from preparatory sketches to the final (unseen) painting is mirrored by the endless manoeuvrings of his model's body into various poses. *La Belle Noiseuse* also dramatises the replacement of one muse by another, and of a star face (Jane Birkin as Liz, the painter's wife and former model) by a star body (Béart as Marianne). This culminates in the sequence where the artist paints over an old sketch of Liz's face with a view of Marianne's naked body, at which the former exclaims *'Tu as remplacé ma gueule par une paire de fesses!'*[12]

Béart is indeed naked in nearly all the scenes set in the painter's studio, and at his demand assumes innumerable contorted poses, which are usually seen from the rear. These scenes in fact structure the narrative and seem to assume a similar function to the sexual 'numbers' in the porn film. However, in contrast with Sylvia Kristel's poses in the *Emmanuelle* series,[13] Béart's poses in *La Belle Noiseuse* are not eroticised. Never coy, masked or soft-core, the nudity here is frank, direct and, above all, repetitive. The star face – the focus of Sylvia Kristel's star image, as we have seen, and more generally the usual index of film stardom[14] – is neglected (almost never seen in close-up) while the star body is not gradually revealed in a striptease but already naked, then twisted, manipulated, pushed and pulled into position like a doll. The contrast with *Manon des sources* is stark: where Béart as Manon incarnated natural, innocent and artless beauty, free to wander through the Provençal countryside, as Marianne she is a naked puppet, passive and static, her body simply the raw material for a piece of work, endlessly manoeuvrable until it fails under the strain (in the fourth pose her foot goes to sleep; in the fifth, she complains that her body hurts as if it is being pulled; in the sixth she gets cramp). Marianne is often exhausted by the end of a session, and the poses become increasingly twisted, as the painter speaks of tying his models up, of breaking toys, of dislocating his wife's shoulder. In the final pose of Part One, Marianne is all but crucified as the painter tells her he wants

---

11• 'a pasteurised Manon', Lalanne, op. cit., p.20.

12• 'You have replaced my face with a pair of buttocks!' Despite her eroticised image (thanks mainly to her duets with Serge Gainsbourg, including *'Je t'aime . . . moi non plus'*), Birkin is very much a star face and a star voice rather than a star body. She contrasts with Béart in this respect, and one could read the scene in question as a comment on this fact.

13• See Chapter 6.

14• See, for instance, E. Morin, *Les Stars*, 3rd edition, Paris, Editions du Seuil, 1972, p.120.

to pull her to pieces. Her body ends up being dispersed in the numerous paintings and sketches around the studio. Béart's star image is also dislocated, dispersed, twisted and put out of place. Through her unremittingly physical and often resistant performance, she ensures that her previous, pliant, 'pasteurised' image cannot be put back again.

La Belle Noiseuse also comments on star labour in general. The modelling sessions in the film are analogous to the hidden work behind the setting up of the sex numbers in soft-porn cinema, and to the invisible labour that occurs between takes in most mainstream cinema. As Edgar Morin notes, '*Sur le plateau, les acteurs sont [. . .] de la matière première non spécialisée sous la direction de vrais* techniciens *[. . .]. Ils peuvent être même réduits à la condition d'objets.*'[15] The analogy in *La Belle Noiseuse* between modelling and screen acting is underlined when Marianne is told not to look directly at the painter, just as actors are taught not to look directly at the camera. The length of the scenes and the physical difficulty of the work suggest that star labour can be both tedious and arduous. Moreover, the repeated assumption of poses in the studio reveals Béart's apparently freer, more natural scenes (breaking off for a coffee, getting drunk, slouching and, above all, '*ce signe clé du "naturel": allumer une cigarette*')[16] as similarly posed. Marianne is always acting, as her triumphant assumption of a new role at the end of the film reveals. Béart, too, is always acting, whether seemingly natural or more explicitly submitting to the painter/director's commands. Indeed, the star is always acting whether on screen or off, whether 'just being herself' or posing for the press, since '*la façon de vivre d'une star est elle-même marchandise*'.[17] If *La Belle Noiseuse* suggests as much, it presents above all a sustained picture of the star actor as a body under duress, a body *at* work. It reveals stardom as labour and calls into question one of the founding myths of stardom, namely that it is 'all play and no work.'[18]

SEXUALITY AND THE FEMALE STAR: MOTHER OR VAMP?

Despite Béart's prominent nudity, *La Belle Noiseuse* in a sense demythologises her body, emptying it of eroticism. The film disperses the star body and seeks the actress underneath, with the painter demanding '*Plus de seins, plus de ventre, plus de cuisses, plus de cul!*'.[19] This is in direct contrast with the famous opening sequence of *Le Mépris* (Godard, 1963), in which Brigitte Bardot's star body is fetishised, its constituent parts celebrated by the camera as Bardot asks: '*Tu les aimes mes genoux? [. . .] Et mes cuisses? [. . .] Tu les trouves jolies mes fesses? [. . .] Et mes seins, tu les aimes? [. . .] Et mes épaules tu les aimes?*'

15· 'On the set, actors are a non-specialised raw material under the direction of real *technicians*. They can even be reduced to the level of objects', ibid., p.111, italics in original.

16· 'that key sign of "being natural": lighting a cigarette', ibid., p.114.

17· 'a star's way of life is itself a form of merchandise', P. Baechlin, *Histoire économique du cinéma*, cited in ibid., p.100.

18· Paul McDonald, 'Supplementary Chapter: Reconceptualising Stardom' in R. Dyer, *Stars*, London, BFI Publishing, 1998, p.195.

19· 'No more breasts, no more stomach, no more thighs, no more arse!'

[. . .] Et mon visage?'[20]. Nonetheless, Emmanuelle Béart is, like Bardot, a highly sexualised star. In 1995, *Empire* magazine placed her at number thirty-two in its list of the hundred sexiest stars of film history. Like Bardot, and indeed most female stars, Béart is also subject to '*le mythe de l'amour*'.[21] Romance and sex inform her star image via her on-screen performances, but also via her private life, which has conformed to another myth of stardom, that '*La star doit, de préférence, aimer la star.*'[22] In 1993 Béart married Daneil Auteuil, her co-star in *Manon des sources* and *Un coeur en hiver*, having had a daughter by him the previous year. Two of Béart's key performances from the early nineties, the period of her marriage to Auteuil, dramatise the tension in the sexualised female star's image between the archetypes of the mother and the vamp.

The archetype of the vamp, the embodiment of predatory female sexuality, has its filmic origins in Danish silent cinema before the First World War.[23] Once established in Western cinema, the vamp became a more comic figure after the coming of sound and the concomitant increase in realistic characters. Her erotic charge informed other female character types, while '*La vamp, semi-fantastique [. . .], ne peut plus s'adapter sans ridicule au nouveau climat réaliste. [. . .] son long fume-cigarettes, ses regards fatals sont devenus comiques.*'[24] It is to this caricatural, fantastical and partly comic form of the vamp that Béart's performance in *L'Enfer* (Chabrol, 1993) refers. She plays Nelly, a happy and beautiful wife and mother whose husband fantasises that she is betraying him and having numerous affairs. Béart presents two distinct performance styles for the two women: the devoted wife/mother is played realistically, with a vivacious energy and freedom of movement that relates back to her star-making role as Manon, but also with a devotion and eagerness to please that seem too good to be true. (The wedding scene is, for example, immediately followed by a baby sequence in which Béart beams exaggeratedly while pushing the pram.) As the imaginary vamp, she is more overtly stylised and more static, with the focus much more on her face (often in close-up, with prominent lipstick and eye make-up) and on the props she uses (cigarettes, a glass of brandy) as she pouts at her lovers. However, despite the difference in performance style (and in the use of lighting and sound, both of which become more stylised in the fantasy sequences), there remains enough common ground in Béart's performance as each archetype to suggest that they are both acts. The dutiful and slightly coquettish wife, always ready to kiss or cajole her husband, is perhaps just as much a fantasy as the predatory vamp. This has several implications for Béart's star image. Firstly, it carries a certain self-reflexivity about acting and stardom that can also be found in *La Belle Noiseuse* and in *La Répétition* (2000), where Béart plays a theatre actress. Secondly, it

---

20• 'Do you love my knees? And my thighs? Do you think my buttocks are pretty? And do you love my breasts? And do you love my shoulders? And my face?'. See the scenario of *Le Mépris* reproduced in *L'Avant-scène cinéma*, 412/413 (May/June 1992), pp.15–16. For more on Bardot, see Chapter 2.

21• 'the myth of love', Morin, op. cit., p.40.

22• 'A star should, preferably, love another star', ibid., p.61.

23• See ibid., p.184.

24• 'The vamp, half fantastical, can no longer adapt to the new, realistic climate without ridicule. Her long cigarette holder and her fatal looks have become comic', ibid., p.27.

suggests that her star image (and indeed, perhaps, the personality behind that image) welcomes splits, schisms and opposites, as observed in several interviews and features.[25] The reconciliation of opposites is, for the star theorists Edgar Morin and Richard Dyer, an essential function of stardom.[26] But when it is expressed via archetypal female roles, such as the mother and the vamp, as here, it also seems to have third implication, that a star's image can draw attention to the artificiality of the forms that it is asked to inhabit.

Those very forms – the mother and the vamp – are present again in *Une femme française* (Warnier, 1995), which adds a further layer of self-reflexivity by starring Béart and Daniel Auteuil as a married couple. Whereas in *L'Enfer* the wife's/mother's serial adultery was imagined, in *Une femme française* it is real. Béart's role as Jeanne involves an increasingly rapid and traumatic oscillation between the two poles of stereotyped female sexuality: the good mother and the scarlet woman. Because Béart's style of performance is, for the most part, consistent across the two roles, the dichotomy is symbolised mainly by costume. In the pre-credit sequence, Jeanne is identified with idealised motherhood when she cradles a dying man in her arms. The costume (she is dressed in blue, the colour of the Virgin Mary) and the pose (a *pietà*) suggest that Jeanne is a kind of Madonna. (This strong maternal image reminds us of Béart's role as Manon, but also prefigures her maternal role in a much more unexpected, political context that was to redefine her star image in the late nineties.) Motherhood is represented throughout *Une femme française* by the colours white and blue, and centres on domestic scenes of Jeanne with her young family; but juxtaposed with these sequences are various affairs that threaten her marriage, culminating in a collision between sexual desire and maternal duty as Jeanne has sex with her lover while her young son is locked in the next-door room. As in the conventions of the soft-porn film, Béart's face is shown in close-up to signal her sexual pleasure at orgasm, while her son's cries call her back to the realm of the domestic and the maternal. The film concludes with a melodramatic evocation of the impossibility of escaping the archetypes at stake. Jeanne's status as a bad mother is confirmed when she neglects her children in order to vamp it up with her lover. In a deliberately exaggerated performance, Jeanne drinks and dances before him in red lipstick and a red dress, presenting herself as the scarlet woman incarnate. Like a modern-day Madame Bovary, Jeanne ultimately dies because she is suffocated by the roles that are offered to her. But as we shall see, Béart's star image successfully reconciles the roles of vamp and mother, and their collision fuels rather than destroys her continuing stardom.

'BELLIQUEUSE MADONE': BÉART AND THE *SANS-PAPIERS* AFFAIR

Already in 1991 certain sections of the French film press had glimpsed something else underneath Béart's reassuring early star image. *La Revue du cinéma* commented that

---

25· See, for example, L. Le Vaillant, 'Belliqueuse madone', *Libération*, 10 December 1996, p.44, and J. Béglé, 'Emmanuelle Béart: la femme libre', *Paris Match*, 23 August 2001, pp.68–72.

26· See Morin, op. cit., pp.31–2 and Dyer, *Stars*, p.82.

'*Emmanuelle Béart est à cent lieues de l'image rassurante et immuable que les medias donnent d'elle. On l'imagine sage, elle est turbulente; on la soupçonne tendre, elle est insoumise*'.[27] This perception was to be borne out by events five years later, when Béart launched herself into political activism in a radical move that repositioned her star image and allegedly lost her the Dior fashion contract. The epithet attached to her character in *La Belle Noiseuse* seemed increasingly appropriate, as Béart became known as a beautiful troublemaker. However, even at this controversial point her star image remained complex, and drew on the earlier maternal, tender and reassuring elements within a tougher and more committed profile. This is best expressed by the title of a *Libération* feature on her from December 1996: '*Belliqueuse madone*'.[28]

What became known as *l'affaire des sans-papiers* began in March 1996, when a church in Paris was occupied by 315 African immigrants who lived and worked in France but had no official documentation allowing them to stay.[29] They subsequently moved to the church of St Bernard where, on 5 July, ten of them began a hunger strike '*pour réclamer la régularisation de leur situation*'.[30] In the weeks that followed, an increasingly tense stand-off developed as the government refused to grant authorisation to the *sans-papiers*, while members of the public and certain celebrities began to visit the church to support the hunger strikers. *Libération* reported visits by Danielle Mitterrand (widow of the former president), by the actress Marina Vlady and by Emmanuelle Béart, of whom it later said, '*[elle] était venue à l'église avec une amie comédienne; elle n'est plus repartie*'.[31] The newspaper published photos of several supporters of the hunger strike in a special feature. Alongside students and teachers are a young couple crouched on the street, captioned as '*Emmanuelle et son frère Olivier, comédiens*'.[32] Béart is here represented as simply an ordinary Parisian, making a personal gesture of solidarity, and as an actor rather than a star. Her surname is not mentioned, although this does not render her practically anonymous, as it does with the other individuals in the feature. Her (literally) street-level appearance contrasts with the photo of Danielle Mitterrand in *Libération* the day before. Where Béart appears as a private and ordinary person, Mitterrand is clearly a public personage on a political visit: rather than squatting on the pavement, she stands at the centre of a crowd, shaking the hand of one of the *sans-papiers* while bodyguards and cameramen jostle around her. She looks like a media star, where Béart is just a supporter. Mitterrand's very public pose is matched by a quotation in which she says that the laws should be changed.[33] Béart,

---

27• 'Emmanuelle Béart is nothing like the enduring and reassuring image that the media give of her. We imagine she's well-behaved, but she's wild; we imagine she's tender, but she's rebellious', Roth-Bettoni, op. cit., p.67.

28• 'aggressive madonna', Le Vaillant, op. cit., p.44.

29• Their precarious situation was often blamed on the infamously hard-line immigration laws (*les lois Pasqua*) and the *code de la nationalité* introduced by Charles Pasqua in 1993/4. See, for example, the editorial in *Libération*, 31 July 1996, p.2.

30• 'to demand that they be granted official authorisation', ibid., p.1.

31• 'she came to the church with an actor friend; she never left', *Libération*, 13 February 1997, p.4.

32• 'Emmanuelle and her brother Olivier, actors', *Libération*, 19 August 1996, p.2.

33• See *Libération*, 17/18 August 1996, p.11.

meanwhile, simply declares herself to be a member of the human race: '*On est venu pour eux et pour nous, en tant que citoyens et êtres humains, et on reviendra tant qu'on pourra.*'[34]

Béart remained closely associated with the protests throughout the summer of 1996. When it was suspected that the police were about to move in, she was among those supporters who handcuffed themselves to hunger strikers. She was photographed holding an immigrant's baby, imploring the police to leave the *sans-papiers* alone, and became a maternal figurehead for the protests. As *Libération* acknowledged,

> *l'image d'Emmanuelle Béart a connu un drôle de torsion. La jeune star à l'ancienne, l'actrice de talent à la beauté très française, s'est retrouvée bombardée madone de Saint-Bernard et vierge à l'enfant noir.*[35]

As well as demonstrating her newfound political activism and providing a positive image of inter-racial solidarity,[36] the photo of Béart with a black baby also conformed to a certain tradition of star image. Classic star iconography, as Morin explains, includes representations of '*la Vierge à l'enfant*' (Virgin and child). Such photos '*nous enseignent que, profondément humaine, la star est toujours prête à verser le lait de la tendresse maternelle sur tout ce qui est innocent, faible, désarmé.*'[37] This maternal, humanitarian iconography tended to soften the otherwise militant and defiant image of Béart that the *sans-papiers* affair generated. She was represented as both an idealised mother figure (the Virgin with the blue eyes holding the black baby) and an aggressive (and hence less stereotypically feminised) fighter. *Libération* noted that two photos taken during the *sans-papiers* affair reveal this dichotomy, but only one (conforming to the conventions of the female star as idealised 'white maiden') was widely reproduced in the media:

> *L'une, connue, la voit lever un visage implorant vers les policiers qui la cernent. L'autre, moins diffusée, la montre bravant une escouade de CRS, regard fier et poings serrés. La combattante vampant la compatissante . . .*[38]

By the next spring Béart was being described as 'France's most politically committed actress' and 'the figurehead of resistance to France's immigration laws'.[39] New hard-line

---

34• 'We came for them and for us, as citizens and as human beings, and we'll come back as often as we can', *Libération*, 19 August 1996, p.2.

35• 'the image of Emmanuelle Béart has undergone a strange twist. The young classic star, the talented actress with a very French style of beauty has found herself catapulted into the role of the Madonna of Saint-Bernard, the virgin with the black child', Le Vaillant, op. cit., p.44.

36• Contrast the hysterically negative tone used to describe the racial ambiguity surrounding Jean Seberg's supposedly black baby — see Chapter 8.

37• 'tell us that the star is deeply human, and always ready to offer the milk of maternal kindness to all who are innocent, weak or vulnerable', Morin, op. cit., pp.59–60.

38• 'The well-known photo shows her looking beseechingly at the police officers surrounding her. The other one, less widely published, shows her defying a squad of riot police, her gaze fierce and her fists clenched. The fighter trumping the bleeding heart', Le Vaillant, op. cit., p.44.

39• S. Herbert, 'Béart's political profile too high for Face of Dior', *The Daily Telegraph*, 1 April 1997, p.7.

proposals, known as the *loi Debré*, had become the subject of mass protests and petitions in February 1997, after a group of film-makers launched a manifesto calling for civil disobedience against them. Béart, herself a signatory to the actors' petition (along with Auteil, Deneuve and many others) became the public face of the movement. When 100,000 protestors marched in Paris against the *loi Debré*, it was she who launched the event, by reading the film-makers' manifesto. Consequently, 'pictures of her brimming eyes, unbrushed hair and scruffy raincoat dominated coverage' of the march.[40] This street-level militancy was a long way from Béart's previous image as 'Nelly the elegant'.[41] Her contract with Dior was not renewed at the end of the year; Isabelle Adjani was lined up as Béart's successor. Adjani, no stranger to controversy about racial issues, had signed the petition but not marched. Posters seen at one of the demonstrations had jokingly celebrated her ethnic origins and her beauty, declaring 'I want to shelter Adjani'.[42] Béart, meanwhile, had become the target for hate mail because of her political stance.[43] Her star image had, it seemed, been changed irrevocably.

CONCLUSION: IMAGE REGAINED

However, just as Adjani's image had been recuperated after the racial hysteria of the mid-eighties, so Béart's was recuperated after the political activism of the mid-nineties. Once again she was seen as part of a grand tradition of French stars, rather than as a troublesome outsider. Comparisons with Deneuve were reactivated by her performance in the adaptation of Proust's *Le Temps retrouvé* (Ruiz, 1999). Deneuve had first billing for her role as Odette; Béart had second billing as Gilberte, her daughter. A sense of star genealogy was thus regained; and in terms of genre, Béart had returned to the heritage film, the secure, official cinema of the period, just as Adjani had with her late 1980s comeback, *Camille Claudel*.

The *sans-papiers* affair and the loss of the Dior contract are still mentioned in interviews, but Béart closes them off as areas of discussion: '*Je n'ai pas envie de parler de ça. Ca ne m'intéresse plus*'.[44] Of the two sides to her star image that the street politics threw into relief, it is the mother rather than the campaigner that dominates. Hence we are told in *Paris Match* that Béart is most proud of her two children, and wants to adopt a third. But the vamp is present again, too. Béart is described as '*cette femme fatale qui fait l'apologie de la maternité*'.[45] The feature is accompanied by photos that display her body as she poses in

---

40• Ibid.

41• This is the title of a feature on Béart from the previous spring. See *Time Out*, 20 March 1996, p.19.

42• This refers to the most controversial article of the *loi Debré*, which criminalised anyone who had sheltered an immigrant without official papers. For more on Adjani's racial origins, see Chapter 8.

43• See L. Payron, 'Qui en veut à Emmanuelle Béart?', *Voici*, 495 (5–11 May 1997), pp.8–9.

44• 'I don't want to talk about that. I'm not interested in it any more', cited in Béglé, op. cit., p.73.

45• 'this *femme fatale* who praises motherhood'. An analogy is also drawn with Béart's role in *Une femme française*. See ibid., p.71.

lingerie – on a bed, on the beach, dripping wet against a tree. Sexuality seems to have replaced politics. The star body, obscured during her political activism, also makes a return on screen. As the stage actress Nathalie in *La Répétition* (2001), Béart presents '*un mélange d'exhibition (cuisses, seins, dos) et de brusque affolement à l'idée de se montrer*'.[46] The *Libération* feature entitled '*Belliqueuse madone*' is glimpsed in the film, but is emptied of its political context, and expresses instead the contrariness of Nathalie's star persona.

It is this contrariness, the prerogative if not the very definition of the star, which informs Béart's mature image too. *Paris Match* finds that '*Parfois elle joue les cover-girls, parfois elle rêve d'être libraire dans une ville de province ... Emmanuelle Béart est une créature hybride, fille d'un mannequin et d'un poète*'.[47] She is both mother and vamp, blonde and brunette. Whereas Deneuve is always blonde and Adjani always dark, Béart fluctuates between the two in very quick succession.[48] She reconciles opposites and cultivates extremes. Playing the maid in *8 femmes* (2002), François Ozon's homage to French star actresses, she gives a dynamic performance of the 1960s hit '*Pile ou face*', thereby expressing the carefree synthesis of opposites in her star image (she lives her life by 'head or tails') and also re-animating a classic pop song. Béart is the star as reconciler of polarities and as national treasure.

46• 'a mixture of display (thighs, breasts, back) and of sudden panic at the idea of displaying oneself', O. J., 'Eloge de ... Emmanuelle Béart', *Cahiers du cinéma*, 558 (June 2001), p.23.

47• 'Sometimes she plays the cover girl, sometimes she dreams of running a book shop in a small town ... Emmanuelle Béart is a real mixture, the daughter of a model and a poet', Béglé, op. cit., p.72.

48• The promotional photos in *Cosmopolitan* and *Cahiers du cinéma* for *La Répétition*, a film in which she appears as a brunette, show her as a dyed blonde.

CHAPTER 11

New stars on the front pages: Laura Smet, Laetitia Casta, Monica Bellucci.

Conclusion: stardom in the new millenium

COMIC STARS

France has a long tradition of producing well-loved cinematic clowns, from Max Linder in the silent era and Fernandel in the thirties, to Bourvil, Louis de Funès and Jean-Paul Belmondo in the 1950s, 1960s and 1970s.[1] Male comic stars in particular have tended to prove extremely successful at the box office. For the period 1956–1990, the three French stars who attracted the most spectators were either largely or exclusively comic in appeal: de Funès, Bourvil and Belmondo.[2] Yet there remains a common perception that, for all their box-office appeal, comic stars are neglected by the film press and by the festivals and award ceremonies organised by the film industry. Speaking of Bourvil and de Funès, Belmondo has declared that '*Le défaut de la France a toujours été de mal traiter ses comiques.*'[3] The same argument was recently mobilised by *Paris Match* magazine when Christian Clavier was ignored in the César nominations for 1995, despite attracting five and a half million spectators to watch him alongside Gérard Depardieu in the comedy *Les Anges gardiens*: '*Faire rire reste le péché originel. Le pays de Molière, de Feydeau et de Louis de Funès, lui, ne comprend pas pourquoi ses saltimbanques les plus doués sont privés de lauriers.*'[4]

Clavier's popularity is manifest not only in his phenomenal box-office record, but also in the 1996 *Paris Match* survey, which saw him voted the best comic star of the day.[5] After establishing the *café-théâtre* troupe *Le Splendid*, with Thierry Lhermitte and Gérard Jugnot, Clavier became a screen star in the 1980s, notably thanks to his role as the transvestite Katia in *Le Père Noël est une ordure* (1982). His hyperactive performance style,

---

1. For accounts of Linder and de Funès, see G. Vincendeau, *Stars and Stardom in French Cinema*, London and New York, Continuum, 2000, pp.42–58 and 136–57. For Belmondo, see Chapter 5, above.

2. See ibid., p.27. Fernandel is at number 5 in the list, behind Jean Gabin.

3. 'France has always been at fault by mistreating its comedians', cited in J. Strazzula and S. Leduc, *Belmondo: L'histoire d'une vie*, Paris, Editions Ramsay, 1996, p.79.

4. 'Making people laugh is still the original sin. But the country of Molière, Feydeau and Louis de Funès doesn't understand why its most gifted entertainers are never rewarded', I. Giordano, 'L'Oublié des Césars, c'est lui', *Paris Match*, 7 March 1996, p.65. The theatrical tradition of Molière and Feydeau is an important facet of Clavier's star image: like Belmondo, he has been extremely popular in comic stage roles as well as cinematic ones.

5. See ibid., p.65. Josiane Balasko was second.

repeated pratfalls, rabid delivery and willingness to play the most ridiculous and idiotic characters, are seen to best effect in the massive hit comedy *Les Visiteurs* (1993), which attracted 13.6 million spectators and proved to be the second most successful French film of all time.[6] Clavier plays Jacquouille, a medieval serf who ends up in the late twentieth century, and who responds to his new environment by energetically using an umbrella as a spit to roast meat, and by washing his face in the toilet bowl. Accompanied by Jean Reno as his master Godefroy, Clavier was deemed to have expressed the essence of the national self-image, embodied in '*le héros noble*' (Godefroy) and '*le prolo débrouillard*' (Jacquouille).[7] These two archetypes are combined in the figure of Astérix, the diminutive Gallic warrior created by Goscinny and Uderzo's comic books. With Depardieu as Obélix, Claiver has starred in both Astérix movies so far, *Astérix et Obélix contre César* (1998) and *Astérix et Obélix: Mission Cléopâtre* (2002). But the success of the latter – generally praised as a much more successful film – has been credited not to the star duo, but to the young comedian Jamel Debbouze.[8]

ETHNICITY AND GENDER

In *Mission Cléopâtre*, Jamel (as he is known) plays the Egyptian architect Numérobis. The role, expanded from the original comic book, showcases his rapid-fire delivery and wide-eyed, gestural acting style. As is usual for any male comic star in France, Jamel has been compared with the legendary de Funès and, unlike Clavier, has not been found wanting.[9] It has been claimed that the success of *Mission Cléopâtre* lies in its willingness to reflect '*le rire métisse et varié*' at the heart of modern French humour.[10] The term '*métisse*' (mixed) is used here as a deliberate and celebratory reference to Jamel's ethnic origins as a second-generation French Algerian. As a DJ, comedian and actor, Jamel's star image is 'heavily rooted in France's multi-ethnic *banlieues*'.[11] However, his portrayal of Lucien, the timid grocer in the nostalgic, sentimental, and decidedly uni-cultural version of Paris offered by *Le Fabuleux Destin d'Amélie Poulain* (2001), was attacked in some quarters for 'the apparent obliteration of [his] ethnicity'.[12] The character's name (a French rather than Arabic one), his personality (unable to stand up for himself without help from the white protagonist) and Jamel's restrained performance all serve

---

6• *Les Visiteurs* beat Speilberg's *Jurassic Park* at the French box office by a factor of two to one. The number one French film remains *La Grande Vadrouille* (1966), starring Bourvil and de Funès.

7• 'the noble hero' and 'the crafty pleb', Patrice Ledoux, film producer at Gaumont, cited in A. Ferenczi, 'Le business Jacquouille', *Télérama*, 2510 (18 February 1998), p.24.

8• See, for instance, C. Mury's review in *Télérama*, 2716 (30 January 2002), pp.42–3.

9• See ibid., p.43. For a critique of Clavier in comparison with de Funès, see P. Murat's review of *Les Couleurs du temps: Les Visiteurs II* in *Télérama*, 2510 (18 February 1998), p.25.

10• 'mixed, varied humour', A. Ferenczi, 'L'arène de Chabat', *Télérama*, 2716 (30 January 2002), p.41.

11• A. Hargreaves, 'Postcolonial minorities in contemporary French cinema: from margins to mainstream', paper given to *World Cinemas Conference*, Leeds University, 27 June 2002. The *banlieues* are the ghettoised suburbs of major French cities like Paris and Marseilles.

12• Ibid.

to render him '*un beur désarabisé*',[13] a safe, whitewashed, neutered representation. This interpretation of *Amélie* as a racist revisioning of multicultural France was, however, an exception to the generally positive reception of the film (see below); and with *Mission Cléopâtre*, Jamel's comic dynamism and his ethnicity – both suppressed in *Amélie* – are very much on display.

Like Jamel, the actor Samy Nacéri is a second-generation French Algerian who has recently become a screen star in France; and, again like Jamel, Nacéri has played both marked ethnic roles and non-marked ones. Alec Hargreaves has called this phenomenon 'trans-ethnic plasticity', and points out that it tends to operate in one direction only: hence we find *beur* actors (Jamel, Nacéri, one might add Isabelle Adjani) playing white roles, but not white actors playing *beur* roles.[14] Nacéri is best known for his performances as Daniel, the apparently white cabbie in *Taxi* and *Taxi 2*. As Hargreaves notes, 'Nacéri's relatively light skin colour enables him to play such a role convincingly', despite the fact that most of the French audience for the films will simultaneously be 'aware of the actor's real-life ethnic origins'.[15] This acceptance on the part of spectators and fans of a star's ability to occupy two distinct ethnicities (one on screen and one off) allows 'trans-ethnic plasticity' to function successfully.

Taxi positions Daniel as a non-marked Frenchman, pitting him and his Peugeot against German criminals known as 'the Mercedes gang'. Similarly, in *Taxi 2*, he is confronted by Japanese villains. Nacéri/Daniel is thus a national icon rather than an ethnic one, an embodiment of France (especially the Latin identity of Marseilles, where the two films are set), who concludes the first film by literally representing his country in a red, white and blue Formula One racing car. The mix of comedy and action in the *Taxi* series, and Nacéri's warm, charismatic performance, balanced between lawlessness and order, positions him as a potential successor to Belmondo. This possibility was underlined by *Paris Match* in 2001, when it reported that Nacéri was to play the young boxer in a television remake of *L'aîné des Ferchaux*, a role taken by Belmondo in the original sixties film. The magazine noted that Belmondo was to play Nacéri's mentor in the new version, and printed a photo showing the two men together, with their arms around each other and fists raised.[16]

As we saw with regard to Isabelle Adjani, however, images of marked ethnicity in France, and particularly of the Arab population, are generally very negative.[17] The media representation of France's large Muslim community (numbering about four million and originating from Tunisia, Algeria and Morocco, known collectively as the Maghreb) has been attributed to three factors:

13· 'a non-Arabic Arab', S. Kaganski, '*Amélie* pas jolie', *Libération*, 31 May 2001, p.7.

14· Hargreaves, 'Postcolonial minorities'.

15· Ibid.

16· See *Paris Match*, 23 August 2001, p.53. For more on Belmondo, see Chapter 5.

17· See Chapter 8.

the unhappy legacy of decolonisation in North Africa, the heightened visibility of anti-western Islamic states in international politics, and feelings of personal insecurity linked to [. . .] economic restructuring [. . .] since the 1970s.[18]

The demonising of the Muslim community in France (in the *foulard* affair of 1989, or the rhetoric of Jean-Marie Le Pen) has been, to a certain extent, qualified by the apparent integration and undoubted popularity of *beur* film stars such as Jamel and Nacéri, as well as star footballers such as Zinedine Zidane, whose number 10 shirt is worn by Nacéri/Daniel in *Taxi 2*. But why are there no similarly successful female ethnic stars? In the sports arena, there is the troubled but celebrated runner Marie-Jo Pérec; but in the cinema, only Isabelle Adjani stands out as a star *beur* actress. Apart from *Ishtar* and *La Repentie* (two films in twenty-five years), Adjani has played consistently unmarked, white roles. This, along with her famously pale appearance and the persistent valuing of whiteness in female stars, may explain why she has as yet no obvious *beur* successor.[19] Moreover, in a sharp contrast with Hollywood, France has no major black film stars at all, and despite a flourishing French rap scene, there has as yet been no real crossover of black rap stars to cinema, as there has been in the USA with Ice Cube and Will Smith. Black actors such as Alex Decas (*Trouble Every Day*) and Firmine Richard (*8 Femmes*) are relatively well known, but the case of Richard in particular illustrates the difficulty of breaking into the predominantly white realm of French film stardom. Best known for her warm performance in the romantic comedy *Romuald et Juliette* (1985), Richard was chosen to play the single black character among a host of white stars – Catherine Deneuve, Emmanuelle Béart, Fanny Ardant, Isabelle Huppert and others – in *8 Femmes* (2002). However, not only was she typecast as a servant (her role in *Romuald et Juliette* was as a cleaner), but the director also seems to have chosen Richard not to celebrate her own image, but to recreate the classical Hollywood stereotype of the black nanny.[20]

ACTRESSES, MODELS AND AMATEURS

The new, white faces of female stardom in France at the turn of the millennium are Monica Bellucci, Audrey Tautou, Virginie Ledoyen and Laetitia Casta. The most experienced actress among them is Bellucci, whose screen career began in 1990 and who has made twenty-five films, mainly in France and her native Italy. She and her husband Vincent Cassel, who came to prominence in *La Haine* (1995), now form a powerful star couple, and have co-starred in several films, including the controversially explicit

---

18· A. Hargreaves, 'The challenges of multiculturalism: regional and religious differences in France today', in W. Kidd and S. Reynolds (eds), *Contemporary French Cultural Studies*, London, Arnold, 2000, p.106.

19· In a review of current French actresses, *Positif* magazine mentions a number of *beurs*, none of whom is as yet anywhere near becoming a major star. See G. Valens, 'Raison et sentiments', *Positif*, 495 (May 2002), p.55.

20· See F. Ozon, 'Femmes sous influences', *Télérama*, 2717 (6 February 2002), p.40. Ozon refers to Douglas Sirk's southern melodrama *Imitation of Life* (1959) as a key source in this regard.

Irréversible (2002). Tautou was an unknown actress until she appeared with Jamel and Matthieu Kassovitz (a rare example of a star director turned star actor) in *Le Fabuleux Destin d'Amélie Poulain*, which drew an audience of over eight million and was credited with helping to make 2001 a boom year for French cinema.[21] Despite the totemic significance of *Amélie*, however, it is Ledoyen and Casta who are, at the time of writing, the key female stars in France.

Casta and Ledoyen are of a similar age (the latter is the elder by eighteen months), but they have very distinct star images, despite the fact that both have been compared to Brigitte Bardot. Like the early Bardot, Casta has an eroticised persona that is associated with nature, the body and the outdoors (notably the beach). She was famously discovered by a photographer on a beach in Corsica at the age of fifteen, before embarking on an extremely successful first career as a super-model. Five years later, when she was at the point of abandoning modelling for the cinema, a magazine feature on sex symbols showed her topless on the cover, and in a bikini on an inside page: in both cases she was photographed on the beach. [22] Her screen appearances (notably as Falbala in *Astérix et Obélix contre César*) have thus far been few, but Casta is already, at the age of twenty-five, a national and a global icon, chosen to replace Catherine Deneuve as the new face of Marianne (personification of the French Republic) for the year 2000, and voted the sexiest woman in the world by *Rolling Stone* magazine in the USA. By contrast, Ledoyen's image and celebrity have developed more gradually. She was not eroticised in early performances such as *L'eau froide* (1994) and *La Cérémonie* (1995), and comparisons with Bardot were only made when she starred in *En plein cœur* (1998), a remake of *En cas de malheur* which had starred Bardot thirty years previously. By 2001, however, the slender Ledoyen was rated second behind the more voluptuous Bellucci in a *Paris Match* survey into fantasies about female stars.[23]

Ledoyen's star image has been summarised thus by François Ozon, who directs her alongside Deneuve, Béart and Richard in *8 Femmes*: 'Virginie is the classic *ingénue* heroine [. . .]. She looks very pretty, natural and simple. But underneath she's more perverse than you can imagine'.[24] Hence, in *8 femmes* Suzon (Ledoyen) is the first character introduced to the audience, and acts as part guide, part detective, in the whodunit that follows. Dressed in pink throughout, she incarnates youth and romance, at one point even serenading a teddy bear. But as Ozon acknowledges, beneath the impression of innocence is a sterner and darker edge, represented in the film by Suzon's secret, illicit pregnancy (a theme we also find in Ledoyen's role from *La Cérémonie*).

21· See, for example, E. Lequerret, 'Jusqu'ici tout va bien', *Cahiers du cinéma*, January 2002, pp.11–12. The title of this article refers to a famous line from Kassovitz's film *La Haine* (1995).

22· See *L'Evènement*, 765 (1 July 1999), pp.1 and 75. For more on Bardot, see Chapter 2.

23· See *Paris Match*, 28 June 2001, p.60.

24· Cited in X. Brooks, 'Di Caprio? I wouldn't wish his life on anybody', *The Guardian (Review)*, 15 November 2002, p.6. The title of this interview indicates that Ledoyen is best known to Anglophone audiences for her role opposite Leonardo Di Caprio in *The Beach*.

In opposition to the star system that has seen Casta and Ledoyen follow Bardot and Deneuve into the hall of fame, a recent trend in French cinema has sought to replace stars, and indeed all professional actors, with amateurs. This trend away from stardom and towards authenticity and naturalism in performance has been influenced by Ken Loach and Mike Leigh in Britain (who have been assumed in France to use amateurs even when they use professional actors!), by the Dogme 95 movement (see below) and by a return to realism in recent French *auteur* cinema. Its general principle is expressed by film-maker Bruno Dumont: '*On a tous envie de démocratie à l'écran, c'est-à-dire d'en finir avec l'aristocratie des stars*'.[25] This desire infamously triumphed at the Cannes festival of 1999, when the male and female leads in Drumont's *L'humanité* and the female lead in the Dardenne brothers' *Rosetta* all won awards for best actor. The amateurs concerned – Emmanuel Schotté, Séverine Caneele and Emilie Dequenne – were booed by sections of the press and public as a result. Dequenne has gone on to act opposite Cassel and Bellucci in the popular blockbuster *Le Pacte des loups* (2001), but Caneele and Schotté have disappeared back into obscurity.

While Dequenne is attempting to follow 1980s 'discoveries' like Sandrine Bonnaire and Béatrice Dalle into stardom, the vast majority of amateur actors do simply return to their day jobs. Indeed, this is the point of using amateurs, according to the key originator of this form of anti-stardom, Robert Bresson. Throughout the 1960s and 1970s, Bresson used amateurs in his films, calling them 'models'. His theory on their function, given in *Notes sur le cinématographe*, declared that the same models were not to be used twice by the same director, since they would no longer be believable or authentic.[26] Moreover, far from having an off-screen persona in the way that stars do, or inhabiting a character as professional actors do, Bressonian models are required to relate solely to their director. This discourse of malleability and passivity can be linked to the fact that most models (both in Bresson's work and in that of more recent film-makers) are female. The male amateur tends to be represented as participating in a much more dynamic, active process, as mythologised by the trajectory of amateurs-turned-stars such as Jean Gabin, Lino Ventura and Alain Delon.[27] Bresson's most well-known model, Anne Wiazemsky, made only one film with him – *Au hazard, Balthazar* (1966) – but did go on to make several films with Jean-Luc Godard – *La Chinoise* (1967), *Weekend* (1967), *One plus one* (1968) – and was briefly a counter-cultural star of the late 1960s. But the basic purpose of the model-as-actor (as opposed to the model-turned actress, à la Casta), expressed by Bresson in the 1970s and reiterated by Drumont in 2000, is to appear on screen in a single, unique incarnation.

HARD-CORE PORN STARS

Another recent development in French film is the flourishing of hard-core pornography for the first time since the 1970s. During the 1980s, porn had retreated from French

---

25• 'We all want democracy on the screen, that's to say we want to do away with the star aristocracy', E. Gouslan, 'Quand les amateurs narguent les pros', *L'Evènement du jeudi*, 11 May 2000, p.32.

26• See Bresson cited in ibid., p.32.

27• See Chapter 5. Fashion models-turned-actresses (Aurore Clément, Carole Bouquet) tend to be female.

cinema but prospered on video and on television. In 1985, the satellite-encrypted channel Canal + broadcast the hard-core 1970s film *Exhibition*, and later developed a regular porn film series, '*Le Journal du hard*'. The gradual re-legitimisation of hard-core porn also involved increasingly effective marketing, and the appearance of hard-core stars on television chat shows. Finally, in the 1990s, hard-core porn returned to the big screen in France, first obliquely with the presence of the porn star Tabatha Cash in *Raï* (1995), then explicitly with a graphic sexual performance from Rocco Siffredi in Catherine Breillat's *Romance* (1998). Male *auteurs* such as Cedric Klapisch, Marc Caro and Gaspard Noé have started to follow Breillat into hard-core film projects, but video and DVD remain the foundations of the porn industry, with 30% of all cassettes and DVDs sold in France rated X.[28] The result is apparently that hard-core porn stars such as Siffredi and Cash '*sont devenues aussi populaires que celles du rap ou du ballon rond*'.[29]

The interplay of Kristel and Dallesandro that we noted in *La Marge* (1976)[30] suggested that heterosexual porn stardom is not always as exclusively female as has been, at times, suggested. Alongside porn actresses such as Coralie and Ovidie, the principal new star of the last decade has been the Italian actor and director Rocco Siffredi, described in the French press as '*la superstar du X*'.[31] Both Siffredi and Ovidie (a self-proclaimed feminist who defines herself and her colleagues as 'sex workers')[32] were winners at the 2002 porn awards, '*les Hot d'or*', which now run alongside the Cannes film festival. The 'Hot' press conference at Cannes in 2001 was, however, cancelled after pressure from the festival organisers. This was perhaps a sign of things to come, as the future of pornographic cinema in France appears threatened by what has been termed the 'new moral and sexual order',[33] led by the centre-right government elected in 2002. A proposed 93% supertax on porn production has been abandoned, but cable and pay-TV stations are being targeted in a new campaign against the broadcasting of pornography. Nonetheless, as *Cahiers du cinéma* pointed out in an attack on the 'hypocrisy' of the 2001 decision, the Cannes festival remains largely populated by pornographic images, whether real or virtual.[34]

DIGITAL STARDOM, VIRTUAL STARDOM

Digital technology is currently having an impact on the representation of star actors, and indeed on the generation of potential rivals in the form of virtual stars. At the low-budget

---

28• See G. Dutilleul, 'Le porno sort du ghetto pour envahir les écrans', *L'Evénément du jeudi*, 21–28 June 2000, p.11.

29• 'have become as popular as rap stars or footballers', ibid., p.11.

30• See Chapter 6.

31• 'the hard-core superstar', Dutilleul, op. cit., p.9.

32• See E. Poncet, 'Major de l'X', *Libération*, 8 January 2002, p.42.

33• Marcela Iacub cited in J. Henley, 'French war on immorality targets porn, prostitutes and pay-TV', *The Guardian*, 26 October 2002, p.19.

34• See C.T., 'Off Croisette', *Cahiers du cinéma*, 558 (June 2001), p.39.

end of the industry, lighter, quicker and cheaper means of shooting films are afforded by digital video cameras. The use of DV cameras has expanded in parallel with recent trends towards realism in European film, notably the 'return to the real' in France and the even more influential Dogme 95 movement established in Denmark by Lars von Trier and Thomas Vinterberg. The Dogme film-makers' 'Vow of Chastity' includes the following declarations:

> The camera must be hand-held. Any movement or immobility attainable in the hand is permitted. [. . .] Special lighting is not acceptable. [. . .] Optical work and filters are forbidden. [. . .] My supreme goal is to force the truth out of my characters and settings. I swear to do so by all the means available and at the cost of any good taste and any aesthetic considerations.[35]

This has implications for the way actors, and in particular stars, are represented on screen. Framing and lighting are not to be used to celebrate the star's image, indeed such 'aesthetic considerations' are anathema. A good example is von Trier's photographing of Catherine Deneuve in *Dancer in the Dark* (2000).[36] Deneuve, so often the immaculately lit focus of the camera's attention, is here often caught on the edge of the frame, shifting in and out of shot as the hand-held camera shudders and twists. Her normally radiant appearance is absent, and yet she seems warmer and more earthy in the neutral tones of the natural lighting. The intimacy of the camerawork, the wan lighting and the naturalistic setting all deglamorise the star to concentrate on the emotion of the character, as Dogme intends (and in complete contrast to Ozon's celebration of Deneuve's star image in *8 femmes*).

Since the early days of cinema, film stardom has required living human beings (such as Deneuve) or dead ones (James Dean) to incarnate values for their audience. This tradition currently faces a potential challenge from the creation of the first virtual stars. During the last twenty years, increasingly sophisticated computer-generated imagery has been showcased in films from *Tron* (1982) to *The Matrix* (1999). In France, CGI has been used to create settings or extras in *La Cité des enfants perdus* (1995), both *Astérix* films, and even historical dramas such as *Vidocq* and *L'Anglaise et le duc* (both 2001). But the creation of life-like human protagonists has long been a stumbling-block for CGI. The year 2001 saw this frontier crossed, with the release of *Final Fantasy*, the American film version of a best-selling video game. The star of the film is Aki, a virtual character who has been hailed as '*la première cyber-actrice réaliste*',[37] and whose human appearance is down to the detail of the digital imagery out of which she is formed: it has been widely reported that each of her 60,000 hairs was constructed individually. Despite the fact that Aki is a character, not an actor, the distinction between the two categories has become blurred by descriptions of

---

35• See C. Fowler (ed.), *The European Cinema Reader*, London and New York, Routledge, 2002, p.83.

36• This is a Dogme film in all but name. It only uses special lighting and non-diegetic music in the half a dozen musical sequences, only one of which features Deneuve.

37• 'the first realistic cyber-actress', P. Fabre, 'L'odyssée du virtuel', *Studio Magazine*, September 2001, p.100.

her as a 'cyber-actress', by shots of her posing in a bikini for a men's magazine, and by the use of an interview with her as part of the film's marketing campaign.[38] Comparisons were made not just with previous CGI creations, but with real-life stars, such as Brigitte Bardot; hence the tag-line used to accompany the bikini shot: 'God created woman ... or was it a computer nerd?'.[39] Moreover, as *Studio* magazine pointed out, Aki is genuinely ageless (where Deneuve is only apparently so): '*en quatre ans de tournage, elle n'a pas pris un ride*'.[40] The nearest French equivalent to Aki is Clara, '*la cyber-bombe*'[41] from *Thomas est amoureux* (2001) and the creation of digital studio Sparx, who also contributed the fantasy sequences for *Ma vie en rose* (1997). Guillaume Hellouin, the head of Sparx, has described Clara as '*de loin le personnage le plus sophistiqué créé par un studio européen*'.[42] Also officially launched in France in 2001 was Eve Solal, not a film character but a free-standing virtual personality with her own website, interview appearances, biography and ambitions (to be a film star).[43]

So, does the advent of the virtual star spell the end for real actors and stars? Clearly not. Virtual stars do not fulfil the same functions as real ones (rarely appearing opposite them in live action films, for example) and are rarely used to replace them. A recent experiment to create a digital version of the French actor Richard Bohringer for a version of *20,000 lieues sous la mer* was abandoned. It is currently much more common for virtual stars to be generated without reference to an identifiable human model. The technique of motion capture instead relies on the activity of mimes and stunt actors, whose movements are recorded before being dissociated from the person who made them, to create '*une sorte de mouvement pur, dématérialisé*'.[44] Moreover, every virtual character still needs a human voice, for which stars are often in demand. In the new millennium, the glamour and importance of film stars is unlikely to fade.

38• See *Studio Magazine*, September 2001, pp.26 and 100, and *Maxim*, August 2001, p.42.

39• See ibid. The single shot of Aki used by *Maxim* was reported to have cost $40,000 to create.

40• 'in four years of shooting, she didn't get one wrinkle', Fabre, op. cit., p.100.

41• 'cyber-sex bomb', ibid., p.101.

42• 'by far the most sophisticated character created by a European studio', cited in ibid., p.101.

43• See www.evesolal.com

44• 'a sort of pure, dematerialised motion', R. Hamus-Vallée, 'Motion capture', *Repérages*, July/August 2001, p.57.

Index

Note: page numbers references in italic refer to pictures.